and a Funeral. He ... s inc ... ... the
Actor, a highly ... ... med bio; ...
biographical trilogy of Orson ...
parts have now been published) and *Love is Where it Falls*, an
account of his friendship with the great play agent Peggy
Ramsay. His most recent book, *My Life in Pieces*, won the
Sheridan Morley Prize in 2011. He lives in London.

From the reviews of *Charles Dickens*:

'Vivid and exuberant … Callow … has immersed himself for
nearly 15 years in the minutiae of [Dickens's] life … This
book, with its fresh angles and out-of-the-way sources, is the
harvest of that dedication. Its take on Dickens's psychology is
not the standard one … [Callow's] book is a celebration'
JOHN CAREY, *Sunday Times*

'A brilliantly original account … Callow does not merely spot-
light his hero's secondary career on the boards but enters the
lime-lit prism through which he believes Dickens saw himself'
ANDREW BILLEN, *The Times*

'Captures with colour and verve Dickens's boundless energy
and restless pursuit of new experiences … an entertaining
read'   MARTYN MCLAUGHLIN, *Scotland on Sunday*

'[Callow's] book is lively, likeable and wise, its tone refresh-
ingly welcoming'   JONATHAN BARNES, *TLS*

'It is one of the many virtues of this book that Callow not only
admires his subject, but has got inside him'
DAVID EDGAR, *Guardian*

engaging account of Dickens's essentially theatrical view of the world, which Dickens himself was very well aware of. He shows why Dickens's histrionic streak runs away with his pen at times, makes sense of the contradictions that sometimes threaten to destroy the fiction, and answers very convincingly the question why Dickens, with his passion for the theatre, never wrote a good play. Callow [makes] him exciting, alarming, and alternately loveable and appalling as he was to his friends; the self-styled "Sparkler of Albion" springs to life before our eyes'   CATHERINE PETERS, *Literary Review*

'A lively account of the great Victorian novelist's life … [written] with breathless élan and palpable fondness'
                                              ANDRZEJ LUKOWSKI, *Metro*

'Who better than Callow to inhabit the great man's spirit and bring it vividly to life?'   *Belfast Telegraph*

'Simon Callow provides an excellent guide to the world of one of our best-loved novelists in this brief, lucid biography … A deeply affectionate tribute'   *Metro*

CHARLES DICKENS

SIMON CALLOW

HarperPress
An imprint of HarperCollinsPublishers
77–85 Fulham Palace Road
Hammersmith, London W6 8JB

This HarperPress paperback edition published 2012

1

First published in Great Britain by HarperPress in 2012

Copyright © Simon Callow 2012

Simon Callow asserts the moral right to
be identified as the author of this work

A catalogue record for this book
is available from the British Library

ISBN 978-0-00-744531-8

Typeset in Minion by G&M Designs Limited,
Raunds, Northamptonshire
Printed and bound in Great Britain by
Clays Ltd, St Ives plc

MIX
Paper from
responsible sources
FSC™ C007454

FSC™ is a non-profit international organisation established to promote
the responsible management of the world's forests. Products carrying the
FSC label are independently certified to assure consumers that they come
from forests that are managed to meet the social, economic and
ecological needs of present or future generations,
and other controlled sources.

Find out more about HarperCollins and the environment at
www.harpercollins.co.uk/green

CONTENTS

This book is dedicated to a friend whose loss only gets worse with the passing years, Simon Gray (1936–2008), superb dramatist, sublime diarist, intoxicating conversationalist, who was more alive to Dickens, and in whom Dickens was more alive, than anyone I ever knew. Much of what is in this book was first floated during hours and hours of Dickensian chat in restaurants across the city during twenty-five golden years of friendship.

FOREWORD

When he was a young graduate, Michael Slater, the current doyen of Dickens studies, was asked by his tutors at Oxford what he wanted to study for his PhD. When he said 'Dickens', they looked at him aghast. Dickens was simply not part of the accepted canon. After vainly trying to dissuade him, they sent him off to Another University for advice and guidance, after which he then commenced his life's work, to the benefit of all Dickensians everywhere. Half a century later, the situation is entirely reversed: there is a non-stop tsunami of scholarly studies of Dickens from every possible angle. Dickens and Women, Dickens and Children, Dickens and Food, Dickens and Drink, Dickens and the Law, Dickens and Railways, Dickens and the Americans, Dickens and Europe, Dickens and Homosexuality, Dickens and Magic, Dickens and Mesmerism, Dickens and Art, Dickens and Stenography, Dickens and Publishing. As yet, I have not come across a book on Dickens and Dogs, but it can only be a matter of time: a perfectly interesting and not especially slim volume is just waiting to be written.* The multifariousness of Dickens makes him virtually inexhaustible as a subject. These studies have run alongside and to some extent been the outcrop of the huge transformation in academic attitudes to Dickens, particularly with regard to the later novels, which were largely dismissed by critical opinion in his lifetime.

* I have since discovered that just such a book is on the stocks: *Curs and Companions: the Dog in the Dickensian Imagination* by Beryl Gray. I eagerly look forward to it.

There has also been a magnificent procession of major biographies, from Edgar Johnson in the 1950s to Fred Kaplan in the 1980s, Peter Ackroyd's sublime act of creative self-identification with Dickens in the 1990s, Michael Slater's revelatory account of, as he puts it, a life defined by writing, to the most recent, Claire Tomalin's vivid survey of the Life and Work. Dickens has never been more present. So it takes some cheek on the part of one who is by no means a Dickens scholar to offer yet one more account of the man who called himself Albion's Sparkler. I dare to do so because my relationship to the great man is a little different from anyone else's. In an exchange that Dickens himself might have relished, the late dramatist Pam Gems went to see one of her plays performed by that fine actor Warren Mitchell. She noticed that one or two lines in the text had changed. Reproached by her, Mitchell replied, 'Pam, Pam: you only wrote 'im. I've *been* 'im.' I have, over the years, been Dickens in various manifestations, from reconstructions of the Public Readings on television, to one of Dr Who's helpers; I have also been involved in telling his life story, through the wonderful play that Peter Ackroyd wrote for me, *The Mystery of Charles Dickens*. Presently I am involved in performing two of his monologues, *Dr Marigold and Mr Chops*, and his solo version of *A Christmas Carol*. In order to do all of this, I have needed to find out what it was like to be him, and what it was like to be around him. I have immersed myself, on an almost daily basis, over a period of nearly fifteen years, in the minutiae of his life, above all seeking out personal reminiscences and his own utterances rather than exegetic texts.

Over the years, since a thoughtful grandmother thrust a copy of *The Pickwick Papers* into my hands as I repined in the itchy agony of chicken pox – from the moment I started reading, I never itched again – I have read virtually everything he has written, with the mixture of joy and frustration that all readers of Dickens except for fundamentalists experience. But it is not the writing that is the focus of the present book: when the content of a novel is autobiographical (which to one degree or another many of them are), I have of course discussed it, but my primary concern has always been to convey the flavour of one of the most remarkable men ever to walk the earth: vivacious, charismatic, compassionate, dark, dazzling, generous, destructive, profound, sentimental – human through and through, an inspiration and a bafflement.

Inevitably, as the title of the book declares, I have focused on the theatre in Dickens's life. In recent years there has been an exceptional sequence of books that analyse the influence of the theatre on Dickens's work in subtle and deeply illuminating ways – books by Robert Garis, Paul Schlicke, Deborah Vlock, Malcolm Andrews, John Glavin. Again, this is not the territory of the present book, which looks at the histrionic imperative so deeply rooted in Dickens, but beyond that is interested in Dickens on the stage of life, as he would certainly have thought of it. I have always been concerned with the peculiar quality of his personality, described with remarkable consistency by his contemporaries as theatrical. The books, therefore, to which I have had most recourse are the ones that have given me the man as he lived and breathed: Forster's richly moving three-volume *Life*, the very first biography, written by the man who knew him better than anyone else, and whose perpetual sense of astonishment at his friend sings out on every page; the glorious twelve-volume *Pilgrim Edition of the Letters*, wherein Dickens speaks again, fresh, funny, tortured by turns; the *Speeches*, edited by Fielding, all improvised but faithfully transcribed to give a unique sense of Dickens the public man; Philip Collins's wonderful collection of reminiscences and interviews; and the superb and constantly illuminating chronology by Norman Page, which in its dry way gives as well as anything written a sense of the sheer amount of abundant living that Dickens crammed into his rather short life. In the end, of course, this biography, as with any other, is a selection of the man: playing Dickens, and performing his work, has been like standing in front of a blazing fire. If I can convey any sense of that, I will have succeeded in my aim.

OVERTURE

A very small, rather frail child is escorted into a pub in Chatham, in Kent, by a plump, lively man. This chap, exchanging affable words with the population of the pub, who all know him well, places his child on a table and enjoins him to recite. Though afflicted with a slight lisp, which he will never entirely lose, the child gives a startlingly vivacious rendition of that noted improving lyric, 'The Sluggard', one of the *Divine Songs for Children* from the prolific pen of the Revd Dr Isaac Watts.

> 'Tis the voice of the sluggard; I heard him complain,
> 'You have waked me too soon, I must slumber again.'
> As the door on its hinges, so he on his bed,
> Turns his sides, and his shoulders, and his heavy head.
>
> 'A little more sleep, and a little more slumber;'
> Thus he wastes half his days, and his hours without number;
> And when he gets up, he sits folding his hands,
> Or walks about saunt'ring, or trifling he stands …
>
> I made him a visit, still hoping to find
> He had took better care for improving his mind:
> He told me his dreams, talk'd of eating and drinking;
> But he scarce reads his Bible, and never loves thinking.

Said I then to my heart, 'Here's a lesson for me,'
That man's but a picture of what I might be:
But thanks to my friends for their care in my breeding;
Who taught me betimes to love working and reading.

The rendition was a great success: 'the little boy used to give it to great effect, and with *such* actions and *such* attitudes,' said the family maid, Mary. It was a modest debut for the greatest literary entertainer of all time, but the seven-year-old Charles Dickens obviously took the moral of the poem to heart: no human being on the face of the earth ever filled his waking moments to better effect than he, cramming his fifty-eight years with an astonishing variety of performances in a multiplicity of arenas.

ONE

Paradise

Dickens's arrival in the world was announced with a flourish in the Portsmouth newspapers on Monday, 10 February 1812: 'BIRTHS: On Friday, at Mile-End Terrace, the Lady of John Dickens, Esq. a son.' The phrase has a certain gallantry about it, archaic even for the time, an almost chivalric floridity entirely characteristic of John Dickens. He was born, in 1785, in Crewe House in London and grew up in Crewe Hall, the stately Jacobean mansion in Cheshire in which his father William had been the butler. William died before John was born, but his widow Elizabeth remained housekeeper, a pivotal figure in the running of the Crewe family's various splendid and extensive establishments. Crewe Hall was a very grand household, and a hotbed of Whiggish political activity; among the regular guests were the politicians Charles James Fox, George Canning and Edmund Burke, the playwright Richard Brinsley Sheridan and the painters Joshua Reynolds and Thomas Lawrence: some of the greatest men of the age. As a boy and a youth, John Dickens would inevitably have been involved in his mother's work, becoming a player, if only in a bit part, in the highly theatrical enterprise of running a great house: the daily routine is a carefully staged perform-ance, with sharply defined spheres of backstage and onstage, rigidly maintained roles and a script to be departed from only in exceptional circumstances.

Certainly John Dickens emerged from that world with an orotundity, above all an elaborate sense of language, that his boy Charles relished and reproduced ever after, affectionately

1

quoting him almost to the last – 'as my poor father would say …' John seems not to have had an official job till 1807, when, at the relatively late age of twenty-two, he had gone to work as an 'extra' clerk in the Navy Pay Office in Somerset House, off the Strand in London. Patronage was the usual route to civil service appointments, and it seems very likely that John Dickens's had been arranged by no less a figure than the high-flying Treasurer to the Navy, John Crewe's political associate George Canning, soon to be Foreign Secretary and then, briefly, Prime Minister. At any rate, the following year the now twenty-year-old 'extra' clerk was thought presentable enough to be chosen to accompany Sheridan's wife on a coach-ride from Portsmouth to London – the ever-versatile dramatist, his theatrical career long behind him, then being Receiver of the Duchy of Cornwall. The fact that John was from Crewe Hall would have naturally encouraged the Sheridans' confidence in him: *The School for Scandal* is dedicated to Mrs Crewe, whose housekeeper, John's mother, Elizabeth, would have been well known to Mrs Sheridan. She was a formidable figure, this Elizabeth Dickens, with a lifetime of service in great houses; before her marriage, she had been Lady Blandford's maid at Grosvenor House. She was responsible for her large staff, answerable directly to Mr and Mrs Crewe; but off-duty, she had a particular gift for storytelling, and her employers' children would seek her out in the housekeeper's room, sitting spellbound at her feet as she spun her yarns. A lifetime later, 'inimitable' was the word that Lady Houghton, one of those children, used of Elizabeth Dickens: an adjective that would immortally attach itself to her grandson.

Meanwhile, her son John had fallen in love with Elizabeth Barrow, his colleague Thomas's sister; their father, Charles Barrow, was John's superior in the Navy Pay Office, rejoicing in the magnificent title of Chief Conductor of Monies in Towns – or at least he did, until he was discovered conducting large sums of government monies into his own pocket, at which point he fled the country, later creeping back to the Isle of Man, where he ended his days. Dodgy money thus makes an appearance very early on in Dickens's saga; money, in one form or another, always featured prominently and tiresomely in his life.

Charles Barrow was caught with his hand in the till in 1810, a year after John and Elizabeth had got married, in some style, at the Church of St Mary-le-Strand, just up the road from Somerset House, John's head office. John was transferred to Portsmouth, where he and Elizabeth set up house. John Dickens's Lady, just like his mother, was a renowned story-teller, famous for the sharpness of her observation and the unerring accuracy of her ear: 'on entering a room, she almost unconsciously took stock of its contents', said a friend, 'and if anything struck her as out of place or ridiculous, she would afterwards describe it in the quaintest manner.' Not necessarily someone you would want to come visiting every day. 'She possessed,' her friend remembered, 'an extraordinary sense of the ludicrous.' She equally commanded a sense of the pathetic, effortlessly reducing her listeners to tears. Above all, she was noted for her vivacity. She liked to say that she had been danc-ing all night the day before Charles was born; diligent research has shown that the ball took place four days earlier, which only goes to show what a spoilsport diligent research can be. Whatever the timing, dancing all night when you're nine months gone suggests a certain commitment to fun.

Charles was born in a small but pleasant newly built terraced house in Portsea, a suburban outgrowth of a wildly prosperous wartime Portsmouth that was bursting at the seams. In that famous year of 1812, the war with Napoleon was raging on land and at sea; just seven years earlier the Battle of Trafalgar had triumphantly established that Britannia did, indeed, rule the waves, and there was a lot of work to be had building, equipping, and maintaining the Fleet. John's job was solid and decently rewarded. Charles was the second child but the first boy, which may partly account for the exuberance of the newspaper announcement. The birth itself took place, as John Dickens's proud announcement notes, on Friday, 7 February. Charles Dickens had occasion to observe that pretty well anything of importance that happened in his life thereafter, happened on that day of the week. The household into which he was born that particular Friday consisted of his mother and father, his two-year-old sister, Fanny, the sixteen-year-old housemaid, Mary Weller, whom we have already met as Charles's first reviewer, and another, older, maid, Jane Bonny. Pleasant though the house and its surroundings were, there was no running water, which may have been what encouraged the family to move, four months after Charles was born, to a house in Hawke Street, which did have that precious commodity on tap, and was in a no less agreeable vicinity, with the added advantage of being minutes away from the Navy Pay Office.

John's salary had been steadily rising to a very comfortable £230 per annum, so their next move, eighteen months later, was to leafy Southsea, in a roomy house with a nice little front garden; it represented a distinct step up the social ladder for them. There they were joined by the latest and newest young Dickens, Alfred, and Elizabeth's much-loved sister, Mary, nicknamed Aunt Fanny, whose husband had died in action at sea. By now, the tide of the war had decisively turned for Napoleon, who was defeated and exiled in April 1814: good news for the world, but not for Portsmouth, and certainly not for John Dickens, who was called back to London in January 1815, thus losing his Outpost Allowance, and suffering a substantial reduction of salary to £200. It was the first major financial setback in a lifetime of increasing pecuniary embarrassment.

The family, now reduced in size after the loss of little Alfred from hydrocephalus (water on the brain), found its first London address in Norfolk Street, now Cleveland Street, just off the Marylebone Road in Fitzrovia – a good bustling area: it was within toddling distance of two great institutions, the Theatre of Variety and the workhouse. They were the alpha and omega of the young Charles Dickens's life, heaven and hell in the same street. Just round the corner from Norfolk Street lived John's mother, Elizabeth Dickens Sr, now retired from domestic service. Visits to her, according to Dickens's lightly disguised accounts forty-five years later, were intimidating affairs, with none of the cosy under-stairs storytelling in which her employers' children had so delighted. The 'grim and unsympathetic old personage of the female gender, flavoured with musty dry lavender, dressed in black crape ... with a fishy eye [and] an aquiline nose' certainly held him spellbound, but the tales she span for him were of serial killers with missing ears and people slaughtered and turned into pies. Even getting a present from this 'adamantine woman' was an alarming event. On one occasion she took him to the World of Toys, shaking him on the way, from time to time, and insisting on wiping his nose herself 'on the screw principle'. When they got to the bazaar, he was told to choose a present for half a crown; finally he settled on a Harlequin Wand. It proved to be a disappointment, however: it had no effect whatever on the rocking horse; it failed to produce a live clown out of the beefsteak pie at supper; and could not even influence the mind of his parents 'to the extent of suggesting the decency and propriety of their giving me an invitation to sit up at dinner'. In time, he would amply make up for this first disappointing performance as a magician.

An even greater mystery was why his far from indulgent grandma had given him a present at all. For many years, he says, he was unable 'to excogitate the reason'. At last he got it:

'I have now no doubt she had done something bad in her youth, and that she took me out as an act of expiation.'

Charles was three at the beginning of his first metropolitan sojourn, and five when it ended. It seems that at some point during their time in Norfolk Street, John had been obliged to borrow money from his mother (in her will she mentions having given him advances); he must have been very glad, one way and another, to be transferred away from London to Sheerness in Kent, restored to his former salary, or rather better, a whopping £289 per annum.

In Sheerness it seems they lived in the racy Blue-town district, which had the immeasurable attraction of being the location of a thriving theatre; it is reported that the Dickenses' house was so close to it that they could overhear the shows in their front room. The theatre was in Victory Street, and victory was very much in the air: performances habitually ended with rousing choruses of 'Rule Britannia' and 'God Save the King', which presumably echoed round their parlour. But the days of Sheerness's theatre were numbered: it was pulled down to make way for an expansion of the dockyards, and, on the crest of this wave of expansion, John Dickens was transferred again, this time to Chatham, the 'wickedest place in the world', according to a fellow naval clerk. Wicked it may have been – as any self-respecting town with an itinerant population of soldiers and sailors was in honour bound to be – but it was the scene of incomparably the happiest days of Charles Dickens's life. Here he lived for five years, between the ages of five and ten; here he immersed himself in nature; here he learned first his alphabet, then the rudiments of English and Latin, at his mother's knee; here he had his first – very nearly his only – formal education, initially at a Dame's school, and then at the hands of the local Nonconformist Minister's highly qualified son, William Giles, freshly down from Oxford. From here he was taken to see his first plays; here he discovered the

Aladdin's Cave of his father's modest library; here he and his sister sang their little songs, shepherded by their father, at the Mitre Hotel, which was run by family friends; here he was admired and approved of, encouraged and rewarded; here he was loved; here his inner life was everywhere richly nourished, and the matrix of his imagination set.

He was, at first, a sickly child, subject to spasms and incapable of active exertions; a lucky circumstance, he always said, because it pushed him to read while his contemporaries were throwing themselves around the sports field. While they ran about, he sat there, on his bed, he said, reading, 'as if for life'. 'Oh, he was a terrible boy to read,' said Mary Weller. The books in his father's little library were the great picaresque English novels of the eighteenth century – *Roderick Random*, *Peregrine Pickle*, *Humphrey Clinker*, *Tom Jones* – with their witty, thrustful, middle-class heroes outwitting a gallery of rogues and rivals; *Robinson Crusoe* and *Don Quixote* (not ALL of *Don Quixote*, surely?); and *Gil Blas* (Smollett *à la française*). There were collections of essays from Joseph Addison's great eighteenth-century magazines, *The Tatler* and *The Spectator*; and then there were two books of immeasurable delight which entered deep into his imagination: *The Arabian Nights* and the *Collected Farces* of the eighteenth-century actress and playwright, Elizabeth Inchbald (these last read over and over again). All rather grown-up stuff, some of it quite risqué, but 'whatever harm was in some of them, was not there for me; *I* knew nothing of it.'

His visits to the theatre, the little Theatre Royal at Rochester, were undertaken under the aegis of a young lodger, James Lamert – the son of Aunt Fanny's new husband – who had taken warmly to the bright, odd, intense little boy. These excursions brought to living, breathing reality the visions he had already encountered between the covers of his books. He was wildly excited by what he saw; the world of the theatre, its mysteries and its absurdities had seized him by the throat:

Many wondrous secrets of Nature did I come to the knowledge of in that sanctuary: of which not the least terrific were, that the witches in *Macbeth* bore an awful resemblance to the Thane and other proper inhabitants of Scotland; and that the good King Duncan couldn't rest in his grave, but was constantly coming out of it and calling himself somebody else.

Once home, he demanded that the kitchen be cleared so that he and the little boy next door could act out scenes from the plays they'd just seen; he then sat down and knocked off *Misnar, Sultan of India: A Tragedy*, his literary début, as far as we know; after its short run in the kitchen in Chatham, it disappeared. Later, on two consecutive Christmases, he was taken up to London to see the greatest clown of the age, Joey Grimaldi. Best of all was the invitation to sit in on rehearsals of the amateur productions staged by his friend Lamert: the making of theatre became a passion for the eight-year-old boy, a passion that would endure till very nearly the day he died.

The house into which the Dickenses moved when they first went to Chatham was at 2 Ordnance Terrace; it was commodious – on three floors – but only just big enough to hold the now swarming family, to which over the next two years were added three more children, Letitia, Harriet and Frederick, joining Fanny and Charles, Elizabeth and John, as well as the two servants and Aunt Fanny. The house commanded 'beautiful' views across the surrounding countryside, promised the auction announcement, taking in the river, and, just beyond, the noble fourteenth-century spire of Rochester Cathedral; it had its own garden and yard. It was, the announcement proclaimed, 'fit for a genteel family', which is how Charles and the rest of the family never ceased to think of themselves, whatever adverse circumstances life might throw up.

Some of those circumstances – brought about by a combination of his father's fecklessness and the peculiar salary structure of employees of the Naval Pay Office – caused them to move, in May 1821, when Charles was nine. The new house, at St Mary's Place, was known as The Brook; it was a little smaller, and there was no beautiful view any more; but he was so utterly caught up with his imaginative life that the loss of a room here or a view there would scarcely have registered with him. Certainly he would have known nothing of his father's inexorable accumulation of debt. Most often he was to be found in the room where his father's books were kept, either reading them for the twentieth time, or acting out scenes from them; or else he was at school, eagerly absorbing whatever Mr Giles could tell him; or he was out playing with his friends. He was sturdier now, happily giving himself over to the games he had quickly mastered. The town offered constant diversions: he keenly watched 'the gay bright regiments always going and coming, the continual paradings, the successions of sham-sieges and sham-defences.' In Rochester, he was held up high by his mother to catch a glimpse of the Prince Regent on a tour of inspection; every St Clement's Day he saw the saint's pageant, with Old Clem chaired through the streets by local men in lurid masks. As a special privileged treat, he would go up and down the Medway in naval vessels with his father; together they took epic walks across the fields all the way over to Rochester and back. Near the village of Higham they came upon a house that fascinated little Charles. It was called Gad's Hill Place. And he told his father that one day he would like to live there; and his father promised him that if he worked very very VERY hard, he would.

And so it came to pass. But not before our hero had undergone many, many trials, to the first of which he was about to submit.

It's worth stopping for a moment to look at the ten-year-old Charles Dickens. He was high-spirited, imaginative, amusing, dreamy, affectionate, at times a little over-emotional; he read a great deal, he loved the theatre and dressing up and playing games; as a pupil he was eager and apt; he was good-looking, polite and charming, confident in the love both of his parents and of his siblings, of his extended family and his many friends. He was the crown prince of his little kingdom. He can have had nothing but optimism for the future. In all of these things, he was like many, many children who go on to live perfectly ordinary lives. What happened to him next all but destroyed his life, but it turned him into Charles Dickens. Had he not been the ten-year-old that he was, with that strong base of love and confidence and approval, it would surely have finished him off.

TWO

Paradise Lost

John Dickens was summoned back to Navy Pay Office head-
quarters at Somerset House in June 1822, not a moment too
soon; despite the improvement in his salary, his alarmingly
mounting debts were becoming difficult to deal with. He sold
up the family's effects at The Brook, such as they were, and
they headed west, finding accommodation in Camden Town
in the north of London, near King's Cross. Charles was not
with the family: his schoolmaster, William Giles, had asked
for him to be allowed to stay behind to finish his final term of
work; which he duly did, lodging with Giles. At some point in
the autumn he made his own way to London. It was not an
encouraging start:

> As I left Chatham in the days when there were no railroads in
> the land, I left it in a stage-coach. Through all the years that have
> since passed, have I ever lost the smell of the damp straw in
> which I was packed – like game – and forwarded, carriage paid,
> to the Cross Keys, Wood Street, Cheapside, London? There was
> no other inside passenger, and I consumed my sandwiches in
> solitude and dreariness ... and I thought life sloppier than I had
> expected to find it.

His arrival at Camden Town in the north of London only
confirmed this perception. 'A little back-garret', he called his
room. In fact, No. 16 Bayham Street was a relatively new
dwelling, part of a development scheme completed ten years
earlier, not unlike the houses they had occupied in Chatham;

all the other houses were occupied by professionals of one sort or another – an engraver, a retired linen draper, a retired diamond merchant, and so on. There were fields behind the houses where in summer hay was still made. The area was semi-rustic, the houses having been built on part of the former gardens of the Mother Red Cap tavern, an old highwayman's inn. It was, in fact, village-like.

But to the boy, after populous, bustling Chatham, the street must have seemed bleak and woebegone: 'as shabby, dingy, damp, and mean a neighbourhood as one would desire not to see,' he wrote, thirty years later. 'Its poverty was not of the demonstrative order. It shut the street doors, pulled down the blinds, screened the parlour windows with the wretchedest plants in pots, and made a desperate stand to keep up appearances.' As with the council estates of the 1950s, the price of amenities was the loss of community. The easy openness of Chatham seemed far way: this was the heartless Metropolis. In his former existence, misfortune had been handled discreetly – he himself had known nothing about his father's troubles – but here

> to be sold up was nothing particular. The whole neighbourhood felt itself liable, at any time, to that common casualty of life. A man used to come into the neighbourhood regularly, delivering the summonses for rates and taxes as if they were circulars. We never paid anything until the last extremity and Heaven knows how we paid it then.

Any possible sense of gentility had disappeared. There were, he said, no visitors 'but Stabber's Band, the occasional conjuror and strong man; no costermongers.' There were a few shabby shops – a tobacconist, a weekly paper shop. And at the corner, a pub. 'We used to run to the doors and windows to look at a cab, it was such a rare sight.'

This isolated little outpost was no more than thirty minutes' walk from his old lodgings in bustling Norfolk Street in Marylebone, but to the ten-year-old boy, it evidently felt like some kind of abandoned urban village. London was in the process of expanding, and Camden was one of the points on the pioneer trail. It was not a slum; not at all. But it lacked roots, identity, humanity. No. 16 itself, with only four rooms, was horribly cramped. There were six children and their two parents, plus a servant girl they had brought with them from the workhouse in Chatham, and James Lamert. Charles had nowhere to go and nothing to do. There were no more agreeable visits to the Mitre to be held up for admiration; he knew no one of his own age with whom to dress up and put on a play; and above all, he had no schooling, which he missed bitterly. His appetite for learning had grown and grown in Chatham. His so obviously not attending school proclaimed the family's poverty to the world; his pride was stung. John Dickens seemed, he said, 'to have utterly lost at this time the idea of educating me'. For want of anything to do, he was reduced to cleaning his father's boots and running 'such poor errands as arose out of our poor way of living'. His only diversion was the toy theatre that his friend James had built for him: he spent hours and hours intensely absorbed in it. It was, Lamert said, 'the only fanciful reality in his present life'. John Dickens was naturally distracted by his financial situation: with the loss of the Outpost Allowance, his salary had declined from £400 to £350; and new debts were mounting. He had not paid the rates, and had been running up bills with the local tradesmen. And yet somehow they managed to find the thirty-eight guineas a year for twelve-year-old Fanny, whose musical gifts had gained her a place at the Royal Academy of Music, to board from April of 1823. Charles loved his sister deeply, but this must have been a slap in the face to him: to see such thought, care and money lavished on her while his needs were entirely ignored acutely enhanced his sense of abandonment.

The speed with which everything that had made life good had disappeared was shocking enough. John was clearly power-less to do anything about it; and Charles's mother – sharp, witty, vivacious Elizabeth – was perhaps not the person to turn to for comfort; besides, she had her hands full. This was the beginning of a very swift growing up for the boy, the start of a premature assumption of responsibility for his own life that was to be the making of him. Or at least, of 'Charles Dickens'.

As a distraction, he was packed off to his mother's brother, Uncle Thomas, who lived over a bookseller's in Soho, about forty-five minutes away; the bookseller's wife let the book-hungry boy loose in the shop for hours at a time. More ambi-tiously, the eleven-year-old boy walked the seven miles to the house of his godfather Christopher Huffam, a certified naval rigger, in Limehouse, in Dockland. Huffam and his friends encouraged Charles to perform his repertory of comic songs for them, which cheered him up no end – an audience again at last. One of Huffam's chums declared the boy 'a progidy'. He then walked the seven miles back home to Camden. Here in the vast metropolis he began his life-long career as a walker, pounding the streets of London, looking at nothing, he said, but seeing everything. Early in 1823, not long after the Dickenses had returned to London, he was taken to see the Church of St Giles-in-the-Fields with its notorious attendant slums, which would in time become one of his favourite haunts. On this occasion, he somehow got detached from the adult responsible for him, and wandered aimlessly across the whole of London, eking out the one-and-fourpence in his pocket. He told himself that he was Dick Whittington and would soon be called upon to be Lord Mayor of London, then changed plan, determining instead to enlist in the army as a drummer boy. He ate a pie here and a bun there, then as darkness fell, he spent sixpence on a visit to the theatre, where for a few hours he managed to forget himself and his woes. Finally, when night had fallen, he admitted the truth to himself, and ran round crying out to whoever would listen, 'O, I am lost! I am lost!' until a watchman in a box took pity on him and somehow got a message to John Dickens, who retrieved the boy, now fast asleep.

As recounted by Dickens thirty years later in an essay he called 'Gone Astray', the story has a whimsical charm, but the reality of a particularly tiny, not especially healthy, eleven-year-old wandering alone and untrammelled across the dangerous, desperate city would have been at least as alarming in 1823 as it is in 2012; but the young Charles was rapidly discovering uncommon resources within himself. He had to. 'I fell into a state of dire neglect, which I have never been able to look back upon without a kind of agony.' His anguish was the least of his parents' worries.

With financial ruin looming more threateningly each day, Elizabeth, determined to, as she said, 'do something', had an inspiration: they would open a school. Of course! They would be rich! Mrs Dickens's Establishment, they would call it. They would need to find premises, of course, which they duly did in a brand new and rather splendid development at the top end of Gower Street, parallel to the Tottenham Court Road. Brushing the dust of Bayham Street off their feet, they moved into magnificent new accommodation at No. 4 Gower Street North at Christmas, 1823. They screwed the brass plate on the door and settled back for the queues of eager students to start forming. Charles was deputed to stuff circulars through the local letter boxes. Inexplicably, 'nobody ever came to the school, nor do I recollect that anybody ever proposed to come, or that the least preparation was made to receive anybody.' This insane last gamble delivered the final *coup de grâce* to the Dickenses' fragile finances.

It was at this point that Charles's life changed irrevocably. What followed was so painful for him to contemplate that he never spoke of it to anyone whatsoever, until in March of 1847 – when he was thirty-five and already a national figure, universally admired as the author of *The Pickwick Papers*, *Oliver Twist*, *Nicholas Nickleby*, *The Old Curiosity Shop*, *Martin Chuzzlewit*, and *A Christmas Carol* – his close friend John Forster casually recounted to Dickens a conversation he had had with a former acquaintance of Dickens's father. The man had mentioned that Charles had been employed as a boy in a warehouse off the Strand. Was there anything in it, Forster wondered. Dickens fell very silent, and a few days later sent his astonished friend – swearing him to strictest secrecy – a lengthy letter in which he detailed, in language of meticulous precision and iron control, a chapter of events in his early life that had branded him for ever.

What had happened was this: James Lamert, Charles's theatre-going friend from Chatham, who had stayed with them for a while at Bayham Street (and indeed, tried to cheer the boy up there by making him a toy theatre), had – 'in an evil hour for me, as I often bitterly thought,' Dickens wrote in the letter he sent Forster – entered into business with a cousin who had set up a shoe-polish factory called Warren's at 30 Hungerford Stairs on the Charing Cross Embankment. Lamert was made general manager of the factory, and in that capacity told the Dickenses, whom he knew to be in desperate straits, that he could offer Charles a reasonably paid job (six shillings – or was it seven? Dickens couldn't quite remember) which would help relieve the pressure on the family finances. What did the job consist of?

Covering the pots of paste-blacking; first with a piece of oil-paper, and then with a piece of blue paper; to tie them round with string; and then to clip the paper close and neat, all round, until it looked as smart as a pot of ointment from an apothecary's shop. When a certain number of grosses had attained this pitch of perfection, I was to paste on each a printed label; and then go on again with more pots.

He was to do this ten hours a day, six days a week.

The bright, imaginative eleven-year-old listened dumbfounded as his parents accepted the offer with alacrity. 'My father and mother were quite satisfied. They could hardly have been more so, if I had been twenty years of age, distinguished at a grammar school, and going to Cambridge.' He was, of course, writing after twenty-five years of anguished brooding; but why would he not have felt all those things at the time: the young prince thrown into a dungeon with the smiling co-operation of those on whose protection he should most have been able to rely? It is every child's darkest nightmare. 'It is wonderful to me,' he wrote to Forster,

> that I could have been so easily cast away at such an age. It is wonderful to me, that even after my descent into the poor little drudge I had been since we came to London, no one had compassion enough on me – a child of singular abilities, quick, eager, delicate, and soon hurt, bodily or mentally – to suggest that something might have been spared, as it certainly might have been, to place me at any common school.

The sense of the injustice of things – of life – was born in him, and it would only grow and grow.

He reported for work in September 1823, aged eleven and a half. The blacking warehouse was the last house on the left at old Hungerford Stairs, more or less where Embankment tube station is today.

It was a crazy tumble-down old house, abutting of course on the river, and literally overrun with rats. Its wainscoted rooms, and its rotten floors and staircase, and the old grey rats swarming down in the cellars, and the sound of their squeaking and scuffling coming up the stairs at all times, and the dirt and decay of the place, rise up visibly before me, as if I were there again.

James Lamert was a decent man; all this had been done out of kindness. He must have had some sense of the outrage to the sensibilities of the boy – whose imaginative intensity he knew first-hand, at the theatre, in the rehearsal room, poring over the toy theatre he had built for him with his own hands – so he arranged for Charles to do his wretched repetitive work in the counting house, near his own desk, with a view of the coal-barges and the river. One of the lads from downstairs came up to show him the ropes; his name was Bob Fagin.

James Lamert had promised to give Charles school lessons during the lunch-hour, but inevitably this plan proved impractical; equally inevitably, little by little, Charles found himself working downstairs with his fellow labourers – Fagin, and an aggressive lad called Paul Green, who was assumed by everyone, including himself, to have been christened Poll. Charles got on perfectly well with the other boys, but his conduct and manners, he said, 'put a space between us'. Thanks to his connection with James, and the deference of the adult workforce (who, heartbreakingly, he tried to entertain with 'the results of some of the old readings which were fast perishing out of my mind'), he was generally referred to as 'the young gentleman'; on one occasion, Poll rebelled against this usage, but was speedily put in his place by Bob Fagin. 'No words can express the secret agony of my soul as I sunk into this companionship; compared these everyday associates with those of my happier childhood; and felt my early hopes of growing up to

be a learned and distinguished man crushed in my breast.' He
felt, he said, buried alive. He told Forster all those years later
that he found it almost impossible to write about

> the sense I had of being utterly neglected and hopeless – of the
> shame I felt in my position – of the misery it was to my young
> heart to believe that, day by day, what I had learned and thought
> and delighted in, and raised my fancy and emulation up by, was
> passing away from me, never to be brought back any more.

His whole nature, he said, 'was so penetrated with the grief
and humiliation of such considerations that, even now –
famous and caressed and happy – I often forget in my dreams
that I have a dear wife and children – even that I am a man –
and wander desolately back to that time of my life.'

He quickly understood that to show any of what he felt
would be fatal. 'I never said to man or boy how it was that I
came to be there, or gave the least indication of being sorry
that I was there.' Instead, he did his work, soon becoming 'at
least as expeditious and as skilful with my hands as either of
the other boys'. The child of singular abilities – quick, eager,
delicate, and soon hurt, bodily or mentally – adapted brilliantly, rapidly learning the skills to survive this onslaught on
his identity. He was learning to wear a mask, to conceal his
inner life, to rise above his circumstances. He had always
found acting fun; now he had to learn to do it in deadly
earnest. This was character-building, in the most literal sense
of the phrase. He was quite unsupported; he knew that he
would have to do it all on his own. 'No advice, no counsel, no
encouragement, no consolation, no support, from anyone
that I can call to mind, so help me God.'

As if to confirm this, his father – who had been so very little
use to him since they had come to London – was now finally
arrested for debt and taken to the sponging house, a sort of

clearing house, prior to being formally committed to the Marshalsea Prison. During the hours when he was not tying pieces of string round pots of polish and sticking printed labels onto the jars, he ran errands for his father, delivered, as Forster says, 'with swollen eyes and through shining tears', until at last John Dickens, unable to raise a single penny of collateral, was committed to debtors' jail, breaking his son's heart, Dickens reports, with the words that later emerged immortally from Wilkins Micawber's mouth: 'The sun has set upon me forever.' Elizabeth and the rest of the family prepared to join him in the Marshalsea. The household furniture was sold for the family benefit. A sale was held at Gower Street North. 'My own little bed was so superciliously looked upon by a Power unknown to me, hazily called "the Trade", that a brass coal-scuttle, a roasting jack, and a birdcage, were obliged to be put into it to make a Lot of it,' he wrote thirty years later, 'and then it went for a song. So I heard mentioned, and I wondered what song, and I thought what a dismal song it must have been to sing!'

Charles visited John at the Marshalsea, where he received some memorably expressed economic wisdom that also later emerged from the mouth of Micawber; soon enough, the family went to live with him there. Charles, the only bread-winner, did not. The boy – and one has to keep reminding oneself that he had only just turned twelve – was, for a small consideration, put into the care of Mrs Roylance, a not especially good-natured old lady in Little College Street in Camden Town, just round the corner from the Dickenses' old residence in Bayham Street; two other children in similar circumstances were likewise accommodated. Charles thus walked to work every day from North London – about an hour – to the black-ing warehouse, and then at the end of the day, he would walk another hour back to Camden Town. On Sundays he would fetch Fanny from the Royal Academy of Music in Hanover

Square, and they would go to the prison together and spend the day there.

He was always hungry. He had to feed himself out of his six shillings a week: a pennyworth of milk and a cottage loaf for breakfast before he left Little College Street, and a small loaf and a quarter of a pound of cheese when he got back at night. The autobiographical fragment is filled with descriptions of meals dreamed of and food yearned after, with the occasional rash indulgence that left him short for the rest of the week, despite his hopeless attempts to divide his six shillings up, one for each day. He lounged about the streets, insufficiently and unsatisfactorily fed, he said. He bitterly missed family life, once so abundant, and loathed going home every night to what he called 'a miserable blank'. He decided not to take it lying down, and confronted his father with it the following Sunday night, 'so pathetically and with so many tears' that, as Dickens, with or without irony, says, 'his kind nature gave way'. Astonishingly, it seems never to have crossed John Dickens's mind that Charles might be unhappy. It was the first time the boy had ever made any complaint about his situation, 'and perhaps it opened up a little more than I intended', he says. The lessons that he learned from this confrontation with John must have been deep: he saw that it was necessary to get his father to think about his child's situation, to face up to it, to try to imagine what he was feeling. He was powerless, he knew, to act on his own behalf, but it was possible, he discovered, to shame his father into behaving like a parent.

A back-attic was quickly found for him in Lant Street in Southwark, round the corner from the Marshalsea, and from then on Charles had breakfast with the family every morning, and supper every night, in the prison. He notes that they seemed perfectly comfortable there, with their little orphan servant from the warehouse looking after them; indeed, he told his friend and future biographer Forster, they seemed rather more comfortable in prison than they had done for a long time out of it, and greatly enjoyed the society of John's fellow prisoners. His mother had winkled their stories out of them, and entertained Charles and the rest of the family with recounting them, no doubt with her famously vivid mimicry. But the damage done to Charles was not so easily made good: his childhood nervous ailments returned in full force, causing him excruciating pain down one side; one night he had to be looked after all night by the manager of his lodgings in Lant Street. It happened again one day at the warehouse, and there it was Bob Fagin who tended him, easing the savage pain by slipping empty blacking-jars filled with hot water under him, as he rested on an improvised straw pallet. When Charles was well enough to go home, Bob insisted on accompanying him, but Dickens, unable to bear the shame of him knowing about the prison, walked up to the door of a rather posh house as Bob went his way and knocked on it, asking whether a Mr Robert Fagin was in.

His great consolation was to go down the Blackfriars Road of a Saturday night to seek out the travelling show-van, and 'with a very motley assemblage' marvel at the Fat-Pig, the Wild-Man and the Little-Lady; this carnival world of oddities and rejects now became part of his mental landscape. The little boy wandered all over the West End, buying himself a glass of ale, keenly studying life around him. 'But for the mercy of God, I might easily have been, for any care that was taken of me, a little robber or a little vagabond.' And then, quite suddenly, under the terms of the Insolvent Debtors Act, John was released from the Marshalsea, and the family were reunited, all of them moving in to Mrs Roylance's in Little College Street, where Charles had stayed before moving to Lant Street. A rare family outing took them all to the Royal Academy, to watch Fanny getting a prize. Charles must have had the afternoon off from the blacking warehouse, and the contrast between his situation and his sister's overwhelmed him: 'I could not bear to think of myself – beyond the reach of all such honourable emulation and success.' He wept. 'I prayed, when I went to bed that night, to be lifted out of the humiliation and neglect into which I had fallen.' He notes that 'there was no envy in this'; it simply sharpened the pain of his daily existence.

A new refinement had been added to his misery at Warren's: the warehouse was moved from the dingy, dank obscurity of the Hungerford Stairs to Chandos Street in smart, bustling Covent Garden, just on the other side of the Strand; the boys were required 'for the light's sake', to do their work in a room in which the window gave onto the street. The boys were very nimble at their task, and soon they found that a little audience would gather every day to watch them, like monkeys in a cage. One day, John Dickens happened to pass by and saw Charles on display. John said nothing at the time, but a short while later, he gave Charles a letter to deliver to James Lamert, who opened it in Charles's presence, erupting so angrily when he read it that Charles cried 'very much' – partly because of the suddenness of the outburst, but mostly because Lamert was 'violent' about John. He told the boy, not unkindly, that he could no longer work there. The foreman said he was sure it was all for the best, and Charles went home, 'with a relief so strange that it was like oppression', no doubt because, just as he had not been able to understand why he had been sent to the blacking warehouse, he was scarcely more able to comprehend why he had been removed from it.

It was an extraordinary little piece of theatre that John Dickens had staged: instead of seeking Lamert out himself and airing his grievances with him, he sent the letter via Charles, knowing that Lamert would open it in front of the boy, become furious, and send him home. Perhaps the explanation lies in what happened next: Elizabeth went to Lamert the following day and asked him to take Charles back; this he agreed to do. No doubt John knew that Elizabeth would never approve of him going directly to Lamert and withdrawing Charles, so he had engineered a situation from which there could be no honourable retreat. And indeed, he dismissed Lamert's placatory offer, loftily declaring that it was time for the boy to resume his schooling. The nightmare had come to an end, but Charles Dickens was changed utterly. As Forster magisterially remarks, though Dickens was deprived of teachers when he arrived in London 'he was at another school already, not knowing it. The self-education forced upon him was teaching, all unconsciously as yet, what, for the future that awaited him, it most behooved him to know.' It was indeed the perfect training to become the greatest novelist of his time. But at what price?

He had learned the lessons of solitude and self-dependency. He had known hunger, neglect, fear, loneliness, humiliation. He knew what it was to be powerless, and that to be free, he must acquire power. In the blacking warehouse he conceived, said Forster, a passionate resolve *not to be* what circumstances were conspiring to make him'. He had taught himself to overcome his engulfing sense of worthlessness and failure, and to put on a brave face. He had suffered terrible injustice, he knew that. He had learned how to survive, by working hard, by not complaining, by making people laugh. He felt that he had been snatched from Eden, that what had seemed a natural state – his birthright, indeed – was a temporary benison that could not be depended upon. He was in mourning for this paradise he had lost, which as he turned it over and over in his mind became more and more important to him; it sustained him, but the memory of its loss was also a source of piercing anguish to him. To counter it, he had learned, at an astonishingly early age, how to nourish his inner life, by observing and responding to the world around him.

More than anything else, his twelve months' hard labour at Warren's Blacking Warehouse taught him that he could rely on no one but himself, not kindly, theatre-loving cousins, not father, not mother. James Lamert, though a well-intentioned fellow, filled with fantasy and fun, had so little understood Charles that he had proposed him for this brain-killing, soul-destroying labour. His father – though 'as kind-hearted and generous a man as has ever lived in the world' – had proved deeply unreliable in every important crisis Charles had faced. But with his mother, it was worse. 'I never afterwards forgot, I never shall forget, I never can forget,' he wrote to Forster, 'that my mother was warm for my being sent back.' That when he had at long last been reprieved, when the malign spell had finally been lifted from him, she should seek to cast him back into the scene of his misery, was incomprehensible to him. This betrayal – this utter inability to understand anything at all about him – permanently skewed his relationship with her, and rendered his attitude to women in general peculiarly complex. The relationship between him and his parents had lost its innocence, because now there was something unspeakable between them: 'From that hour, until this, my father and my mother have been stricken dumb upon it. I have never heard the least allusion to it, however far off and remote, from either of them.' But then, neither did he ever allude to it. He knew that to survive he must banish from his consciousness the period of pain and despair he had lived through, and that he must never mention it to anyone. The strength of mind, the self-control! – to batten down the hatches and forever lock off the sharp pain. 'I have never, until I now impart it to this paper,' he told Forster in a resoundingly theatrical image, 'raised the curtain I then dropped.' The denial came, of course, at a price. 'All the danger he ran in bearing down and over-mastering the feeling, he did not know,' said Forster. 'A too great confidence in himself, a sense that everything was possible to the will that would make it so, laid occasionally upon him self-imposed burdens greater than might be borne by anyone with safety.'

He had dramatized his experience, establishing a dynamic that would thereafter underpin everything he ever wrote or did. 'I do not write resentfully or angrily,' he remarked, whether entirely honestly or not, of the autobiographical fragment he gave Forster, 'for I know how these things have worked together to make me what I am.' He was fourteen but he was already what he was. The spring was wound up, and it unwound with ever-increasing velocity over the next forty years.

THREE

Beginning the World

School, so longed for, the *summum bonum* of his youthful dreams, turned out not to be all it was cracked up to be. Perhaps it was the particular school: certainly the Wellington House Academy for Boys on the Hampstead Road in Camden Town was not Eton or Westminster. Indeed, Dickens claimed that the headmaster, William Jones, a Welshman, was 'the most ignorant man I have ever had the pleasure to encounter and one of the worst-tempered men perhaps that ever lived.' He was obsessed with ruling ciphering books with a bloated mahogany ruler, 'smiting the palms of offenders with the same diabolical instrument, or viciously drawing a pair of pantaloons tight with one of his large hands and caning the wearer with the other'. (Dickens, as a day-boy, was spared the rod, which was specially reserved for boarders.)

Despite Jones's barbarity, Wellington House Academy was generally considered a rather good school, one of the very best in the area. Perhaps Dickens had already decided that, as with everything else in life, if he wanted to be educated, he would have to do it for himself. He said of himself that he won prizes at school for Latin, and that he was the First Boy; Forster says that his contemporaries pooh-poohed these claims, though, apart from his occasional anarchistic inclinations, one would have thought that Dickens was very much head-boy material. His schoolfellows recollected him with affection, noting that he was small but well-built, curly-haired and handsome, with 'a more than usual flow of high spirits'. No doubt after his year in limbo, simply being around boys of his own age with time on their hands must have been a joyful release. Almost to the end of his life, he played games with manic exuberance, sometimes becoming quite rough, even with – especially with – young women.

He held his head more erect, it was noted, than boys are wont to do, and was generally rather smart, choosing to wear instead of the usual frill a turn-down collar, 'which made him look less youthful in consequence'. No one would ever accuse him of being a 'poor little drudge' now; he was acquiring a peacock quality that would become more pronounced with time. He started writing small tales that circulated among the boys ('though,' sniffed one of his contemporaries, 'I cannot recollect anything that then indicated that he would hereafter become a literary celebrity') and he made up an imaginary language – 'the lingo' – which his fellows learned and joined in with. Needless to say, he participated passionately in school plays. These were evidently done in some style: that quintessential Gothic melodrama, *The Miller and His Men*, which Dickens directed, was designed by little William Beverley, later to become one of the most famous scene painters of the age, and the explosion of the mill at the end was achieved with a thrilling outburst of firecrackers.

The fifteen-year-old Charles even made extracurricular appearances, at a small playhouse in Catherine Street, parallel to Drury Lane, right in the heart of the then theatre district. It was one of the so-called Minor Theatres, where amateurs would pay to be allowed to appear in the plays; child performers were presumably not charged. Perhaps they were even paid; that would have been welcome, since John Dickens, though out of the Marshalsea, was already in financial trouble again. Charles also seems to have been the moving spirit in a form of street theatre in which he and half a dozen of his school chums would disguise themselves as beggars, pestering passers-by for money, an odd parody of what he felt might so easily have been his actual destiny. It was all high-spirited, wholesome, boyish stuff, a thousand light years away from the rat-infested Hungerford Stairs, about which he must never speak to anybody, but the memory of which was boiling away quietly inside him. In one edition of the school paper, he wrote an amusing squib that might have contained a foundation of truth: 'Lost – by a boy with a long red nose and grey eyes: a very bad temper. Whoever has found the same may keep it, as the owner is better off without it.' Anger was an emotion he struggled to keep in check, but it was never very far from the surface.

He left Wellington House Academy a month after his fifteenth birthday, having been there for more or less two years, which brings the sum total of years that he spent in education to three. The school had served its purpose, though. 'I won prizes at school, and great fame,' he told a correspondent who had asked for details of his life in 1838, shortly after his first great writing triumphs, 'and was positively assured that I was a very clever boy. I distinguished myself (as at other places) like a brick.' He had left school 'tolerably early', he told the same correspondent, because his father was not a rich man 'and I had to begin the world'.

The bit of the world he chose to begin was not at all congenial to him and came about thanks to an intervention by his mother, but it furnished him with a subject he would never tire of: the law. He was first very briefly employed by the solicitor Charles Molloy, in Chancery Lane, but he moved quickly on from there. His second boss was the solicitor Edward Blackmore. Writing about his youthful employee, Blackmore used a word many people reached for in describing Dickens: prepossessing. He was a bright, witty, well-turned-out lad – almost military in his bearing – and discharged his tasks so efficiently that another lawyer unsuccessfully tried to poach him from Blackmore. He was increasingly something of a peacock, and took to wearing a Russian sailor jacket and military-looking cap, but he was no fop, and when someone satirically hailed him with the words 'Hello, Sojer', he punched him in the face, and was punched back in return. The would-be wit learned what many people in future years would learn, to their cost: don't mess with Charles Dickens.

Mostly, though, he made people laugh, with wicked impersonations of everyone around him: clients, lawyers, clerks, even the cleaning woman. When *Pickwick Papers* came out, his former colleagues realized that half of them had turned up in its pages. His eyes – eyes that everyone who ever met him, to the day he died, remarked on – beautiful, animated, warm, dreamy, flashing, sparkling – though no two people ever agreed on their colour – were they grey, green, blue, brown? – those eyes missed nothing, any more than did his ears. He could imitate anyone. Brimming over with an all but uncontainable energy, which the twenty-first century might suspiciously describe as manic, he discharged his superplus of vitality by incessantly walking the streets, learning London as he went, mastering it, memorizing the names of the roads, the local accents, noting the characteristic topographies of the many villages of which the city still consisted. And when he wasn't pounding the streets, he was at a show. He claimed that for at least three years he went to the theatre every single day of his life.

The theatre of the late 1820s was pitched somewhere between Las Vegas and weekly rep, highly physical, spectacular, comic, sentimental and from time to time sublime. Great roaring actors roamed the boards, accompanied by sometimes as many as a hundred extras, in bastardized versions of the classics, clowns of genius purveyed surreal scenarios of mind-boggling illogic, raddled old actresses pretending to be seventeen-year-olds wrung the audience's withers in scenes of heart-breaking pathos. Punters would theatre-hop, catching an act here, a song there, a curtain call somewhere else. They gave instant verdicts on the performances, shrieking their disapprobation, howling their praise. It was an entirely inter-active experience, with actors giving quite as good as they got, though sometimes, in the face of overwhelming rejection, they made heartfelt apologies for their performances from the stage. All the great writers wrote for the theatre – Byron, Shelley, Walter Scott – and on the whole what they wrote for it was fundamentally untheatrical. It was an age of huge personalities, of stupendous scenic effects, of patriotic senti-ment and radical satire, supposedly tightly censored but slip-ping rapidly out of control. And Dickens loved every second of it. It was mother's milk to him. He offered an explanation some years later for the popularity of the theatre he grew up on: he was writing of pantomime, but he might as well have been writing about the whole experience:

> that jocund world … where there is no affliction or calamity that leaves the least impression, where a man may tumble into the broken ice, or dive into the kitchen fire, and only be the droller for the accident; where babies may be knocked about and sat upon, or choked with gravy spoons, in the process of feeding, and yet no Coroner be wanted, nor anybody made uncomfort-able; where the workmen may fall from the top of a house to the bottom, or even from the bottom of a house to the top, and sustain no injury to the brain, need no hospital, leave no young children; where everyone, in short, is so superior to the accidents of life … that I suspect this to be the secret … of the general enjoyment which an audience of vulnerable spectators, liable to pain and sorrow, find in this class of entertainment.

As a particularly vulnerable spectator himself, one liable to pain and sorrow, his joy in escaping from the realities of life was intense. He also relished melodrama, the dominant form of the age, with its schematic opposition of good and evil and its ruthlessly plotted outcomes, in which the characters' destinies are manipulated by the puppet-master dramatist. All this he rejoiced in. But there was one form of theatre, and one particular performer, he prized above all others. Charles Mathews – in his fifties when Dickens first saw him – was an absolute original, both as writer and as performer. His *monopolylogues*, farces in which he played all the characters, were fixtures of the season; he invariably took the town by storm with them. 'As good as half a dozen plays distilled,' said the dandyish critic Leigh Hunt. They sit somewhere between Sheridan and the *Goon Show*. In *Youthful Days*, Mathews played, in rapid succession, changing costume at dazzling speed as each character came and went, a servant, a French organist, a knight from the shires, an outrageous dandy, a stout Welshman, and then, finally, a skinny snooker player and his wife. They had names like Sir Shiveraine Scrivener, Monsieur Zephyr, ap Llewellyn-ap Lloyd, and Mark and Amelrose Moomin. Major Longbow was a great favourite:

'How do, Major?' 'How do I do? How should I do, eh? Better than any man living – there's muscle! – strongest man living – How do I do? – pho! – no man so well as I am. I am reckoned the finest piece of anatomy that was ever sent upon the face of the earth. Upon my life, it's true. What will you lay me it's a lie? Hit me with a sledge-hammer if you like – can't hurt me – there's muscle!' 'Are you inclined to go up, Major?' said I. 'Up what, in that thingummy, a balloon? Why, I can walk up higher than you'll go in that thing. When I was in India, I walked up an inaccessible mountain; walked for five days running, for four hours every day; took me seven days coming down, run the whole of the last day, and danced at the Governor's Ball at night. Upon my life it's true. What will you lay it's a lie?'

It could so easily have been a generalized blur of stereotypes, but surprisingly the quality for which his contemporaries most admired Mathews was his verisimilitude. He more or less invented character acting; and his repertoire of dialects, especially London dialects, was astonishing. Dickens loved him, attending his shows again and again, learning the monopolylogues by heart and practising them over and over at home.

In the offices of Ellis and Blackmore, he would lay on impromptu performances for his fellow clerks, unerringly imitating not just Mathews but all the great popular singers of the day, and all the leading actors – Cooke, Charles Kean, Macready – and 'he could give us Shakespeare by the ten minutes'. Clerks from other offices came in to be entertained; even officers of the Court couldn't resist. He and one of his fellow clerks, Potter, used to go to the theatre together; according to Blackmore, they appeared in the minor theatres, like Goodwin's in the Strand, and any number of others in Vauxhall, paying to play parts. This interesting activity – a sort of Thespian karaoke – was perhaps a step towards some sort of professional involvement in the theatre, always a temptation. He certainly wanted to find a way of making a living other than the law. Later he described the Inns of Court, and Gray's Inn, where Ellis and Blackmore had their offices, specifically, as

> generally … one of the most depressing institutions in brick and mortar known to the children of men. Can anything be more dreary than its arid Square, Sahara Desert of the law … when my travels tend nowadays to this dismal spot, my comfort is its rickety state. Imagination gloats over the fullness of time when the staircases shall have quite tumbled down.

For the time being he was stuck with the law, but an example from an expected quarter suggested a different possibility.

While he was still in the Marshalsea, his father had, very sensibly in a pre-emptive strike, tendered his resignation to the Navy Pay Office on medical grounds before they could sack him, thus protecting his pension. He had subsequently found employment as a journalist, an activity in which he had lightly dabbled back in Chatham. In order to facilitate his career as a reporter, he had mastered what David Copperfield calls 'the savage stenographic mysteries' of Brachygraphy, Gurney's tortuously arcane shorthand system. John's dedication in learning it is initially somewhat surprising, revealing an aspect of his character his son always affirmed: his capacity for hard work. His essential failing was a sense of financial unreality; one which his son did not share. Indeed, Charles had learned in the hardest possible way how incompatible such a sense was to a tolerable existence, and he fixed his mind beadily against it from an early age. Now, after eighteen months at Ellis and Blackmore's on subsistence wages, he determined to try to get a job as a Parliamentary reporter, for which he needed to be able to write shorthand. Charles had certainly inherited John's capacity for work, in overplus, and he mastered the Byzantine complexities of Gurney in a cool ten weeks, which, in November 1828, got him, if not the job he wanted, then at least the right to work as a freelance shorthand reporter for the proctors of Doctors' Commons, one of the arcane byways of the English legal system, a part of the Consistory Court, the diocesan court of the Bishop of London, 'where they grant marriage-licences to love-sick couples, and divorces to unfaithful ones; register the wills of people who have property to leave; and punish hasty gentlemen who call ladies by unpleasant names.' Its days were numbered; thirty years later it was gone. The sixteen-year-old Charles worked in the death-like hush of the Prerogative Office of Doctors'

Commons, and was very bored, not realizing, perhaps, how perfect a training ground it was for a satirist.

He was not very well paid, and the work was intermittent. which made him start to think of the theatre as a possible career 'in quite a business-like way'. He prepared himself for it with every bit as much intensity as he had applied himself to mastering Gurney. He was fanatical in his attendance at performances, studying the form, assiduously tracking down the best acting, always seeing Mathews 'wherever he played'. He practised on his own 'immensely' (such tricky but critical matters as how to walk in and out of a room, and how to sit on a chair); he often did this for four, five, or six hours a day, shut up in his own room or walking about in a field. He worked out a system for learning parts, a large number of which he committed to memory. And then, when he finally judged himself ready, towards the end of 1831, when he was nineteen, he sat down in his little office at Doctors' Commons and wrote a letter to George Bartley, Charles Kemble's manager at the Covent Garden Theatre. He told him how old he was, and exactly what he thought he could do: he had, he said, 'a strong perception of character and oddity, and a natural power of reproducing in my own person what I observed in others'. A very sensible letter, from someone who clearly has no idiotic ideas about the theatre, who knows his own worth but makes no exaggerated claims for himself. And, once Covent Garden had got their forthcoming sensation, *The Hunchback*, up and running, Bartley wrote back offering him an audition to perform anything of Mathews's he liked (presumably he'd mentioned his admiration for the mono-polylogues). He planned to sing as well, and lined up his sister Fanny to play for him. But on the day of the audition, he went down with a bad cold and inflammation of the face (the beginning of a persistent earache), and asked if they could re-arrange the audition for the following season. And then, while the old season was still running its course, his uncle William Barrow, another of his mother's brothers, offered him a job as a reporter on *The Mirror of Parliament*, a would-be rival to Hansard that Barrow had established. Charles accepted with alacrity, working side by side with his father, a brace of Bracygraphers, toiling away together. He took his place in the House of Commons for the first time early in 1832, just around the time of his twentieth birthday, and – for the time being – his dreams of working in the theatre melted away.

Going to work for *The Mirror of Parliament* was when he really 'began the world', when his course was set, and after which his career proceeded like an arrow shot from a strong-bow. Whether being a writer, or a novelist, was his ambition, we simply don't know. He never spoke of it. It simply followed as day follows night. He had been in training for it, whether he knew it or not, cultivating the 'patient and continuous energy which then began to be matured in me'. This patient energy, he knew, was the source of his subsequent success. David Copperfield put it very well many years later:

> I do not hold one natural gift, I dare say, that I have not abused. My meaning simply is, that whatever I have tried to do in life, I have tried with all my heart to do well; that whatever I have devoted myself to, I have devoted myself to completely; that in great aims and in small, I have always been thoroughly in earnest.

His long walks through the city, his nights at the theatre, his painstaking mastery of shorthand, his hours in the British Museum Reading Room, for which he had got a ticket as soon as he was eligible, just two days after his eighteenth birthday, devouring Shakespeare and the historians and the philosophers, his months in the blacking warehouse, his sense of abandonment, of exile from Eden, his hunger, his loneliness, his humiliation, his despair. Everything that had happened to him conspired to make him what he became; every last detail of it fed into his work. The 'strong perception of character and oddity, and a natural power of reproducing in my own person what I observed in others' he had told the Covent Garden Theatre about was as well suited to writing as it was to acting. Recounting the story of his abandoned audition, he told Forster that he had never thought of going on the stage as anything but a way of getting money. After he broke into journalism, he said, and had a success in it, he quickly left off turning his thoughts that way, and never resumed the idea. 'I never told you this, did I?' he asked his friend. 'See how near I may have been to another life?' Another secret, but one that he could talk about, fifteen years after the event.

FOUR

The Birth of Boz

Dickens's passionate appetite for every aspect of life did not by any means exclude the opposite sex. From his earliest years in Portsea and Chatham, he seems to have been drawn to pretty little girls; indeed, many of his co-conspirators in pranks and putting on plays seem to have been girls rather than boys. He writes sweetly in the memory pieces that flowed so prolifically from him in his last decades of a succession of flawless little charmers with names like Olympia Squires, all of whom he idolized. Perhaps he writes a little too sweetly either for our taste in the early twenty-first century or indeed for credibility. Radical in so many of his attitudes, he seems entirely to have subscribed, as a fully grown author of major novels of fathomless complexity, to the Victorian belief that children were adorable, innocent little adults in disguise; nothing amuses him more, for example, than to write a story – 'Boots at the Holly-Tree Inn' – in which two eight-year-olds elope.

It does seem, however, that even as a youth and a young man, he maintained an uncommonly idealizing attitude to young women. His sense of abandonment and isolation during the blacking warehouse years, the lack of warmth he received from Mrs Roylance in the lodgings at Little College Street, and the shattering betrayal (as he saw it) inflicted on him by his mother, may have impelled him to create a countervailing image of an ideal female presence, instinct with kindness, affection, approval and nurture, not maternal but celestial: beautiful, radiant, the sort of vision that illuminates the blackest night of the soul and heals the wounded heart.

The word Angel expresses many of these things, or did in the nineteenth century, and it is a word that he used frequently to describe the women he admired, whether of his own invention, or in life itself.

On his own admission, he was rarely out of love in his early days, and, Dickens being Dickens, it was an overwhelming, an obsessional, a cataclysmic experience. The very phrase 'Dickens in Love' conjures up alarming images, his energies so extreme, his need so great, his resources of charm, of eloquence, of comedy, so inexhaustible that it must have been startling to find oneself on the receiving end. There had been several objects of his affection before he met the twenty-year-old Maria Beadnell, but on none of them did he lavish the same degree of passion, nor indeed did he ever lavish as much again on anyone else. The year was 1830; he was eighteen, and still languishing in Doctors' Commons, only sporadically employed. We have no photograph of the young Maria Beadnell, but there is a charming watercolour of her in the unlikely guise of Dido, Queen of Carthage. In it she is depicted as possessing the huge, limpid, heavy-lidded, almost somnolent eyes that would later feature in so many Victorian depictions of women: deeply passive, unsmiling eyes, surmounting a neat, shapely nose and a tiny red mouth. It is entirely possible that such a woman would stir the loins of a slightly younger man: there is somehow the promise of deep sensual embrace, although the expression on the face itself is oddly inert, which is perhaps part of the charm. It's an amateur daub, and one should perhaps not read into it too closely, but whatever the precise nature of her appeal, Dickens was certainly enslaved by her.

Maria was no doubt confounded by the ardour of her boyish suitor: for his first forty years, Dickens looked absurdly young, and at eighteen (as we see from a charming watercolour of him by his aunt, Janet Ross) he looks almost girlish, big-eyed and bashful, but his passion was torrential. She tried to control the situation, following the time-honoured policy of blowing alternately hot and cold, in rapid succession. This had the entirely planned effect of whipping him up to even greater heights of desperation and desire, utterly at a loss to know how to please. He must have realized almost immediately that she was not offering the luminous celestial balm he had been looking for; she was a fairly average young woman, not an angel. But it was too late; he was hooked.

Then there was the question of the parents: George Beadnell was a banker and somewhat underwhelmed by the flashy, talkative, manically exuberant young man who was clearly not out of the top drawer; the Beadnells deeply doubted Dickens's suitability as a prospective husband for their precious little girl. Whether to relieve the situation or not, they sent her off to France. 'My existence was entirely uprooted, moreover, and my whole being blighted, by the Angel of my soul being sent to Paris to finish her education!' he wrote to Maria when she made contact with him some twenty years later, effortlessly slipping back into the language of adolescent infatuation. At the time, the inevitable crisis in their relationship came when he found out that Maria's best friend, Marianne Leigh, who had purportedly been liaising between them, had been imparting to Maria confidences never meant for her to hear, and he realized that he was being played with by the two girls. He wrote Maria an overwrought good-bye letter.

> Our meetings of late have been little more than so many displays of heartless indifference on the one hand, while on the other they have never failed to provide a fertile source of wretchedness and misery; and seeing, as I cannot fail to do, that I have engaged in a pursuit which has long since been worse than hopeless, and a further pursuit of which can only expose me to deserved ridicule, I have made up my mind to return the little present I received from you some time since (which I have always prized,

as I still do, beyond anything I ever possessed) and the other enclosed mementoes of our past correspondence which I am sure it must be gratifying to you to receive, as after our recent situations they are certainly better adapted for your custody than mine.

He develops a lightly sarcastic manner:

my feelings upon any subject, more especially upon this, must be a matter to you of very little moment; still I *have* feelings in common with other people – perhaps so far as they relate to you they have been as strong and as good as ever warmed the human heart – and I do feel that it is mean and contemptible of me to keep by me one gift of yours or to preserve one single line or word of remembrance or affection from you. I therefore return them, and I can only wish that I could as easily forget that I ever received them.

He ends: 'A wish for your happiness, though it comes from me may not be the worse for being sincere and heartfelt. Accept it as it is meant, and believe that nothing will ever afford me more real delight than to hear that you, the object of my first and last love, are happy.' The most striking thing about this letter is not how deeply felt it is (and there is no doubt that it is) but how conventional the expression is. It could have come from any frustrated young man of the period, or from the pages of any unremarkable contemporary epistolary novel. That is what Maria had done to him. Her conventionally capricious behaviour had forced him to play her game; he was humiliated and toyed with, but worse than that, he was diminished, less than himself. He would never allow that to happen again, with anyone.

But balm was to hand: he was working on a show. He had been writing, directing and acting in plays in his family circle ever since he started work (a little later he wrote a play for them called *O'Thello*, featuring his father in the role of The Great Unpaid), and during all these anguished months of amorous frustration, he had been directing a triple bill consisting of *Clari, the Maid of Milan*, *The Married Bachelor* and *Amateurs and Actors*. The company and cast were all friends, but there was nothing amateur about his work on the show. He was in supreme command, casting it, staging it, stage-managing it, starring in it, seeing to the music, arranging the set, checking the props. A couple of weeks after his passionate valedictory to Maria, he was writing to his chum Kolle, who was engaged to Maria's sister Anne, 'you are, or at any rate will be, what I can never be, that is, happy and contented', briskly adding that 'the corps dramatic are all anxiety. The scenery is all completing rapidly, the machinery is finished, the curtain hemmed, the orchestra complete and the manager grimy.' He was, in short, in his element, and in his letter, the moment he writes about the theatre, he is instantly, unmistakably, Charles Dickens. Lovelorn or not, he had no intention of hiding this particular light under a bushel: he had invited a large audience (including 'many judges'). It was a triumph. Maria and her family came, too, but she sulked. A month later, he sent her one final, final affirmation of his love, and she was coldly reproachful in return. It was finally over.

He was shaken by the affair, nonetheless. He had given her everything of himself. He had lowered his guard, bared his heart. And she had just toyed with him. 'It excluded every other idea from my mind for four years, at a time of life when four years are equal to four times four,' he wrote a quarter of a century later. That the experience of the relationship burned itself into his heart and mind is beyond question, but the contention that it excluded every other idea from his mind will not bear examination. On the contrary. Perhaps the pain was greater precisely because the whole affair dragged itself out over a time when Dickens was first beginning to feel his power in the world, and was exploding in every direction. At the time he met Maria, he was still a shorthand reporter plodding away at Doctors' Commons; by the time their relationship was over, in 1833, he was a star reporter, trembling on the brink of authorship.

The instant he joined *The Mirror of Parliament*, in 1832, the uncommon accuracy of transcription made possible by his phenomenal shorthand skills was admiringly recognized, and his self-confidence soared. At about the same time, he started writing for another new paper, the *True Sun*, and again, his skills were immediately hailed. But he quickly made his mark there in another way, too. When he had joined the staff, the *Sun* was already in trouble. The journalists were at war with the proprietor, and had called a strike. And Dickens, a twenty-year-old tyro reporter, was their chief negotiator. 'I well remember noticing at this dread time, standing on the staircase of the magnificent mansion we were lodged in,' wrote another young *Sun* contributor, John Forster, who had been invited to a meeting of the disaffected workforce, 'a young man of my own age whose keen animation of look would have arrested attention anywhere, and whose name, upon enquiry, I then for the first time heard.' 'Young Dickens', he discovered, had conducted the recalcitrant reporters' case 'triumphantly'.

It is worth briefly freezing the frame at this moment, because it changed both men's lives. Though it would be some years before they finally sat down at a table together, they sensed, at occasional accidental meetings over that time, that there was a profound sympathy between them; when they did sit down together, Forster immediately became Dickens's most intimate associate, which he remained for some decades, his advice sought and taken on matters personal, professional and artistic. Many of Dickens's books and much of his life would have been quite different without Forster's influence. And Forster, despite his ingrained cussedness a natural hero-worshipper, found the great task of his life. The vision of Dickens on the staircase during the *Sun* strike was for him a *coup de foudre*, of which the final and greatest outcrop was the biography, which, flawed and partial though it sometimes is, gave the world Charles Dickens the man as we know him.

Dickens, meanwhile, once the strike was (temporarily) resolved, plunged back into the life of a newsman, *c.*1833. It was a world without technology: neither telephones, telegrams, tape recorders, television, nor indeed trains. 'I pursued the calling of a reporter under circumstances of which subsequent generations can form no adequate conception,' he told a gathering of newsmen in the 1850s. 'There never was anybody connected with newspapers, who in the same space of time had so much express and post-chaise experience as I.' He was reporting on political life in Parliament, often in marathon sittings requiring relays of up to half a dozen reporters to cover them – 'I have borne the House of Commons like a man and have yielded to no weakness except slumber in the House of Lords' – and up and down the country on the hustings. He and his fellow reporter Thomas Beard were conveyed to these far-flung places in the bone-breaking, heart-stopping, life-threatening species of fast coach known as Tally-hos, Taglionis and Wonders: they leapt in and out of a variety of these vehicles, in a multitude of weather conditions, on their way to remote destinations across the British Isles, in order to record for posterity the deathless words of a class of human being for whom he increasingly found he had nothing but contempt. 'Night after night,' he wrote ventriloquially through the mouth of David Copperfield, 'I recorded predictions that never came to pass, professions that were never fulfilled, explanations that were only meant to mystify.' His allergy to Parliamentary democracy in action was quickly established, seeing it as a debased form of theatre: 'I have been behind the scenes to know the worth of political life.' He thought this disposition of his might be due to 'some imperfect development of my organ of veneration'. He had seen elections, he said, and never once been impelled, no matter which party won, 'to damage my hat by throwing it up in the air'. Perhaps, he concluded, he was 'of a cold and insensible temperament, amounting to iciness, in such matters'.

His travels, nevertheless, had a profound effect on him, giving him a detailed insight into the state of the nation, affording him hilarious encounters with innkeepers and fellow travellers and helping to form his political views, which he found, on examination, to be uncompromisingly radical. He was recruited, in 1835, to the *Morning Chronicle*, the great liberal newspaper of the day, under the inspiring editorship of the trenchant Scot, John Black, who had formed a shrewdly favourable opinion of Dickens's qualities. 'Dear old Black!' Dickens wrote of him, 'My first out-and-out appreciator.' As well as inculcating in him the principles of Reformism – these were the politically despairing days after the passage of the wretchedly inadequate Reform Bill of 1832 – Black, sensing Dickens's potential, relieved him of the obligation of filling the dog days of the recess with the book reviewing or theatre criticism or attendance at public meetings with which other reporters were burdened, and encouraged him to write about what interested him – which turned out, of course, to be pretty well everything, though with a marked preference for the London he had obsessively scrutinized since being so rudely de-rusticated there, some ten years earlier.

Thus appeared, in 1834, only a month after he had started work as a reporter for the *Chronicle*, the first piece under the heading of Street Sketches, signed with the sparkish byline of Boz. He had already put the name (borrowed from his youngest brother, Moses, whose nickname it was) to some sketches written for the *Monthly Magazine*, which had a year before published his very first literary effort, 'A Dinner at Poplar Walk'.

> I had taken with fear and trembling, to authorship. I wrote a little story in secret, entitled 'A Sunday out of Town', which I dropped stealthily one evening at twilight into a dark letter box, in a dark office, up a dark court in Fleet Street. It appeared in all the glory of print in the December 1833 issue of *The Monthly Magazine*, its name transmogrified to 'A Dinner at Poplar Walk', on which occasion – how well I remember it! – I walked down to Westminster Hall, and turned into it for half-an-hour, because my eyes were so dimmed with joy and pride, that they could not bear the street, and were not fit to be seen there.

This pleasant, if perhaps overlong, sketch features the first dog in Dickens (Dickens does love a dog), the first eating scene (the food, alas, not described), and a little in-joke (the central figure works at Somerset House, where both Dickens's father and disgraced grandfather Barrow had worked). It also appears to contain a mildly malicious portrait of a household that may bear some resemblance to that of the Beadnells, the in-laws that never were. Renamed 'Mr Minns and His Cousin', the piece re-appeared in book form in *Sketches by Boz*; but the pieces for the *Chronicle* speak in an altogether different voice, the immediately recognizable voice of Charles Dickens, playful, fiery, fantastical, witty, suddenly grave – verbal Hogarth, with more than a touch of Rowlandson. Piercing observation is joined to a rising and irrepressible hilarity; the mood is one of benevolence and affection for the foibles of the city, a tenderness towards ordinary life that could perhaps only have come from one who had once feared that he would be deprived of one. Even Parliament gets off the hook lightly. Everything is informed with the geniality and ease of the twenty-two-year-old writer rejoicing in his powers, communicating with apparently effortless conversational directness with his readers. Read as a collection, the enjoyment is immense, but the individual articles, as they came out, were as eagerly anticipated as letters from a delightful friend.

Their author was in understandably expansive mood. He rejoiced in the admiration of his peers, having earned the reputation, he playfully boasted, of being 'the best and most rapid reporter ever known, it being generally acknowledged that I could do anything in that way under any sort of circumstances, and often did. (I daresay I am at this present writing the best shorthand writer in the world.)' It had been done with exceptional hard work: he had gone at it with a determination 'to overcome all the difficulties which fairly lifted me up into that newspaper life, and floated me away over a hundred men's heads'. He had done it as if in preparation for his work as a creative writer: he had mastered the technical aspect of writing, strengthening his verbal muscle, so that when he started to use his imagination, he knew exactly how to express himself. And now he was beginning to be known by the general public, and to make decent money.

One of the first uses he put his money to was clothes. He favoured flashy waistcoats, jewellery on his fingers, a florid new hat and a rather handsome blue cloak with black velvet facings, which he threw over his shoulder *à l'Espagnol*. His theatricality was unfavourably animadverted on in some quarters; the phrase 'not quite a gentleman' was murmured in the clubs and the salons, as it would be for the rest of his life. But he wanted to celebrate his achievements – to celebrate himself. At the height of the session, working preposterous hours, he had been able to rake in up to an astonishing twenty-five guineas a week.

It was just as well that he was in funds, because in November 1834, John Dickens, for all his diligent work in the press gallery, had again lost touch with the facts of financial life, and found himself back in the sponging house. There he was visited by Charles. For Dickens, there was no heartbreak, as at the Marshalsea, no sense that the sun had set on his life. It was simply a question of how to clear up the mess: for all practical purposes, his father was now, already, his child. Dickens found out how much was owed, paid it off, located a new, cheaper flat for them (they had been living in genteel grandeur in Bentinck Street at the posher end of Marylebone), and rooms for himself and his brother Fred. It was not easily done – he had to borrow a little, and mortgaged his salary for two weeks – but it was done swiftly and effectively. 'We have much more cause for cheerfulness than despondency, after all,' he told his friend Beard, which might have been the motto for the first half of his career. There seems to have been no sentimentality about it, no reproaches; he just got on with it, as he had just got on with the rest of his life. He had taken them in hand, as he had taken his own life in hand. The disadvantage of being proved so effective was that he was now expected to provide the same service whenever the need arose, and not only for his feckless father but for all the rest of the family who, with the exception of Fanny, seem to have inherited the financially incompetent genes that nature had happily withheld from Dickens himself.

Meanwhile, his career as a writer took another step forward. In January of 1835, the *Morning Chronicle* launched an evening edition, under the editorship of the *Chronicle*'s music critic, George Hogarth, another Scot, who invited Dickens to contribute more of the Street Sketches to the new paper. Dickens proposed that they should be a series, which is what they became, twenty of them appearing over the following eight months, establishing him – or rather, Boz – ever more clearly in the public mind. The two men got on well, Dickens being particularly excited by Hogarth's close friendship with his hero, Walter Scott, who had died only three years before, in circumstances that always haunted Dickens: desperately writing himself to an early grave to repay his debts, a fate Dickens determined at all costs to avoid. Hogarth had been Scott's lawyer, helping him to recover from his financial crash, though he was not so successful in avoiding financial disaster for himself, suffering a total collapse of his affairs not once but twice. Once he moved out of the law and into journalism, he moved onto a more even keel. He invited Dickens to his house in semi-rural Fulham, and Charles soon became a familiar presence there, delighting in the company of Hogarth's three daughters, little suspecting that the girls – Georgina, aged six, Mary, fourteen, and Catherine, nineteen – would between them and in very different ways become absolutely central to his life.

He found himself strongly attracted to Catherine, who had Maria's large sleepy eyes, but was much less pert and altogether more straightforward in her response to him. Before long, she and Charles became engaged. There was no resistance whatever from Catherine's parents: Dickens was hard-working, and a coming man, with admirable prospects, well able to provide for a family. Indeed, so hard was he working, he barely had time for his courtship. Half a century later, Georgina recollected that, during that period, when she was a very young girl, Dickens had once burst through the drawing-room doors in a sailor outfit, performed a vigorous hornpipe, swiftly disappeared, then immediately afterwards come in through the front door in his normal street clothes. The story suggests a certain hectic quality to his wooing, although it might equally suggest a desperation to create a little excitement in the somewhat placid Hogarth domestic environment. No doubt to Dickens it was the most normal thing in the world to do: dressing up and disguising himself was as natural to him as breathing.

However much her father might approve of the dazzling young wordsmith, Kate was not best pleased to find out quite how much of his time Charles gave over to his work, and she let him know it. She had no sympathy whatsoever for his pleas of 'furteeg'. She was not mercurial or scornful, like Maria; instead she was prone to long sulks and being – as she spelled it in her letters – 'coss' with him. But Dickens was having none of it. He had been Maria's slave: he would, in the kindest, nicest possible, way, be Kate's master. 'If a feeling of you know not what – a capricious restlessness of you can't tell what, and a desire to tease, you don't know why, give rise to it – overcome it; it will never make you more amiable, I more fond, or either of us more happy.' Dickens was just four years older than Kate, but already he was writing to her as if he were her father. Kate wrote back asking him to 'love her once more' – and he replies briskly, if unromantically, 'I have never ceased to love you for one moment since I knew you; nor shall I.' When she persists, he uses the ultimate threat: if she doesn't like things the way they are, or him the way he is, 'I will not miss you lightly, but I shall need no second warning.' This masterful tone of his might have seemed quite sexy to Kate: there seems no doubt that he desired her. When he isn't disciplining her, his letters are filled with endearments: Dearest Katie, Dearest Love, Dearest Darling Pig, My Dearest Life, as often as not signed off with the lavish addition of 990,000,000,000,000,000,000,000,000 kisses.

It is impossible to believe that a young man of Dickens's intense vitality was not highly charged sexually. We know virtually nothing of his amorous activity outside of his fertile marriage and the liaison with Ellen Ternan during his final decade (and, in truth, we know very little about that), but he must, by now, at the age of twenty-three, have been in a sexually explosive state. Moreover, he wanted a family, to give to children of his own the things he felt he had lacked: stability, continuity, a sense of nurture. But whether he actually saw Catherine for herself, as she was, is doubtful. He was very turned on by her, and greatly enjoyed his involvement in the

Hogarth family – a much better, stabler model than his own – and their nice house in leafy Fulham. But had he worked out what he wanted from a woman, apart from hearth and home and abundant sex? Did he ever?

Alongside his marital aspirations, the rest of his life was whirling along, professionally and socially. He was now mixing with the young bloods of his day. In particular, he had become friendly with William Harrison Ainsworth, wildly successful author of the highwayman novel *Rookwood* and contributor to the politically provocative *Fraser's Magazine*. Ainsworth was some seven years Dickens's elder, and a brilliant and influential figure on the social scene, witty, elegant, tastefully dandyish. After scandalously leaving his wife and three children, he established a bachelor salon at his rooms at Kensal Lodge, Harrow Road, in North West London, which became the meeting-place of a wide circle of young bloods – Daniel Maclise, the brilliant young Irish painter with a fascination for the theatre, on the brink of becoming a very young Royal Academician; the novelist and political amateur Benjamin Disraeli (his dandyism a rival to Ainsworth's); the best-selling novelist and Member of Parliament, Edward Bulwer-Lytton; and, considerably the oldest of them all, the political satirist, cartoonist and wild man, George Cruikshank. This was Dickens's first exposure to his leading contemporaries. His presence there was something of a coup for Ainsworth as a social impresario. Everyone wanted to meet Boz. He barely had his foot on the bottom rung of the literary ladder, but Ainsworth's brilliant guests welcomed him, exhilarated by his energy and entertained by his mimicry. Apart from Disraeli, with whom he was ill at ease both personally and politically, these men all became his friends and collaborators; and it was here that he met his first publisher.

Being Dickens's publisher, as many people were to discover over the years, was not a restful experience, but the twenty-six-year-old John Macrone, about to reissue Ainsworth's best-seller *Rookwood*, foresaw no complications when he suggested to Boz that his Sketches might make a nice book, and that perhaps his friend Mr Cruikshank sitting over there on the other side of the table might be just the man to provide some illustrations for it; perhaps, too, Dickens might like to consider writing a three-volume novel? Well, of course he might, and in short order contracts were signed, one assigning to Macrone the copyright in *Sketches by Boz*, which appeared soon after, and swept all before it, and the other commissioning a novel, *Gabriel Vardon, the Locksmith of London*, which took a very long time indeed to see the light of day, and pleased almost no one when it finally did.

Things were now happening for Dickens with extraordinary rapidity. More sketches, under a different pseudonym (Tibbs), were appearing weekly in *Bell's Life in London*; he continued reporting up and down the country for the *Morning Chronicle*; and he was working on the libretto for an operetta. He had been approached by his sister Fanny Dickens's Royal Academy of Music contemporary John Hullah, who had an idea for a piece set in Venice called *The Gondoliers*. Delighted though he was at the prospect of writing something for the theatre, Dickens said he couldn't write about gondoliers; he had to write about real people whom he knew and understood, and suggested instead an everyday story of country folk, their love affairs and comic misunderstandings. To this Hullah meekly agreed – an early example of the irresistible force of Dickens's personality in action – and went away to write the music, while Dickens thrashed out the book and lyrics.

He had temporarily moved to Fulham to be nearer to Catherine, who was still pouting a great deal about the lack of time he spent with her, and receiving more callous reproofs from him.

> If the representations I have so often made to you, about my
> working as a duty, and not as a pleasure, be not sufficient to keep
> you in the good humour which you, of all people in the world
> should preserve – why, then, my dear, you must be out of
> temper, and there is no help for it.

There is something inexpressibly depressing about Dickens's
relations with the women he loved – a lack of spontaneity, of
parity, of freedom. He's always somehow being *trapped* by
them into these terrible patterns of behaviour. His exchanges
with Catherine are of a very low grade; it's paltry, piffling stuff.
From time to time fun was had – they loved going to the theatre together, and he was always able to make her laugh. But,
forgivably, she simply didn't understand the sheer amount of
work involved in keeping the Boz bubble going: 'Is it my fault
I cannot get out tonight?' he cried. 'I must work at the opera.'
Such were the communications between them, before they
were married. No great passion, no torrential exchange of
thoughts, no intimations of the sublime, as his ardent nature
would seem to have demanded. No doubt that was the last
thing he wanted; he had quite enough of that for two of them,
and he could communicate with his male friends on that
level. What he needed was stability, comfort, continuity. At
least, that is what he thought he wanted.

Meanwhile, he received a visit that had momentous consequences. As often with Dickens, the encounter had a fated
flavour to it, a sense of the inexorable march of destiny. His
visitor was William Hall, one of the partners in Chapman and
Hall, a newly established publishing firm. When Dickens
opened the door of his new flat at Furnival's Inn in Holborn,
he gasped, because Hall, in his former incarnation as a book-
seller, had sold Dickens the copy of the *Monthly Magazine* in
which his very first story had appeared. Hall had come to
Dickens with a modest proposal: his firm had just had a big

success with their first publication, *A Christmas Squib*, by the noted illustrator Robert Seymour. Seymour had had an idea for a new book based on his pictures of the absurd exploits of some Cockney would-be sportsmen, they needed someone to provide the copy for the pictures, would he be interested? With extraordinary clarity of purpose, Dickens saw an opportunity for something much more ambitious: a story in monthly episodes based on the free-wheeling activities of an eclectic, not to say eccentric, group of friends whose central figure was to be a genial middle-aged man whom Dickens decided should be named Pickwick, borrowing the name of a well-known coach operator just outside Bath that he must have frequently passed on his journalistic hikes around the country. Dickens would not provide copy for the illustrator: he would deliver his copy, and the illustrator would take his cue from that.

Chapman and Hall were swept away by the boldness of Dickens's plans, and made it clear to Seymour that he must fall in with the new thinking. Dickens immediately dashed off two instalments – 'Pickwick is at length begun in all his might and glory!' – and was full of courteous but firm suggestions as to how Seymour might go about his task; even Edward Chapman weighed in with strict notes to the illustrator on how to portray Pickwick, on the basis of the physical appearance of someone he once knew, 'a fat old beau who, in spite of the ladies' protests, would wear drab tights and black gaiters'. Seymour, utterly crushed, went away and did his work, but after a particularly trying night wrestling with some recalcitrant etching plates for the third episode, he blew his brains out.

Neither Dickens nor Chapman nor Hall seemed unduly fazed by this turn of events; they hired another designer, who suspended work on his entry for the Royal Academy, but his etching skills were inadequate, so they sacked him (just after the entry date for the Academy competition had passed); they briefly glanced at the portfolio of a young giant of an aspiring illustrator called William Makepeace Thackeray, and then they struck gold with Hablôt Knight Browne, who, under the pseudonym of Phiz, created some of the most memorable of all visual realizations of Dickens's characters. Perhaps the most extraordinary aspect of this sequence of events is that, despite the splendid and expensive adverts in *The Times* and the *Athenaeum*, the first few episodes of *The Posthumous Papers of the Pickwick Club* were far from successful and the publishers were reduced to halving the print run, but they kept faith. Their young author's confidence carried all before it, and with the arrival in the fourth episode of the Cockney genius Sam Weller, which also happened to be Phiz's first as illustrator, it took off in the words of a contemporary reviewer, 'like a Skyrocket'. And suddenly everybody was reading it. As Forster exuberantly put it: 'Judges on the bench and boys in the street, gravity and folly, the young and the old, those who were entering life and those who were quitting it, alike found it irresistible.' It was that publisher's dream, a book that had in it something for everyone.

For any young writer to have created in his first novel such a complete world, a world teeming with individuals who seem always to have existed, who seem to have come out of the very heart of England, at once real and archetypal, bowling through the contemporary landscape on a journey that might have started at the beginning of time, each strutting his stuff like so many brilliant turns on the stage of life, while blending perfectly into the ensemble, is astonishing enough; that that writer was the same Charles Dickens who only ten years before had thought that his life was over, that he was doomed to a life of humiliation and ordinariness, is simply astounding. The quality that beams out of the book with such golden force is one of optimism and benevolence. That it should do so is a triumph of Dickens's spirit over his circumstances: but it had not been easily won, and in time to come he would struggle to maintain the faith that he so ineffably expresses in the book's final pages:

> And in the midst of all this, stood Mr Pickwick, his countenance lighted up with smiles, which the heart of no man, woman, or child, could resist: himself the happiest of the group: shaking hands, over and over again, with the same people, and when his own hands were not so employed, rubbing them with pleasure: turning round in a different direction at every fresh expression of gratification or curiosity, and inspiring everybody with his looks of gladness and delight.
>
> Breakfast is announced. Mr Pickwick leads the old lady (who has been very eloquent on the subject of Lady Tollimglower), to the top of a long table; Wardle takes the bottom; the friends arrange themselves on either side; Sam takes his station behind his master's chair; the laughter and talking cease; Mr Pickwick, having said grace, pauses for an instant, and looks round him. As he does so, the tears roll down his cheeks, in the fullness of his joy.
>
> Let us leave our old friend in one of those moments of unmixed happiness, of which, if we seek them, there are ever some, to cheer our transitory existence here. There are dark shadows on the earth, but its lights are stronger in the contrast. Some men, like bats or owls, have better eyes for the darkness than for the light. We, who have no such optical powers, are better pleased to take our last parting look at the visionary companions of many solitary hours, when the brief sunshine of the world is blazing full upon them.

In between episodes two and three of *Pickwick*, Dickens got married. He had been emboldened to do so by the success of the recently published *Sketches by Boz*, a success he had done everything in his power to promote, sending copies to anyone of note whom he had encountered along his way – Lord Stanley, for instance, who had once dictated to him an epically long speech when he was still reporting in the gallery of the House of Commons, and Thomas Talfourd, the distinguished barrister, crusading MP and playwright, whom he had met at Ainsworth's. The book had been greeted with a powerful review in the *Chronicle* (by his father-in-law-to-be, as it happens), and another in the *Morning Post*; it was admired not only for its view of the city, but for the range of the material and the variety of forms: stories, fantastical impressions, hard-core reporting. A voice – although an exuberantly polyphonic one – had been established. More startlingly, there was an authority, a perspective of passionate radicalism and a compassion extraordinary in such a young man: 'such sights will make your heart ache,' he wrote of what he had seen in the slums at St Giles's, 'always supposing that you are not a philosopher or a political economist'.

With the *Sketches* and now *Pickwick*, Boz, whose identity was still known only to his inner circle, was the toast of the town; speculation was rife as to who he might be. 'We do not know the author,' said a sharp anonymous review of *Sketches* in the *Metropolitan Magazine*, 'but we should apprehend that he has, from the peculiar turn of his genius, been already a successful dramatist; if he has not, we can safely opine that he may be if he will.' The review strongly recommends 'this facetious work to the Americans ... as it is a perfect picture of the morals, manners, habits of a great portion of English society ... it would be needless for us to particularise any one of these admirable sketches, very many of which would form an admirable groundwork for light comedies and farces.'

He made another pseudonymous appearance early in 1836, this time in the guise of Timothy Sparks, in a pamphlet entitled 'Sunday Under Three Heads', in which he articulated his championship of people's right to pleasure. There was a move afoot in Parliament to ban games on Sundays: Dickens came forth blazingly against it.

The wise and beneficent Creator who places men upon earth, requires that they shall perform the duties of that station of life to which they are called, and he can never intend that the more a man strives to discharge those duties, the more he shall be debarred from happiness and enjoyment. Let those who have six days in the week for all the world's pleasures, appropriate the seventh to fasting and to gloom, either for their own sins or for those of other people, if they like to bewail them; but let those who employ their six days in a worthier manner, devote their seventh to a different purpose. Let divines set the example of true morality: preach it to their flocks in the morning, and dismiss them to enjoy true rest in the afternoon; and let them select for their text, and let Sunday legislators take for their motto, the words that fell from the lips of that Master whose precepts they misconstrue, and whose lessons they pervert – 'The Sabbath was made for man, and not man for the Sabbath.'

Dickens's lack of enthusiasm for organized religion is bluntly expressed.

Look into your churches – diminished congregations and scanty attendance. People have grown sullen and obstinate, and are becoming disgusted with the faith which condemns them to such a day as this, once in every seven. And as you cannot make people religious by Act of Parliament, or force them to church by constables, they display their feeling by staying away. Turn into the streets [on a Sunday] and mark the rigid gloom that reigns over everything around ... all is as melancholy and quiet as if a pestilence had fallen upon the city ...

Dickens was increasingly becoming the Voice of the People.

Sales for *Sketches by Boz* continued brisk, and at last confident that he could support and maintain a family, he formally asked George Hogarth for Catherine's hand and was warmly accepted; no Beadnell-like hesitations here. He was writing round the clock to complete the 12,000 words per instalment for *Pickwick*, plus doing other journalistic bits and pieces, which, to Catherine's continuing dismay, kept him writing till two in the morning. By getting ahead of himself, he had managed to clear the decks for a week's honeymoon, and lived only for the great day. 'Here's another day off the fortnight. Hurrah!' he wrote to Kate.

In the event, the wedding, which took place just before Bozmania had fully got under way, was a subdued affair – surprisingly so, given the general level of excitement in his life at the time, and that nobody loved a party more than Charles Dickens, or more eagerly welcomed an opportunity to dress up. But the wedding, which took place on a Saturday morning at St Luke's Church in Chelsea, the biggest – and tallest – parish church in London, with a nave that was then higher than that of any other London church apart from St Paul's, was strikingly plain: only his family and Catherine's were present (whether this was a first meeting for the two families is unclear). His friend and fellow reporter Thomas Beard was his best man; he had asked John Macrone, the publisher of *Sketches by Boz*, to do the job, but Macrone was married, which disqualified him; he came to the service nonetheless. A significant absentee was Elizabeth Dickens's book-loving brother, Thomas, of whom Dickens was inordinately fond. He had written to this favourite uncle apologizing for not inviting him: it would be impossible, Dickens said, for him to do as a married man what he had been unable to do as a single one, that is, enter a house from which his father was banned. Obviously some drama, now submerged, lay behind this apology: John Dickens was no doubt held responsible for all the disasters and humiliations that had fallen on the family's head. Perhaps it was complications of this sort that encouraged Dickens to dispatch the nuptial business as rapidly as possible. A small shadow, a certain complexity, seems to have fallen over what was supposed to be a day of joyous celebration. After the ceremony, they all repaired to the Hogarths' just up the road, where, according to Fanny's husband Henry, 'a few common, pleasant things were said' at the wedding breakfast, 'healths were drunk with a very few words' – how unDickensian it all is! – 'and all seemed happy, not least Dickens and his young girlish wife'. The carriage took them to Chalk, in Kent, where their married life began, and then, a week later, they took up residence in Dickens's rooms in Furnival's Inn, which he had thoughtfully and thoroughly equipped for his new circumstances.

With them in the flat from the beginning was Catherine's now sixteen-year-old sister Mary, who remained with them for a month after their return from Chalk. This is a little odd. Dickens's 1950s biographer Edgar Johnson was of the opinion that the presence of Mary in their lives right at the very beginning got the marriage off to the worst possible start: the young couple never had time to get to know each other alone. G. K. Chesterton rather more forthrightly suggested that Dickens simply married the wrong sister. Mary adored her clever brother-in-law and was excited by his growing renown ('his literary career gets more and more prosperous every day and he is courted and flattered on every side by the great folks of this great City – his time is so completely taken up that it is quite a favour for the Literary Gentlemen to get him to write for them'). Dickens was equally enchanted by her.

For all her starry-eyed admiration of her new brother-in-law, Mary was scarcely exaggerating the ever-increasing demands on his time; most of his day must have been spent at his desk toiling away. In July he had a read-through of *The Village Coquettes*, the operetta he had written with Hullah; meanwhile he was busy cultivating outlets for future novels, accepting commissions that there was little chance of his having the time to write; he even accepted a commission for a play, *The Strange Gentleman*, a little two-act farce adapted from one of the Boz sketches, which he knocked up more or less overnight. It opened to tepid notices; by the savage standards of the time, though, they were not unkind.

More impressively, he was approached by Richard Bentley to write not one but two novels. Bentley was the successful publisher of Harrison Ainsworth's *Rookwood* and Edward Lytton's *The Last Days of Pompeii*, both runaway bestsellers; after protracted negotiations, he and Dickens struck a deal. In addition, Dickens was contracted as editor of a new magazine, *Bentley's Miscellany*. This was something he was very excited by. He was determined to acquire greater control over his work, and being the editor of a magazine seemed like a good way to do so. Indeed, it would have been, had he had absolute authority over one; but this was not Bentley's intention at all, as Dickens very soon discovered. The young author had no experience whatever as an editor, and, to no one's surprise but Dickens's, Bentley meddled. This was not a good thing to do with Charles Dickens, even at the age of twenty-four; trouble was in the air from early on. As for the contract for the novels, that too proved problematic. One word lay at the heart of the increasingly bitter dissension between Dickens and Bentley: copyright. In the 1830s, publishers owned the copyright in the books on their lists. Writers had no continuing reward from their own work: once they had been paid, that was it. This was, naturally, enshrined in the contract Dickens signed with Bentley, but the more he thought about it, the more it enraged him. In November 1836, however, everything seemed to be going splendidly, and he cheerfully handed in his notice on the *Chronicle*. It was churlishly, not to say sourly, received. Dickens responded tartly: 'Depend upon it, Sir, if you would stimulate those about you to any exertions beyond their ordinary routine of duty … this is not the way to do it.'

The old year ended joyfully, with the production of *The Village Coquettes*, followed by *The Strange Gentleman* as an after-piece. The reviews were poor for the operetta – 'all … blow their little trumpets against unhappy me, most lustily' – but worse for the tenor, who was also the manager. In the packed theatre itself, though, they screamed and screamed for Boz on the night. He briefly trotted on and bowed and then trotted off again; he was excoriated for this, too ('a disgusting new practice'). He couldn't have cared less, and whenever he could get to the theatre during the short run, he was to be found backstage, adoring just being part of it all. Before long, Dickens was somewhat embarrassed by the operetta's naivety: like virtually everything Dickens wrote for the stage, it suffered from his abject adoration of the theatre of his day, which he dutifully reproduced. It would be hard to find a sentence in any essay, novel, story or letter of Dickens's that does not have some authentic flavour, but you will search the plays in vain for a single Dickensian turn of phrase. He was, surprisingly, the most uninspired of dramatists, though the most theatrically obsessed of men. Every episode of *Pickwick* introduced new editions of old stage characters; the spirit of Charles Mathews was everywhere in its pages. Dickens had put all of his love of the theatre, all of his 'strong perception of character and oddity', all of his pleasure in the stage devices of coincidence and contrivance, into it. Before long, other people would respond to the inherent theatrical potential in his fiction and start restoring them to the stage to which, in an important sense, they belonged.

FIVE

The Peregrinations of Pickwick

The New Year began dramatically with the birth, nine months almost to the minute after the wedding, of Charles Dickens's son and heir, Charles Culliford Boz, dutifully named after an ancestor, triumphantly named after a Phenomenon. The precise date of birth was 6 January, Twelfth Night (or rather, to be pedantic, Twelfth Day), a date that would forever thereafter be sacred to Dickens. But the birth was not without its complications: the confinement had been far from easy, and Catherine was unable to breastfeed the child. 'Poor Kate! It has been a dreadful trial for her,' wrote Mary Hogarth to her cousin. 'Every time she sees her baby she has a fit of crying and keeps saying that he will not love her now that she is not able to nurse him.' Catherine, it seems, was in the grip of post-natal depression. 'I think time will be the only effectual cure for her,' continued Mary, wisely, for so it proved, and would prove after each of her many subsequent confinements. 'Could she but forget this, she has everything in the world to make her comfortable and happy.' Dickens, says Mary, 'is kindness itself to her and is constantly studying her comfort in every thing'; both her mother and Charles's were in bustling attendance.

By the end of the month, he was responsible for producing another new child: an orphan, this time. The first episode of *Oliver Twist* (which also had a very difficult birth, one with which he had to cope all on his own) appeared in *Bentley's Miscellany*: Dickens had decided that the article the contract committed him to write every month should be a short serial, then he realized that it should be a novel. He was still writing, for an ever-expanding readership, the monthly instalments of *Pickwick Papers*. That was 12,000 words a month; *Twist* meant another 12,000. A nightmarishly demanding form for most writers, the novel in monthly instalments suited the journalist in him: the rush of adrenalin, the need to focus the mind with absolute clarity, the sense of sending out a dispatch to unknown but eagerly awaiting readers, provided almost ideal conditions for his creativity. There were, too, occasional pieces to be penned for the newspapers, and *en passant* he managed to toss off a quick farce with songs for the St James's Theatre called *Is She His Wife?*, which is really quite seriously silly. Nonetheless it took some thinking about; even the process of sending the pen across the page was time-consuming. But in the case of the novels – two of the most famous novels ever written, their every sentence pored over and analysed by scholars from that day to this – he was functioning at the highest level of imagination and invention of which the human brain is capable. For one mind to have created the radically different worlds of *Pickwick* and *Twist* within it at the same time is a staggering and indeed barely comprehensible phenomenon. Add to it that he was also editing a magazine, a demanding job he had never done before – correcting, re-shaping, advising, consenting – while at the same time helping to look after a new-born baby and an unhappy, perhaps depressed, wife, and that he was just twenty-five years old – well, one might say that he earned the month's holiday he now took. It was a working holiday, needless to say, but at least they were out of town.

When they came back from holiday, they moved into a new house, No. 48 Doughty Street, just off Mecklenburgh Square. It represented a very large step up the social ladder from his digs in Furnival's Inn. There were gates at either end of the street and a uniformed porter on duty. It was, as it happens, less than ten minutes' walk from the office of the solicitor Charles Molloy, where, a semi-educated lad, he had gone to work straight out of school just ten years before. The new house had twelve rooms, on three floors with a basement; Dickens's study was at the back of the house, looking into the garden. But all the action was in the front room next to it: here the family – Dickens's wife Kate, her sister Mary, little Charley, along with Dickens's younger brother Fred – would gather, surrounded by friends and mothers and brothers and sisters-in-law and brothers-in-law; his sister Fanny and her rather intense husband Henry, both musicians, would come round and sing and play. And as often as not, Dickens himself, drawn by the lively sounds, would come through and bring his writing with him, encouraging them to carry on with their chat and their games, sometimes breaking off from his work – as Mozart and Puccini were wont to do – to share with them what he was working on, reading out loud anything he thought particularly funny or moving. Dickens adored parties, and he and Kate threw a number of notably ebullient ones here; he sang comic songs, accompanying himself at the little upright piano, and hurling himself like a madman into dancing – a thing almost impossible to imagine in the modest confines of that little front room, but a well-attested fact.

Just a month after they all moved in, young Mary went to spend the day with her mother in Brompton; when she came back, she, Catherine and Charles went to the St James's Theatre to see *Is She His Wife?* They had a delightfully jolly time, as Dickens always did when Mary was around, and they went home. Catherine retired to bed, and Dickens and Mary chatted until one o'clock. She then went to her bedroom. The moment she entered the room, she uttered a sharp cry. She was all of a sudden very ill. Doctors were sent for; every remedy applied. Dickens held her throughout, comforting her, waiting for the fever to break. And then, without warning, after many hours, suddenly, but calmly, she was dead. Dickens was shattered; when he realized what had happened, he slipped a ring off her finger, and wore it for the rest of his life.

At first, the letters he wrote under the shock of the event were controlled: 'She had accompanied us to the theatre the night before apparently in the best health; was taken ill in the night, and lies here a corpse,' he wrote to Harrison Ainsworth. 'She has been our constant companion since our marriage; the grace and life of our home. Judge how deeply we feel this fearfully sudden deprivation.' To Mary's grandfather, he wrote:

> You cannot conceive the misery in which this dreadful event has plunged us. Since our marriage she has been the peace and life of our home – the admired of all for her beauty and excellence – I could have better supplied a much nearer relation or an older friend, for she has been to us what we can never replace, and has left a blank which no one who ever knew her can have the faintest hope of seeing supplied.

He was deeply fond of the girl, and he was understandably shocked by her sudden death. But there is something intemperate, disproportionate, in his reaction to her death. His suggestion that he would rather have sacrificed someone else in his immediate circle – who, precisely? – is alarming, and the conviction that she was the peace and the life of their home reflects most unhappily on Catherine. His words are the words of a bereaved parent; but he felt no such emotions about his own children when they died. 'Thank God she died in my arms,' he wrote to Thomas Beard, on black-edged mourning paper, 'and that the very last words she whispered were of me ... I solemnly believe that so perfect a creature never breathed. I knew her inmost heart, and her real worth and value. She had not a fault.'

Mary, for Dickens, was the angel he had so long sought for. And now she was gone. He composed her epitaph:

YOUNG, BEAUTIFUL, AND GOOD
GOD IN HIS MERCY
NUMBERED HER AMONG HIS ANGELS
AT THE EARLY AGE OF
SEVENTEEN

He was, remember, just twenty-five. Mary had, of course, been absolutely and unnegotiably unavailable to him as wife or lover, but she was a perfect supplement to the imperfect relationship he had settled for; she made his existence possible. When she died it was as if her death had happened to him personally; as if something terrible had been done to him. He had, he felt, been unimaginably blessed by the presence in his life of this paragon, this faultless creature, this shining antidote to a bad, faithless, unreliable world – and now, for no reason, she had been snatched away from him. It was a blow from which he never entirely recovered.

The extent of his shock can be gauged by the fact that, for the first and only time in his life, he stopped working. He and Kate withdrew to a little farm at the North End of Hampstead Heath for a fortnight; no new numbers of either *Pickwick* or *Oliver Twist* appeared. Rumours abounded as to why *Pickwick* had been suspended: the author was an eighteen-year-old who had run out of material; or had been in prison for years; or was a committee that had broken up. In attempting to console her mother, who, Dickens said, had been 'insensible' with grief, Catherine seems to have rallied herself, but at Collins's Farm, she broke down completely; shortly after she lost the child she was carrying. The air was heavy with hysterical mourning. Mary ceased to be a real young woman and became the abstract of all virtues: of her relationship with her sister, which as far as we know was perfectly ordinary, Dickens wrote that 'not one cross word or angry look on either side even as children rests in judgement against her ...' It is a commonplace that this fetishization of the departed pervades a great deal of his work; when he resumed work on *Oliver Twist*, he found that he couldn't, as he had planned, kill off Rose Maylie, the character fashioned after Mary: 'so mild and gentle; so pure and beautiful; that earth seemed not her element, nor its rough creatures, her fit companions'. Rose was duly spared. Mary is to be found in novel after novel of Dickens's. She had died at exactly the age at which for him a woman was at her most perfect: she never grew fat, dull, tired, tedious. To his inexpressible joy, he was sent a lock of her hair by Mrs Hogarth; that, too, he kept by him always. She fixed for ever for him the ideal of what a woman should be – that is, a girl. It is hard to avoid a sense of arrested development in Dickens. To survive inside, he had had to keep alive in a secret place the twelve-year-old boy that he had been; and Mary was that twelve-year-old boy's salvation.

It was while Charles and Catherine were staying in Hampstead, trying to come to terms with what had happened, that John Forster, whom Dickens had first met at Ainsworth's on Christmas Day of 1836, finally spent some time with him over a meal. They both came away from that dinner feeling as if they had known each other all their lives. Forster, Dickens's exact contemporary, was from Newcastle-on-Tyne; his father had been a cattle-dealer and butcher. He went up to Cambridge, but transferred to London University. The plan was for him to become a lawyer; in the fullness of time he did, but his true bent was for literature, and he became a critic. A big, thickset man, he was, even as a young man, pompous, blunt and assertive, something of an intellectual bully, in fact; in literary circles, his insensitivity was legendary. The reverse side of this coin was his acute awareness of artistic excellence, and his reverence for it in others, which no doubt explains the strong friendships he formed with some of the most interesting and difficult men of his time: Carlyle, Landor, Tennyson, Lamb. He was a prolific writer, but he never attempted fiction or poetry; as a biographer, he was both acute and adoring. Dickens instantly took to him, forming with him one of those intense nineteenth-century male friendships which, though not remotely sexual, achieve intense tenderness; despite being constantly threatened by jealousy and temperament, it endured solidly till Dickens's death. But in May of 1837, and for a long time afterwards, they could scarcely get enough of each other.

Shortly after that dinner – a matter of weeks – Dickens was writing to Forster: 'I look back with unmingled pleasure to every link which each ensuing week has added to the chain of our attachment. It shall go hard, I hope, ere anything but death impairs the toughness of a bond now so firmly riveted.' Forster, for his part, was overwhelmed by his handsome new friend's charisma: he found his face to be uncommonly compelling, 'the eyes wonderfully beaming with intellect and running over with humour and cheerfulness'. But there was something beyond mere animation: 'the quickness, keenness, practical power, the eager, restless, energetic outlook on each several feature, that seemed to tell so little of a student or writer of books and so much of a man of action and business in the world. Light and motion flashed from every part of it.' Dickens cemented his friendship with Forster. He wanted him by him at all times. After a hard morning of writing and editing, he needed the relief of physical exercise, walking, or, even better, riding, ideally all over Hampstead Heath with his best friend and then a good supper and a few flagons of wine at Jack Straw's Castle. The summons would arrive; how could Forster refuse? 'Is it possible that you can't, oughtn't, shouldn't, mustn't, *won't*, be tempted, this gorgeous day!' or 'I start precisely – precisely, mind – at half-past one. Come, come, *come*, and walk in the green lanes. You will work the better for it all week. COME! I shall expect you.' Or 'where shall it be? *Oh where?* – Hampstead? Greenwich? Windsor? WHERE??????' While the day is bright, not when it has dwindled away to nothing! For who can be of any use whatsomdever such a day as this, excepting out of doors?' Or it would just be: 'A hard trot of three hours?' and then, without waiting for a reply: 'So engage the osses.'

Many people were struck by what Forster calls Dickens's 'practical power': his appearance of being a man of action. Jane Carlyle, always, like her husband the great philosopher Thomas, pitiless in judgement, said of his face: 'It was as if it was made of steel.' Carlyle himself wrote to her, rather more comprehensively: 'He is a fine little fellow – Boz, I think,' noting the 'clear, blue, intelligent eyes that he arches amazingly, large, protrusive, rather loose mouth, a face of the most extreme *mobility*, which he shuttles about – eyebrows, eyes, mouth and all – in a very singular manner while speaking. Surmount them with a loose coil of common coloured hair, and set it on a small compact figure very small and dressed à la d'Orsay [a noted dandy of the time, whom Dickens knew and indeed imitated] rather than well – this is Pickwick. For the rest, a quite-shrewd-looking little fellow, who seems to guess pretty well what he is and what others are.' This was not the mask polite society expected: 'What a face to meet in a drawing room!' said Leigh Hunt: 'It has the life and soul in it of fifty human beings!'

Forster's arrival so close to Dickens's heart was not a cause for rejoicing among the rest of his circle, the Ainsworths and the Cruikshanks. They did not take at all well to his brusqueness, his discourtesy, his assertiveness. Quirky, combative, aggressive, he made a point of correcting everyone (even quarrelling with William Macready, the greatest actor of his day, on points of dramatic interpretation). Richard Bentley, who had invited him to a party at Dickens's behest, found that he had insulted many of his guests. But Dickens had a strong instinct that the very faults that sometimes made Forster a social liability could be of great use to him in the sphere of business: his forcefulness, doggedness, the thickness of his skin, to say nothing of his knowledge of the law, made him a very useful negotiator, and Dickens increasingly asked him to take on the role of his unofficial business manager; as far as we know he was never paid for these services. And Dickens made use of them, almost immediately, in his battles with publishers. He currently had three: Macrone for *Sketches by Boz*, Bentley for *Oliver Twist*, and Chapman and Hall for *Pickwick*; each of them at one time or another had to be put in their place. Macrone was simply and rather brutally bought off; Chapman and Hall were behaving impeccably for the time being, throwing a party to celebrate the anniversary of the first number of *Pickwick*, giving Dickens an *ex gratia* payment of £500 and striking a dozen apostle spoons with characters from the novel in place of the saints; but Bentley, with his oppressive contract, had to be punished. And Forster was the man to do it.

The truth is that, despite his unparalleled success – and there had been nothing like it, since, after the publication of *Childe Harold*, Bryon had woken up one morning to find himself famous – Dickens was by no means well-off. When Mary Hogarth died, he had paid for the funeral, and he needed to borrow money to do so. His publishers, by contrast, were becoming very rich on his back, and this disparity deeply rankled with him: it was an injustice and a humiliation, and he had had enough of both in his life. Forster acted brilliantly and cannily for Dickens. But his contribution did not end there. He had considerable critical heft in his own right. He was, after all, the literary editor of *The Examiner*, one of the most valuable and influential of the bewildering plethora of magazines of the period, and Dickens invited him, to an altogether surprising degree, to give his opinion on work in progress; what is more, he often took it. Dickens was notably lacking in preciousness about his work, but no one had a greater influence on it – often for better, occasionally for worse – than John Forster, who was the first reader of everything he wrote from now on, advising and arbitrating; in time he even did Dickens's proof-reading for him, making small changes as he saw fit, almost without exception endorsed by Dickens. And Forster introduced him to his own friends, who, as we have seen, were a formidable bunch.

For Dickens, the prize of all these introductions was not a painter, nor a philosopher, it was Macready, the great tragedian, in the mid-1830s at the very height of his powers as a performer, and widely acknowledged as the man who had restored dignity to the British stage. Dickens had seen everything he had done in the last decade and idolized him, making a determined and ultimately successful effort to bind the actor to him with hoops of steel, at first somewhat to the alarm of the famously formal and reserved Macready. Long after abandoning his dreams of becoming an actor, Dickens remained slavishly devoted to the theatre in all its forms, even putting the somewhat spurious *Memoirs of Grimaldi* into shape, and providing a loving introduction to them out of nostalgia for the sublime clown whom he had twice seen as a little boy; to his amazement, the book proved a bestseller (not that he saw any of the profit from that, either). The fascination with the stage was not all one way: the stage was very interested in Dickens, too. A mere six months after the first number of *Pickwick* appeared, the first pirate adaptation was up and running under the title of *The Peregrinations of Pickwick*; more followed. William Moncrieff's *Sam Weller*, cashing in on the accession of young Princess Victoria to the throne, featured a loyal chorus, during the singing of which a procession of 'Heralds, Beefeaters, Guards etc' are seen passing through Temple Bar to acclaim her. Dickens despaired at the violence done to his work before he had even finished it; but his affection for the theatre stopped him from preventing his friends the actors from trying to earn a decent crust at his expense; in the absence of copyright laws, it was virtually impossible to stop them, anyway. *The Pickwick Papers* had come to a conclusion, and *Oliver Twist* was in its sensational stride, exposing the criminal underbelly of London which he had studied so closely in his endless wanderings in the city. *Twist* was immediately, and wretchedly, adapted to the stage, too. Within the pages of the novel, he had written, more or less *en passant*, an artistic manifesto that frankly acknowledged his dues to the theatre: 'It is the custom on the stage, in all good murderous melodramas, to present the tragic and the comic scenes, in as regular alternation, as the layers of red and white in a side of streaky, well-cured bacon.' The streaky bacon method was to serve Dickens exceptionally well, right to the end. The readers of *Twist* were much more conscious of the tragic scenes, which presented almost unacceptably horrifying images of contemporary life. They were particularly shocking as the next characters to come from the pen of the dashing young author who had just enchanted the world with the great comedians that comprise the cast of *The Pickwick Papers*; his sudden descent into the underworld seemed like a betrayal of his affirmation in the closing pages of *Pickwick* already quoted:

> There are dark shadows on the earth, but its lights are stronger in the contrast. Some men, like bats or owls, have better eyes for the darkness than for the light. We, who have no such optical powers, are better pleased to take our last parting look at the visionary companions of many solitary hours, when the brief sunshine of the world is blazing full upon them.

Night came very suddenly. Dickens's readers needed to fasten their safety belts: it proved to be a bumpy trip. He was intent on deromanticizing the criminal world of which he had such vivid first-hand experience. The all-important thing for Dickens in writing the book was that IT IS TRUE, as he wrote (his capitals) in the Preface. He was describing 'the very scum and refuse of the land', determined to show that there was nothing glamorous about a criminal life: 'What charms has it for the young and ill-disposed, what allurements for the most jolter-headed of juveniles? Here are no canterings on moonlit heaths, no merry-makings in the snuggest of all possible caverns.' This was the life of the urban underbelly: 'the cold, wet, shelterless midnight streets of London; the foul and frowzy dens, where vice is closely packed and lacks the room to turn; the haunts of hunger and disease, the shabby rags that scarcely hold together.' He had been perilously close to immersion in that underworld. Oliver's experience was for Dickens an all-too-probable vision of the horror that his own life might have sunk into. 'But for the mercy of God, I might easily have been, for any care that was taken of me, a little robber or a little vagabond.' He put all his understanding of the danger of the world into his lowlife characters, explicitly identifying them in his Preface: 'Sikes is a thief, and Fagin a receiver of stolen goods; the boys are pickpockets, and the girl is a prostitute.' The blunt use of the last word stopped Dickens's readers dead in their tracks – no wonder Lord Melbourne tried to dissuade the young Queen Victoria (who ascended the throne the year the book started to appear) from reading a book about 'Workhouses and Coffinmakers and pickpockets … I don't like that low debasing style.'

Meanwhile, even as he was exposing the brutality both of so-called charity and of organized child crime in *Twist* to the astounded fascination of the nation, he determined to expose the iniquities of the Yorkshire boarding schools. He had been deeply moved by stories he had read of children abandoned to the untender mercies of these primitive educationalists, so he and Phiz travelled to the North under pseudonyms – how Dickens must have loved that masquerade – and did hair-raising field research. The following month, the first instalment of *Nicholas Nickleby* appeared, fuelled by the furious energy of Dickens's rage at what he had seen; it was read by an astonishing 50,000 readers, and confirmed Dickens as the most compelling literary voice of his time. But the novel did not confine itself to social criticism; like *Pickwick*, its form was loose enough to embrace many aspects of British life on which Dickens wished to comment. En route, for no particular reason, he takes a sizeable detour into the world of the theatre, an astonished Nicholas finding himself recruited into a company of moth-eaten thespians under the titanic leadership of Vincent Crummles (a fate that would have been something of a dream come true for Dickens himself). These sections of the book are Dickens's love letter to the profession, and it is entirely fitting that the novel, when it appeared in hard covers, was dedicated to Macready, a very different actor indeed from Mr Crummles.

It is worth stopping for a moment to consider what the theatre meant to Dickens, since it occupied such a central role in his imagination. Nicholas finds a kindness, a warmth and an inclusiveness in the theatre that contrasts favourably with almost every other stratum of society he encounters. It has room for dwarves and giants and women with beards, for those with one tiny skill and for the preternaturally gifted. It is, as he rightly calls it, 'a little world', but his stress is on the noun, not the adjective: he sees the theatre as an entire world, consistent within itself. Every transaction within its boundaries, on or off stage, is somehow theatrical (even the pony's mother was 'in the business'): it is life lived as a series of plays-within-plays. Nicholas finds it irresistibly charming, the whole gaudy enterprise essentially affirmative. 'Are they very theatrical people here?' he asks Crummles of the folk of Portsmouth. 'Far from it,' reports Crummles, moodily. 'I pity them,' says Mrs Crummles. 'So do I,' Nicholas concurs, 'if they have no relish for theatrical entertainment, properly conducted.'

As an actor, Nicholas responds vividly, as Dickens did, to the heroic act of performance, to rising above your situation, getting on stage and giving it your all, which was essentially, of course, Dickens's own approach to life. It is generous and dangerous and not like normal life. The artificiality of the theatrical environment makes it, paradoxically, more real: it is actually happening before your eyes, people are making it happen for you. The moment of performance, the coming together of the elements, the power of impersonation, are all practical mysteries that heighten experience and charge life with an electrical current of excitement. To enter a theatre for a performance is to be inducted into a magical space, to be ushered into the sacred arena of the imagination. 'Is this a theatre?' doubts Smike one morning when Nicholas slips him onto the stage where Crummles and co. will be playing that night. 'I thought it was a blaze of light and finery,' to which Nicholas gives the superb reply, revealing the measure of Dickens's understanding of the essential nature of the theatre: 'Why, so it is … but not by day, Smike, not by day.' Dickens is not so stage-struck, though, as to be unaware of the practical realities of the business, drily noting the 'remarkable fact in theatrical history, but one long since established beyond dispute, that it is a hopeless endeavour to attract people to a theatre unless they can be first brought to believe that they will never get into it.'

His view of the stage is not unsatirical, but his affection for its denizens and their activities is deep. Crummles's theatre, bordering as it does on vaudeville, and with more than a nod in the direction of the end of the pier, is not exactly, as Paul

Schlicke remarks, the Royal Shakespeare Company, but it is – like most theatre companies – a broad church, able to encompass not only the tumblers, the dancers, and Miss Ninetta Crummles, the Infant Phenomenon herself, but also the 'First Tragedy Man' who, when he played Othello, 'used to black himself all over'. Vincent Crummles is rather in awe of this pioneering Method actor: 'that's feeling a part and going into it as if you meant it. It isn't usual – more's the pity,' he adds, mournfully echoing the general view, frequently expressed in the novel's theatre sections, of the sad decline of the English stage. Everyone in Crummles's group is a readily identifiable theatre type and has his or her counterpart in any modern company. Perhaps the most startling portrait is that of Folair, who dances the part of The Savage. Dickens paints him unmistakably as a bitchy theatre queen, spreading poison wherever he goes; the spirit of Folair, alas, lives still. The theatre is, as has perhaps been too often observed, a family, and all families, as Dickens more than most had cause to know, have their problem children (and problem parents). But a feeling of family was central to the Eden from which he had once been exiled, and for a return of which he ardently hoped, and the theatre supplied it.

Beyond his sense of the theatre-as-world was his sense of the world-as-theatre, of the charivari, the endless parade, each man in his time playing many parts, absurd, grotesque, battered, damaged, ridiculous, briefly glorious. It is a carnival view of life, in which we are all, like members of a theatre company, dependent on each other, all limbs of one body, all human, and therefore all flawed, all beautiful. There are, too, as part of this more or less medieval view of the great theatre of the world, devils and angels, playing havoc with the endless parade, creating a pressing and permanent tension between *Nicholas Nickleby*'s carnival spirit and its morbid sentimentality, a tension highly characteristic of the nascent Victorian era in which it was written, and one which was central to Dickens himself; he never quite resolved it to the end. But for the most part the book is a kind of corybantic frieze of all-too-human mankind, its characters parading unforgettably past us, insinuating themselves permanently into our imaginations, populating our mental landscapes. Its spirit seems to hark back, past Shakespeare to Chaucer, enabling Dickens to embody something quintessentially and irrepressibly English.

Nickleby was of course, adapted for the stage, too, long before the final instalment was written, notably by the prolific William Moncrieff. Dickens struck back in the later pages of the novel itself, speaking of 'a literary gentleman who had dramatised in his time 247 novels as fast as they had come out – some of them faster than they had come out'. Taking this as a personal taunt, Moncrieff (still before *Nickleby*'s serialization was finished) issued an aggrieved statement challenging Dickens to end the book *better than I have done* after which he promised to 'sink into the primitive mire from which I have for a moment attempted to emerge by catching at the hem of his garment'. Punching below the belt, Moncrieff, alluding to the plays the very young Dickens had written, adds:

> having himself *unsuccessfully* tried the drama, there is some excuse for his petulance towards its professors; but it is somewhat illiberal and ungrateful that, being indebted to the stage for so many of his best characters – Sam Weller from *Beasley's Boarding House*, for instance – he should deny it a few in return.

Beasley and his boarding house have disappeared from view, so it is impossible to know what debt the immortal Sam owed them for his existence, but in general terms Moncrieff was not wrong: Dickens owed a great deal to current theatrical conceptions in his creation of character. But he transformed those prototypes out of all recognition, giving them – as in the case of Sam Weller – immortality in exchange for the shallow, cardboard lives they had known before. In any event, despite Moncrieff's hope that Dickens would indulge 'in a little more generosity of feeling towards his humbler brethren of the quill', there was no reply. Pirate adaptation was, after all, a very minor corner of his ever-expanding kingdom of art.

He was increasingly stepping outside of the parameters of his art. Not content with fearlessly addressing, in his novels, the injustices of the day – especially those perpetrated against the young – he was starting to speak on the burning issues of his time in his own person. More and more, he sought the most direct possible contact with his readers, whom he took to be no less than the entire population of the British Isles; to them were soon added the rest of the English-speaking peoples. Not much later, his readership would encompass all of Europe, and beyond. Translation into German and French started in 1838: the same year some episodes of *Pickwick* were rendered into Russian. He was immediately embraced by that huge constituency as a uniquely vivid spokesman for the disadvantaged. His first public speech, to the Literary Fund Anniversary Dinner, did not concern itself with the woes of suffering mankind, however, but with the inequities of his own profession, on whose behalf he now publicly took up cudgels. Throughout his life as a writer, he strove to increase both the financial rewards and the status of his fellow professionals: self-respect was one of the cornerstones of his view of life, and he felt keenly the factors that militated against it. He campaigned tirelessly against the disadvantages under which writers laboured; he also felt deep compassion for those who, like Walter Scott, had fallen on hard times. His speech to the Fund was gracious and modest ('the flattering encouragement he had received from his literary brethren had nerved him to future exertions, smoothed his path to the station he had gained, and animated his endeavour not to do other than justice to their kind praise').

Like every speech he ever made in his life, it was extempore, with no reference to notes. He very soon acquired the reputation of being the best public speaker of his time. He had taken pains to master the art, approaching it with scientific precision. On the morning of a day on which he was giving a speech, he once told Wilkie Collins, he would take a long walk during which he would establish the various headings to be dealt with. Then, in his mind's eye, he would arrange them as on a cart wheel, with himself as the hub and each heading a spoke. As he dealt with a subject, the relevant imaginary spoke would drop out. When there were no more spokes, the speech was at an end. Close observers of Dickens noticed that while he was speaking he would make a quick action of the finger at the end of each topic, as if he were knocking the spoke away. When he listened to the speakers that preceded him, he could be seen following their words with an almost imperceptible action, as if he were taking them down in shorthand.

He was now a central presence on the scene, at twenty-six a national figure, the best-selling author of three extraordinary and extraordinarily different novels, each of which had made a stunning impact, and which had earned him a genuine and notably affectionate popular following, as well as a more than decent living; he was also the father of two children whom he adored: Charley and a new daughter, named – of course – Mary. He was the editor of a highly successful magazine, for which he wrote various occasional pieces; and lesser but delightful books – the *Sketches of Young Gentlemen* and *Sketches of Young Couples* – flowed effortlessly (and anonymously) from him. He was lionized in literary and bohemian circles, and had, at an unprecedentedly early age, just been invited to become a member of the seriously grand Athenaeum Club.

Things had settled into an agreeable sort of pattern, life at Doughty Street comfortable and content, his unceasing literary toil punctuated with annual family holidays in Broadstairs, in Kent, where he could work, if he so desired, as well as play.

It is curious, therefore, that at this golden moment in his life he should suddenly have erupted with such startling ferocity against his publisher, Richard Bentley. Clearly, under all the success and the radiance and the easy charisma, there were rumblings of a deeper discontent.

SIX

Practical Power

'The consciousness that my books are enriching everybody connected with them but myself, and that I, with such popularity as I have acquired, am struggling in old toils, and wasting my energies in the very height and freshness of my fame, and the very best part of my life, to fill the pockets of others, where for those who are nearest and dearest to me I can realise little more than a genteel subsistence –' Dickens wrote to Forster, 'all this puts me out of heart and spirits.' The good humour and self-assurance he habitually displayed masked deep and continuous pressure. 'He never wrote,' said Forster, 'without the printer at his heels.' He often failed to write the requisite number of words. Realizing that he had to extend the instalment, he would dread that his invention had dried up; often it would return only at the last moment. 'I perpetrated a great deal of work yesterday, and have every day indeed since Monday, but I must buckle-to again and endeavour to get the steam up. If this were to go on long, I should "bust" the boiler.' This was slavery, of a sort; and eventually, inevitably, he would turn on the perceived slave-master.

Having agreed to write two novels for Bentley – two new novels, that is, quite separate from the monthly instalments of *Oliver Twist*, which he had chosen to write for the magazine – Dickens now insisted that *Oliver Twist* should count as one of the two novels. Though making other concessions, Bentley refused to accept this; and technically, contractually, he was unquestionably in the right. But Dickens was fighting on other grounds.

'Before God, morally,' Dickens told Forster, 'I hold myself released from such hard bargains.' Arbitrators, including Cruikshank, were brought in. At this point, Bentley, concerned that because of all these ructions, the magazine was being neglected, visited the printers and made some changes to that month's edition. This, of course, set Dickens off volcanically: his authority was being undermined, overruled, questioned. He gave notice that he would cease to edit the *Miscellany* after four weeks. Solicitors were brought in, whereupon Dickens simply stopped writing *Oliver Twist* and filed a piece of amusing padding (*The Full Report of the Mudfog Association for the Advancement of Everything*). Bentley, outwitted, caved in, and agreed that *Twist* would count as one of the two new novels; Dickens, seizing the advantage, pressed for more guarantees concerning his editorial authority. Again, Bentley caved in, only retaining his final veto on what was to be included in the magazine, and the responsibility for payments out. He even agreed to defer the deadline for the new novel – the one remaining new novel he was now due – to the end of October 1838.

All through this period of confrontation, except for the brief *Mudfog* interlude, Dickens continued writing *Oliver Twist* in all its angry, dark, desperate, wildly comic brilliance. It was now that Bentley asked Dickens to edit Grimaldi's *Memoirs*. He agreed, reluctantly and resentfully and without unduly exerting himself; mainly on the strength of his name, it turned into a big commercial success, which of course angered him all over again. Bentley, having been so comprehensively out-manoeuvred, still kept doggedly coming to the *Miscellany*'s office to promote writers he favoured, and developed a sudden interest in the word-count of Dickens's own pieces for the magazine. When, as they occasionally did, they fell short, Bentley took to deducting what he felt to be appropriate sums from his salary. 'Do you think,' rasped Dickens, 'that such treatment is likely to make me wish for a very long continuance of our business connection?' – almost exactly the form of words he used when lashing back at the *Morning Chronicle* after their churlish acceptance of his resignation: with Dickens, humiliation bred resentment.

Before long Dickens realized that he would not be able to write the contracted novel (originally called *Gabriel Vardon* but now known as *Barnaby Rudge*) in time for the agreed October date, proposing instead that it should come out in the *Miscellany* in monthly episodes. Bentley disagreed; then yet again caved in. But Dickens was still chafing. He now demanded a further extension of the date at which episodes would start to appear in the magazine. Bentley agreed, on the not unreasonable condition that Dickens would write for no one else in the interim. That did it. Dickens erupted like a madman, and resigned from the editorship. Ainsworth should take over, he said. He would help him in every way; he would also refrain from writing for any other magazine till the end of the year. There would be no negotiation. Bentley accepted; he had no option. A new agreement was drawn up whereby *Barnaby Rudge* would be delivered on 1 January 1840, for a payment of £4,000; Dickens had originally agreed to write it for £500. Three months before delivery date, he had still only written two chapters, whereupon Dickens angrily made two complaints to Bentley: a novel by Ainsworth (now installed as the new editor) was being linked in advertisements in the magazine with *Oliver Twist*; and Bentley was bringing out cheap editions of three-volume novels before they had begun to sell at full price. Dickens was so upset by these two circumstances, he said, that he found that he could not deliver the book on time; he needed a further extension. Bentley's lawyers demanded to know what compensation he would offer for breaking their agreement. In the event, it never went to law. *Barnaby Rudge* would now be published by Chapman and

Hall, to whom Bentley also wearily signed over all his rights in *Oliver Twist*. Game, set and match to Dickens. Bentley had been humbled, punished, and banished for evermore from Dickens's sphere. This fresh-faced, vivacious, idealistic twenty-seven-year-old was clearly someone not to cross; certainly not if you were his publisher.

Or his father. John Dickens had yet again run out of money, and tried to raise some on the strength of his having sired the illustrious young novelist. His chief target was Chapman and Hall, now Dickens's sole publisher, and he gently but relentlessly tapped them for increasingly large sums of money, colouring the situation with his own unique orotundities: failure to secure the money immediately 'would be productive of fatal consequences'. Soon after, 'the subject is one of settlement by 2 o'clock, and unless I so arrange it, I am lost'. In the next document, marked *Confidential*, he needs, he says, an extra £50 to save him 'from perdition'; the money must arrive 'by 2 o'clock tomorrow' to 'avert the most awful consequences'. Chapman and Hall never murmured a word of any of this to Dickens, but they finally pulled the plug on their donations. John then took to padding round the booksellers, hawking autographs and pages from Dickens's manuscripts. None of this enterprising activity was enough to avert eviction. Shortly after a very merry party to celebrate Dickens's twenty-seventh birthday, the whole set of schemes collapsed and John was obliged to make a clean breast of it. Dickens swiftly decided that his parents must leave town, enabling John Dickens to ignore the tradesmen's bills on a plea, Dickens says, of *non est inventus*, which would place him out of the sheriff's jurisdiction. The legal phrase (meaning 'He has not been found') leaped to his pen effortlessly; no doubt he had heard it often enough during their early years in Camden Town: people at the lowest end of the social scale became experts in loopholes to evade the process of the law.

Dickens's handling of the situation demonstrates the quality Forster so admired in him: the 'practical power' that 'seemed to tell so little of a student or writer of books and so much of a man of action and business in the world'. As soon as he could, he took a coach to the countryside around Plymouth, immediately finding a house to let: Mile End Cottage, in the sweet little twelfth-century village of Alphington, near Exeter. He quickly equipped it with furniture, for the most part second-hand; within days, first his mother, and then his father, with eleven-year-old Augustus and the dog, were dispatched down there.

This is disposing of your family as you would characters in a novel. They were far from grateful. They didn't in the least like being in the dear, quiet little village: they were used to bustling ports, towns, cities. Dickens got an 'unsatisfactory epistle from mother' and 'hateful, sneering letters' from both of them. But they finally settled in, and were allowed to come on family holidays to Broadstairs, where they were observed to be 'less at ease with Charles than with anyone, and seemed in fear of offending him'. Dickens appeared especially to resent his mother when she danced, which she loved to do: 'although she never indulged in it with any partner other than her son-in-law, or with some relation, Charles always looked as sulky as a bear the whole time'. They were finally pardoned in 1842, and allowed to return to the metropolis.

So much for his parents: now for the next round with his publishers. Having thrown off the hated yoke of Bentley, Dickens started looking for a way of avoiding the terrible galley-work of endless monthly or weekly instalments. He conceived a plan for a monthly magazine, of which he would be proprietor, editor and chief contributor; the magazine would feature short pieces on many subjects, essays, stories, factual contributions. The figures of Gog and Magog, mythic guardians of the City of London, would be the masters of ceremonies, introducing other figures from Dickens's back catalogue – Pickwick and Sam and Tony Weller, for example – who would tell stories. The framing device would be provided by an old gentleman and his cronies gathering round his grandfather clock, in which the documents and the stories which form the magazine are concealed; the magazine would be called *Master Humphrey's Clock*. Dickens then told Forster to summon Chapman and Hall; he wrote his script for him:

> You know that I am well-disposed towards them, and that if they do something handsome, even handsomer perhaps than they dreamt of doing, they will find it in their interest and they will find me tractable. You know also that I have had straightforward offers from responsible men to publish anything to a percentage on the profits and take all the risk; but am unwilling to leave them and have declared to you that if they behave with liberality to me, I will not on any consideration, although to certain extent I must surely gain by it ...

Once they had agreed to his plan – and how could they not? he correctly surmised – he would deliver his conditions: he was to get an extra £1,500 for *Nicholas Nickleby*, £50 a week for editing the magazine, take 50 per cent of the profit and bear none of the losses. As Forster observed, as a result of this deal, he would always be, not only a gainer, but the greatest gainer. And he would, at last, have full control. This is Dickens in a new mode: the master manipulator, supremely confident in the cards that he has in his hands, several moves ahead on the chessboard. He got absolutely everything he wanted, of course.

It was a disaster – or very nearly. Cautious Forster had had his doubts, but, he wrote, Dickens could never endure 'the interval between the accomplishment of anything and "its first motion"', adding, 'and he was too ready to make any sacrifice to abridge or end it'. They went full steam ahead, and in April 1840 the first edition hit the shops. It sold 70,000, a stunning figure, 20,000 ahead of the first episode of *Nickleby*. But the readers were disappointed, and that was something Dickens could never tolerate. He had misjudged them: they didn't want titbits: they wanted nourishment. Sales rapidly declined. He knew exactly what he must do: he would give them a new novel in monthly instalments – the very thing *Master Humphrey's Clock* had come into existence to obviate.

What he gave them was *The Old Curiosity Shop*, which became the best-selling book he had written so far. Public interest in the forlorn figure of Little Nell – the climax of all Dickens's morbid sentimentality, though by no means the last example of it – became hysterical, on both sides of the Atlantic, as her life ebbed away. It was Forster who had told Dickens that Nell must die; his argument that she deserved a better fate than a conventional happy ending convinced Dickens, but the terms in which Forster expressed it must have pierced Dickens to the core: 'so that the gentle little pure figure and form should never change to the fancy'. Nell, like Mary Hogarth, would be arrested in her tracks before time could wreak its cruel changes on her. He saw the force of Forster's argument, but he found himself almost incapable of doing the deed. 'Old wounds bleed afresh when I only think of the way of doing it … what the actual doing it will be, God knows.' Correspondents wrote to him, begging for a reprieve. Even Macready put in a word for her. But Dickens knew it had to be done. Nell must not be allowed to live on. Finally he did the deed.

'When I die, put near me something that has loved the light, and had the sky above it always.' Those were her words.

   She was dead. Dear, gentle, patient, noble Nell, was dead. Her little bird – a poor slight thing the pressure of a finger would

have crushed – was stirring nimbly in its cage; and the strong
heart of its child-mistress was mute and motionless for ever.

On coming upon those words it had dreaded reading, the
nation dissolved in uncontrollable sobs. Strong men were
broken by it. The great Irish patriot Daniel O'Connell threw
the periodical in which it was written out of the window of his
railway carriage, exclaiming 'He should not have killed her!'
Nell and her protracted demise have overshadowed an extraordinary and complex novel, which summons up an almost
Wagnerian world with its dwarf and its gold, a cautionary tale
about capitalism. As a counterpoint to this, Dickens intro-
duces a distinctly un-Wagnerian crew of rather dingy show-
people, with waxworks and dancing dogs, as well as giving
free rein to the merry cavortings of Dick Swiveller and the
Marchioness, all beer and cribbage. It is astounding that
Dickens should have whipped up this whole elaborate fable
out of thin air, more or less overnight, quickly extrapolating it
out of a little story that he thought he might write about a
sickly child and her grandfather, in order to keep faith with
his public; he never pleased them more with anything.

He followed it with the very first novel he had been
commissioned to write, which had passed through two titles
and two publishers over five years, with only three chapters so
far to show for it. *Barnaby Rudge*, Dickens's first historical
novel, set in the late eighteenth century, now appeared in
monthly instalments in *Master Humphrey's Clock*, and its long
and halting genesis seems to have subdued Dickens while he
was writing it; it has little of the improvisatory spontaneity of
its predecessors. Forster tactfully noted that 'it has unusually
careful writing in it, and much manly upright thinking', but
when Dickens discharges the full intensity of his personal
violence into the scenes depicting the anti-Catholic Gordon
Riots, they have an astonishing actuality; their aftermath, in

which London is depicted as a sort of Ground Zero, has eerie prescience:

> A dull smoke hung upon the ruin … and the wind forbore to move it. Bare walls, roof open to the sky – chambers, where the beloved dead had, many and many a fair day, risen to new life and energy, where so many dear ones had been sad and merry; which was connected with so many thoughts and hopes, regrets and changes – all gone. Nothing left but a dull and dreary blank – a smouldering heap of dust and ashes – the silence and solitude of utter desolation.

Dickens seemed to connect, on a personal level, with the half-mad Gordon himself: 'he must have been at heart a kind man and a lover of the despised and rejected, after his own fashion,' he wrote in Gordon's defence to Forster. 'He always spoke on the people's side, and tried against his muddled brains to expose the profligacy of both parties. He never got anything by his madness, and never sought it.' And the novel's sequence of sons failed by their fathers may well have had some resonance for Dickens. But the alternation of violence and 'careful' writing did not appeal to readers, and his central character, Barnaby himself, deranged but fantastical, was unlikely ever to become loved in the way that many of the characters in the previous novels had been. It was Dickens's first popular failure, though the character of pretty, witty, sexy Dolly Varden became central to a large number of theatrical adaptations; a few of them, as usual, appeared before the run in serial form had been completed. In his foreword to *Rudge* in book form, perhaps trying to strike a lighter tone, Dickens refers with delicious whimsy to the death of two of his pet ravens, upon whom Barnaby's pet Grip was modelled: no such whimsical note is to be found in the pages of the novel itself.

Barnaby was a hard slog, but Dickens's extraordinary energies were barely subdued by it. Indeed, he seems to have been in a state of inner ferment for some time. Summering at Broadstairs the year before *Rudge*, the Dickenses had invited along, among other people, Eleanor Picken, the pretty young fiancée of his solicitor's best friend. Dickens pretended to be in love with Eleanor and her friend Milly Thompson, and flirted outrageously with them in 'a wholly nonsensical way', which Catherine Dickens apparently found very funny. There was a lot of dancing that summer, and one night Dickens, whom Eleanor discovered to be disconcertingly moody – shifting from playful to withdrawn at a moment's notice – suddenly grabbed her hand and ran with her down to the sea. Once there, he held her tightly round the waist, hanging on to a tall post in the water with his other arm, and proclaimed that they would both drown there in the 'sad sea waves'. She tried to get free, but he went madly on: 'Let your mind dwell on the column in *The Times* wherein will be vividly described the pathetic fate of the lovely EP, drowned by Dickens in a fit of dementia!' She gave a loud shriek, begging him not to get her silk dress – her *only* silk dress – wet. Then she called to Catherine, who implored Charles to stop. 'Talk to me not of dress!' he shouted back. 'When the pall of night is enshrouding us in Cimmerian darkness, when we already stand on the brink of the great mystery, shall our thoughts be of fleshly vanities?' On and on he went; the girl got wetter and wetter; her shoes were ruined; her dress was destroyed. She finally ran free, half in tears, back to her friends. She heard Catherine telling Dickens that he must replace Eleanor's dress. 'Never! I have sacrificed my boots and her finery to the infernal gods. Kismet!' What should have been fun – joyful high spirits – had become hard and driven, almost frightening. After that, Eleanor and Milly gave Dickens a wide berth. One glance at his face, Eleanor said, would tell whether he was in one of his moods. His eyes, she said, were like danger-lamps, warning people to clear the line 'for fear of collision'. She was, she said, horribly afraid of him at such times.

Some profound restlessness was unsettling Dickens; as long as it was absorbed by his work, it was containable. *Barnaby Rudge* was the first book he had written that caused him trouble: he spoke to Forster of 'the extreme difficulty of fixing my thought on Barnaby ... I didn't stir out yesterday, but sat and *thought* all day not writing a line; not so much the cross of a t or the dot of an i ... last night I was unutterably and impossible-to-form-an-idea-of-ably miserable.' It was a book that was torn from his head rather than his heart; for the first time he neither wept nor laughed while he was writing it. He felt the urgent need, even before he had finished the book, to have a complete change of scenery, to get out of England, to be on the move, to meet new people. He needed to get some adrenalin going. Thus, in June of 1841, he impulsively set off for a two-month tour of Scotland with Catherine. Scotland was ready and waiting for him.

SEVEN

Here We Are!

Dickens's reception in Edinburgh was the first of the acclamations that would become such a regular feature of his life. A supper was announced for which three hundred people secured places; seventy were turned away. Dickens was 'besieged', he said, in his hotel room, and hailed wherever he went. His physical appearance astonished the guests: 'a little, slender, pale-faced boyish-looking individual,' observed a Scottish journalist, 'and perhaps the very last man in the room whom a stranger to his portrait could have picked on as being the author of *Pickwick*.' He was introduced by one of the leading lights of the *Edinburgh Review* who described him as dealing, like his heroes Defoe, Smollett and Fielding, with 'the common feelings and passion of ordinary man, in the common and ordinary paths of life'. The supper was an unequivocal triumph, his public speaking universally admired ('it is simple and inartificial, and seems to be suggested by circumstances as they arise, having entirely a conversational tone'). He was alarmed at first to see the guests arranged around him on cross-tables, but as always, his natural instincts as a performer took over: 'I was quite self-possessed however, and not withstanding the enthoosemoosy, which was very startling, was as cool as a cucumber.' With throwaway modesty, he described his aim as an artist to increase the stock of harmless cheerfulness. 'I felt that the world was not utterly to be despised; that it was worthy of living in for many reasons. I was anxious to find … if I could, in evil things, that soul of goodness which the Creator has put in them.'

It was indeed, at a deep level, his purpose to replace darkness with light, and despair with hope, as first articulated in *Pickwick*: to celebrate the triumph of the spirit. But it was always a struggle. Easier, in a sense, to focus on social injustice.

> I was anxious to show that virtue may be found on the by-ways of the world, that it is not incompatible with poverty and even with rags, and to keep steadily through the life the motto, expressed in the burning words of your Northern poet:
>
> > The rank is but the guinea's stamp
> > The Man's the gowd for a'that'

This gracious nod to Burns was greeted with *Loud cheers*, as the transcript records. He mentioned Little Nell, he praised Walter Scott, he honoured his only recently deceased friend the Scottish painter, David Wilkie, and he was cheered and cheered to the echo by the serried ranks of Scottish culture and society. Afterwards even he could scarcely express his amazement that all this attention should be bestowed on a twenty-nine-year-old: 'I felt it was very remarkable to see such a number of grey-headed men gathered about my brown flowing locks.'

During his sojourn in the city, he met, as he said '(I hope) everybody'. He visited Scott's apartments, and was duly moved, while Catherine went off to look at the house where she was born. They were breakfasted, lunched and dinnered; they went to the theatre to see the noted Scottish actor Mclan. On Dickens's arrival the orchestra struck up 'Charley is my darling'. Exciting and gratifying though it was, it was a bombardment, and Dickens was keen to get to the Highlands and get back to work. 'I am a poor slave of the Lamp and tomorrow it will have been rubbed thrice with no response from me,' he wrote to the critic Lord Jeffrey. 'It is impossible to work or think here, and I must fly for my life – or my living, which is the same thing.' He had to write his instalments of *Barnaby Rudge*, and to that end they stayed a few placid days at Lochearnhead, home of the Highland Games, but he was in pursuit of the tremendous, and eagerly surged forward to Ballaculish, glorying in a waterfall there which foamed and crashed down three great steeps of riven rock, 'leaping over the first as far off as you could carry your eye, and rumbling and foaming down into a dizzy pool below you with a deafening roar'. The wind was incessant, the rain drove down relentlessly; it was bitterly cold, and no amount of whisky ('of which I have today drunk about a pint') could warm them up. Dickens was in his element, striding vigorously across the craggy terrain, while poor Catherine cautiously picked her way along, a servant holding an umbrella, and their guide, Angus Fletcher, trying to comfort her. She retreated as often as possible to the carriage, in which they travelled through rivers and up impassable mountain roads. They went through the pass of Glencoe, 'which is perfectly *terrible*,' Dickens exulted, among rocks 'which fell down God knows where, sprinkling the ground in every direction, and giving the aspect of the burial place of a race of giants'. On they went, up to Dalmally, then were driven back by the appalling weather to Glencoe again, where they encountered a *spaet*, with 'torrents rushing down every hill and mountainside, and tearing like devils across the path, and down into the depths of the rocks'. They ate huge Highland meals – 'kippered salmon, broiled; a broiled fowl; hot mutton, ham and poached eggs; pancakes; oatcakes; wheaten bread; butter; bottled porter; hot water, lump sugar and whiskey' – and they never, ever got warm. Once, at a ford, in the midst of a violent storm, Dickens finally managed to persuade Catherine to dismount from their carriage, only for it to be swept away by the torrential flow of the water. 'It made me quite sick to think how I should have felt if Kate had been inside.'

Dickens's letters to Forster from this Highland tour are masterpieces of descriptive writing, whose energy surges almost terrifyingly off the page. His excitement at the savage power of nature, and his need to immerse himself in it, striding on while the elements did their worst all around him, contain an essence of the man. Walking was the quintessential Dickensian activity: it was one of his maxims that a given amount of mental exertion should be counteracted by a commensurate amount of bodily fatigue. Here in Scotland, he gave himself over to pitting himself against nature, or perhaps attempting to identify himself with it in an almost pantheistic way. These heroic walks were the counterpart and in some ways the opposite of his urban walks, where he sought out the hidden world of the city, peering into it and opening himself to it with profound empathy. In the Highlands, he unleashed himself into nature, giving vent to the wildness that was in him, defying it to destroy him. There, in the city, he was receptive, absorbent; here, titanic, dominant. And Catherine was wet, and cold, and perhaps a little frightened. They returned by way of Glasgow, where he gracefully declined a dinner in his honour, and they made their way back to London.

Once back, Dickens finished *Barnaby Rudge* and implemented his decision to pull the plug on *Master Humphrey's Clock*, whose circulation was now down to 30,000 and sinking. There is no record of him acknowledging that it might perhaps not have been such a very good idea after all. And indeed, why should he? *The Old Curiosity Shop* had appeared in *Master Humphrey's Clock*, setting new records for the sale of fiction. He would come back to the idea of the weekly magazine, which was a form he relished, his affection for it inspired by the great eighteenth-century magazines, *Tatler* and *The*

Spectator, which had been such an important part of his child-hood reading. For the immediate future, he wanted to travel. Domestic life in the splendid new house he had rented at Devonshire Terrace, off Regent's Park, was pleasant enough, the family now swollen, with the arrival earlier that year of Walter Landor Dickens, to six (after the birth of Katey, his third child, he had told Macready that she was 'the last'), but he needed stimulation. He was aware that he had recklessly plundered his imaginative resources over the last six years; he needed renewal. He did a deal with Chapman and Hall for a new novel, but not for a year. He was increasingly fascinated by the idea of America. His political radicalism was growing – 'I wax stronger and stronger in the true principle every day!' – as he became more and more impatient with the British democratic system, which seemed incapable of reform. The amended Poor Law of 1834 had made everything worse, not better, as he had gone to some pains to point out in *Oliver Twist*; the Whigs were feeble in power; the Tories beneath contempt. His frustration drove him to verse:

> The bright old day now dawns again; the cry runs
>   through the land,
> In England there shall be – dear bread! In Ireland –
>   sword and brand!
> And poverty, and ignorance, shall swell the rich and grand,
> So, rally round the rulers with the gentle iron hand
> Of the fine old English Tory days;
> Hail to the coming time!

He had been asked by the Whigs of Reading to stand as their Member of Parliament, but he knew that he could be more useful outside Parliament than in. He was still boiling with rage at the horrors revealed in the 1842 First Report of the Parliamentary Children's Employment Commission:

of dark tunnels through which the seven-year-old children dragged loaded carts to which they were chained; of girls clad only in ragged trousers working in the dark, often up to their knees in water and carrying heavy loads of coal up steep ladders a distance exceeding the height of St Paul's Cathedral; of dreadful accidents constantly occurring; of deformed and stunted boys toiling fourteen hours a day, fed on offal, struck with bars, burned by showers of sparks from red hot irons, pulled by the ears till the blood ran down.

He was toying with Republicanism, having been mildly irritated by the fiddle-faddle surrounding the new young Queen – first her ascension to the throne in 1837, then her Coronation (which had interrupted his work) the following year, and finally by the Royal Wedding in 1840. Exasperated by this assertion of everything he thought absurd about Britain, he longed, he said, for 'a democratic kingless country freed from the shackles of class rule'. He wrote some wickedly whimsical letters to friends about the wedding:

Society is unhinged by her majesty's marriage, and I am sorry to add that I have fallen hopelessly in love with the Queen, and wander up and down with vague and dismal thoughts of running away to some uninhabited island with a maid of honour … I think she will be sorry when I am gone. I should wish to be embalmed, and to be kept (if at all practicable) on the top of a triumphal arch at Buckingham Palace when she is in town, and on the north-east turrets of the Round Tower when she is at Windsor – from your distracted and blighted friend.

Part of him simply wanted to go: to leave England for good, Forster wrote, 'carrying off himself and his household gods like Coriolanus to a world elsewhere.' 'Thank God,' Dickens cried, 'there is a Van-Diemen's land! That's my comfort. I wonder, if I went to a new colony with my head, legs and strength, I should force myself to the top of the social milk-pot? What do you think? Upon my word I think I should.' He wanted to connect with a young country, a country where hope, justice and equality were enshrined in the constitution. Catherine wept whenever he mentioned the subject of America, but he was haunted by dreams of going there. Despite his wife's resistance to the idea – *because* of his wife's resistance to the idea – nobody seriously doubted that he would go. 'God willing, I think it MUST be managed some-how.' Apart from anything else, he wanted to correct the condescending reports of the country that had been appearing in Britain: they made the fundamental error, as he saw it, of trying to judge the New World by the standards of the Old. He would write his own book on the subject in celebration of the brave New World, and shame the exhausted Old. In September 1841 he telegraphed Forster I HAVE MADE UP MY MIND (WITH GOD'S LEAVE) TO GO TO AMERICA, and he started to amass books on the subject, and study maps. 'I could light my cigar against the red-hot state of Ohio,' he told a visiting American journalist. He was ready to go, when he was stopped in his tracks by the need to submit to 'a cruel operation, and the cutting out, root and branch, of a disease caused by work-ing overmuch, which has been gathering, it seems, for years'; this seems to have been a rectal fistula. There was no anaes-thetic; the pain and subsequent discomfort were intense.

A further delay in his plans for departure was brought about by an event that caused him worse pain than the opera-tion, taking him back to the complex and tormenting emotions surrounding the death of Mary Hogarth. Catherine's grandmother died; on her deathbed, she had expressed a desire to be buried next to Mary, in Kensal Green Cemetery. At the traumatic time of Mary's death, Dickens had secretly consoled himself with the thought that one day he would be buried next to her, but when he learned of the grandmother's wishes, he conceded that she had the greater claim. He toyed with the idea of secretly moving Mary's remains to the cata-comb, where, in the fullness of time, he could join her, but he knew that this was madness. 'I cannot bear the thought of being excluded from her dust,' he wrote to Forster, 'I neither think nor hope (God forbid) that our spirits would ever mingle *there*. I ought to get the better of this, but it is hard.' He had barely recovered from his recent excruciating operation, and he knew that this was why it disturbed him 'more than it ought', but whatever his rational understanding, the pain was overwhelming; it was, he said, like losing her a second time. Despite his lifelong horror of funerals, he somehow managed to be present at the grandmother's burial next to Mary. He gazed long and hard on her coffin, then locked himself away for three days.

He pulled himself together in time to make preparations for the voyage: he and Catherine bought a large number of clothes for the trip, his rather flashier than hers. The days before their departure were filled with farewell drinks and meals with friends; Christmas 1842 was celebrated in their usual exuberant style. The children were to stay at home for a while under the care of his brother Fred, then to move in with Macready (the dress rehearsal of whose somewhat unseasonal production of *Merchant of Venice* Dickens attended on Christmas Eve); they would be away for five months, a long time in the lives of young children. Charles and Catherine, accompanied by Forster, travelled to Liverpool by train on the second of January; on the fourth, Forster saw them onto the spruce new ocean liner RMS *Britannia*, and they were off. The journey they were about to undertake was epic: criss-crossing a vast land still very much in a state of development. The transatlantic voyage itself was alarming, with a gale at the beginning, and a storm at the end; Dickens did his bit to maintain morale by playing the accordion for his fellow passengers. When they finally and with great relief alighted in Halifax, a huge reception was thrown for him, after which he was immediately and urgently taken to both Houses of Assembly, with poor Kate, who had a painfully swollen face, reluctantly dragged along in his wake. The scale and warmth of the reception were something of a surprise. Before leaving England, he had notified everyone he knew in America of his visit, and the British press had extensively reported his departure, but he had not in the least expected the scenes of overwhelming excitement his arrival generated. Before the Dickenses could disembark, editors, carrying copies of their own newspapers, came on board; at first Dickens thought that they were selling the papers. In Boston, he was literally mobbed: the crowd was so huge and eager for him that it was actually dangerous. But he was only exhilarated by the welcome he got: he had wanted adrenalin, now he had it, in spades. He positively ran towards it.

As he bounded into the hotel lobby, he cried – in the immortal catchphrase of the circus clown – 'Here we are!' Once he got to his room, he found letters and invitations from all over America waiting for him, from both individuals and institutions. Outside the room, there were people quietly waiting for him, too. 'I have had deputations from the Far West, who have come from more than two thousand miles: from the lakes, the rivers, the backwoods, the log-houses, the cities, factories, villages, and towns,' he wrote to Forster. 'It is no nonsense', his friend William Ellery Channing, the leading Unitarian preacher of his day, wrote to him, 'and no common feeling. It is all heart. There never was, there never will be, such a triumph.' Dickens was inclined to agree with him: but in the midst of all the fanfares and the fireworks, his first thought, he confessed to Forster, was of Mary Hogarth:

> I feel, in the best aspects of this welcome, something of the pres-
> ence and influence of that spirit which directs my life, and
> through a heavy sorrow has pointed upward with unchanging
> finger for four years past. And if I know my heart, not twenty
> times this praise would move my heart to an act of folly.

Just as well; it could have seriously turned a young man's
head. But Dickens had, to an uncommon degree, an inbuilt
capacity to be untouched, at the deepest level, by either
acclaim or its opposite.

He had a splendid time in Boston. After the huge welcoming party, he and the young Earl of Mulgrave whom he had
befriended on board the *Britannia*, were shown around the
streets of Boston. Dickens was in such a state of exhilaration
that he ran round the snowbound streets at night, roaring
with laughter for the pure joy of it. The following day he and
Kate went to the Tremont Theatre, sitting in a gaily decorated
box, to watch a pirate adaptation of *Nicholas Nickleby*; he even
managed to enjoy that. The show was followed by the intrigu-
ingly titled *Boz: A Masque Phrenologic*, while newly composed
Boz waltzes played in the foyer and during the entr'actes. The
following day, he sat for his portrait: the studio was invaded
by women who tried to cut snips off the fur on his coat; he
was chased all the way into his hotel room. On the recom-
mendation of the portraitist, he hired a secretary, George
Putnam, who came to the studio every morning while Dickens
signed autographs on cards, as a sculptor and a painter did
their work on either side of the room.

Everyone wanted to meet him. He was keenly scrutinized;
not all of his visitors were equally impressed by what they saw.
The sculptor William Wetmore Storey found him to have a
considerable touch of 'rowdyism' in his manner, but the eyes,
he thought, were fine, and 'the whole action of the mouth and
lower part of the face beautifully vibratory. People eat him

here!' Longfellow took to him, detecting 'a slight dash of the Dick Swiveller about him' – a slightly equivocal compliment, perhaps. Richard Henry Dana, author of the recently published *Two Years Before the Mast*, resisted him on first meeting, but found over supper that he was the '*cleverest* man I ever met', adding in an elaborate but precise military metaphor,

I mean he impresses you with the alertness of his various powers. His forces are all light infantry and light cavalry, & always in marching order. There are not many heavy pieces, but few sappers & miners, the scientific corps is deficient, & I fear there is no chaplain in the garrison.

There were widespread doubts about his breeding: his green and crimson velvet waistcoats raised eyebrows, as did the prominence and profusion of gold watch-chain. Dining at a grand mansion, he saw in the mirror that his hair was awry, so, to sharp intakes of breath, he combed it at the table then rather naughtily remarked of two famous London hostesses, that though Mrs Norton was the more beautiful, the Duchess of Sunderland was the more kissable. Not quite a gentleman: London's verdict was repeated in Boston, which came to the conclusion that Mrs Dickens 'showed signs of having been born and bred her husband's social superior', in which judgement they were not wrong. All in all, Boston's *beau monde* handed him on to New York with some relief.

But the Young Men of Boston, who had arranged a sumptuous banquet for him (with a choice of forty dishes) thought differently: 'How we did hurrah, we young fellows,' wrote James Fields, 'when Dickens stood up at last to answer for himself, so fresh and handsome with his beautiful eyes moist with feeling, and his whole frame aglow with excitement.' Dickens spoke to them of dreaming 'by day and night, for years, of setting foot upon this shore and breathing this pure air'. Lauding America's classless society, he said that he believed that 'Virtue shows quite as well in rags and patches as she does in purple and fine linen ... I believe that she goes barefoot as well as shod ...' He spoke of Nell, of course, and of Oliver; and he ended with a toast: '*America and England! And may they never have anything but the Atlantic between them.*' The Young Men of Boston cheered till they were hoarse, but that is not what the newspapers chose to report. Just before the end of his speech, he had made a light and graceful plea for America to adopt international copyright law. The following day, every newspaper denounced him for 'discourtesy' in raising the matter. It was, it seemed, a matter of constitutional faith with the American people that authors – above all foreign authors – had no rights in their own work (just as their descendants believe in their god-given right to download music from the Internet). With his comments on copyright law Dickens had, unwittingly or wittingly, let a genie out of the bottle; it would grow, over the course of his visit, to quite disproportionate size.

The furore it engendered threatened to derail Dickens's entire trip; but for the time being there was New York to look forward to. The first part of the journey was by train, a new experience for Dickens. To his alarm, wherever the train stopped, heads were incontinently thrust in, bawling out, 'Is Mr Dickens here?' At one point he overheard someone say, 'What's the matter? What's it all about?' 'They've got Boz in there,' someone else said. 'Got Boz?' 'Why, it's Dickens,' the first man said. 'They've got him here!' 'Well, what's he been doing?' 'He ain't doin' nothin'. He writes books.' 'Oh! Is that all? What do they make such a row about that for?' They stopped at Worcester, Massachusetts, and stayed overnight with the Governor; then carried on the journey, rather more privately, by steamboat to Hartford, Connecticut; that night, when they arrived at their hotel, the students serenaded them.

The following day, 7 February, was Dickens's thirtieth birth-day, and he spent it exactly as he would most have wished, visiting the insane asylum, the Institution for the Deaf and Dumb, the State Penitentiary, and finally, the jail for untried offenders. He was not impressed by any of them, though he refrained from saying so. The eye he cast on such institutions was an expert one: it was his practice to visit them wherever he went in Britain, and he was abreast of all the latest think-ing. He had high hopes for American attitudes to mental health and penal management, but they were disappointed. Elsewhere on the trip, he was nauseated by what he saw, sometimes to the point of physical sickness.

Next day there was another stupendous banquet, and more speeches of welcome. His reply was graceful, modest, noble:

> we cannot hold in too strong a light of disgust and contempt, before the view of others, all meanness, falsehood, cruelty and oppression, of every grade and kind. Above all, that nothing is high because it is in a high place, and that nothing is low because it is in a low one.

There were cheers, and loud applause. And then, telling them that he had sworn that he would never refrain from raising 'a certain topic', he said 'I would beg leave to whisper in your ear two words, International Copyright'. He quickly rose above a whisper, speaking passionately: if there had been International Copyright Law, he thundered, Scott would not have died in penury. His friends had advised him to leave the subject alone, which made it absolutely certain that he would address it. 'I wish you could have heard how I gave it out,' he wrote to Forster. 'I felt as if I were twelve feet high when I thrust it down their throats.' The anticipated howls of rage from the press only made him 'iron upon this theme, and iron I will be here and at home, by word of mouth and in writing as long as I can articulate a syllable or hold a pen'. It was a matter, as always with Dickens at his greatest, that was both intensely personal and a matter of principle, one in which he felt he spoke for his fellow human beings, in this case, his fellow workers, the writers of both England and America.

But the response to his campaign was making him slightly less starry-eyed about the supposed Utopia he was about to explore. He had dark premonitions: 'I do fear that the heaviest blow ever dealt at Liberty's Head will be dealt by this country, in the failure of its example to the earth.' Now that he had experienced at first hand America's brand of injustice, in a matter that concerned him directly, the whole sham was revealed to him. Free speech was a charade here. He decided that there would be no more public appearances after the ball and the banquet already agreed to in New York. The decision was not a sulk on his part: he flung himself into the life of the city as eagerly as ever, fascinated by its fashions, the huge ice blocks used by the restaurants, the pigs in the streets. He also discovered the price of celebrity: a man came up to him, claiming to have been the first person in that city to have sold his books. The man told him that he was financially distressed, while Dickens was obviously revelling in luxury. Dickens sympathized, but offered no money, at which the man told him that he thought it rather strange that the man who wrote *Nickleby* should be utterly destitute of feeling. Dickens was amused by this, and keenly interested in every aspect of American life. But his illusions were rapidly evaporating.

What was not in doubt was the ability of Americans to stage a spectacle. The Boz Ball at the Park Theatre in New York on 14 February was certainly that. Tiers of boxes draped in white muslin trimmed with gold served as a background for the arms of the individual States under a trophy of English and American flags; there were medallions representing each of Dickens's works and, in the centre, a portrait of Dickens hung, brooded over by a golden eagle with a crown of laurel in its beak. Three thousand people crowded in at seven thirty; at nine o'clock the band at last arrived, playing 'See, the Conquering Hero Comes!', and Dickens appeared at the side of General George Morris, who was wearing full military dress uniform. Escorted by Macready's American friend David Colden, Kate followed, staggering under the weight of an enormous bouquet. There were speeches, and then everyone went twice round the room to the accompaniment of the Grand March, then there were tableaux, quadrilles, and waltzes. There was serious threat to life and limb as the couples whirled, or tried to whirl, round the monstrously overcrowded room. Dickens was a little irritated to discover from the next day's newspapers that he had been awed by the proceedings, that he was never in such society as he had seen in New York, and that its high and striking tone could not have failed to make an indelible impression on his mind. 'For the same reason I am always represented, whenever I appear in public, as being "very pale", "apparently thunderstruck"; and utterly confounded by all I see,' he told Forster. 'You recognise the queer vanity which is at the root of all this?' It was never wise to patronize Dickens. Such was the success of this epic event, however, that a repeat performance was planned for two days later, but Dickens, unsurprisingly, had a sore throat, and declined to attend. He was no doubt preserving himself for the Grand Dickens Dinner on the eighteenth, a splendid but less gaudy event, on whose committee every distinguished man of letters in New York sat; there were 250 guests. The chairman was Dickens's friend, Washington Irving; they had been in mutually admiring correspondence since the late 1830s. Irving, as he had predicted he would, broke down in his speech, which had anyway been inaudible, and blurted out the toast to Dickens to general hilarity.

Dickens made an insouciantly brilliant speech, provoking waves and waves of laughter, in which he paid affectionate tribute to Irving, and ventured a risqué joke at Catherine's expense: 'Why, gentlemen,' he said, 'I don't go to bed two nights out of seven, as I have a credible witness very near at hand to testify' – at which, the *New York Herald* tells us, 'Boz gave a funny Sam Weller *sort* of side look out of one eye half round at his wife', at which, said the *Herald*, Catherine laughed, blushed, hid her face in her handkerchief, and laughed again – 'I say, gentlemen, I do not go to bed two nights out of seven without taking Washington Irving under my arm upstairs to bed with me.' [*Uproarious laughter.*] Dickens rhapsodized deliciously upon Irving's work, proving his intimate acquaintance with it, and teasingly seemed, right to the end of the speech, on the brink of mentioning 'a certain topic', but never actually did so. Instead, Irving himself ringingly proposed the toast: 'To International Copyright!', to which Cornelius Matthews responded, in a very hard-hitting pro-copyright speech. Next day, there was no press comment on Matthews's speech whatever, except from Horace Greeley in the *New York Tribune*: 'Who should protest against robbery but those robbed?' he asked. 'Why is America trying to bribe Dickens from criticism with acres of inflated compliments soaked in hogsheads of champagne?'

That was, indeed, the last public speech Dickens gave in America during that visit. Over the next few days in New York, he visited the asylum, the penitentiary, the workhouse and the notorious Tombs, the house of detention; he went out all one night with two of the New York Precinct's most famous constables: 'started at midnight and went into every brothel, thieves' house, murdering hovel, sailors' dancing place, and abode of villainy, both black and white'. From New York he and Catherine went to Philadelphia, where he met Edgar Allan Poe, on whose behalf he promised to speak to an

English publisher. Kate was already desperately homesick; both of them were longing for letters from home with news, above all, of the children, but there was no sign of any. Before they left Philadelphia, Dickens visited the Penitentiary, where he was shocked at the widespread use of solitary confinement, sometimes for as long as twenty years. The prisoners wore hoods, without holes for eyes, nose or mouth. Dickens contemplates 'the utter solitude, day and night'. And then, in one of those characteristic shafts of insight with which he suddenly penetrates to the core of another's being, he wonders: 'Are they haunted by ghosts?' After Philadelphia, they went by boat, train, steamboat and train again, to Washington, where Dickens was presented to the President, John Tyler, who said, on seeing him for the first time, 'Is *this* Mr Dickens?' 'It is, sir.' 'I am astonished to see so young a man, sir,' the President said, adding, 'I am happy to join with my fellow citizens warmly in welcoming you to this country,' after which they sat by the stove in silence and looked at each other, while the Presidential staff spat prolifically in the background. Dickens excused himself, certain, he said, that the perennially embattled President had more pressing business to attend to. Dickens visited both the House of Representatives, delivering it a petition concerning International Copyright, and the Senate, to which he returned several days running, riveted by one particular senator, 'an evil-visaged man, looking', he said, 'as if he had been suckled, Romulus-like, by a she-wolf, with a great ball of tobacco in his left cheek,' who, on being called to order, replied, 'Damn your eyes, sir, if you presume to call me to order, I'll cut your damnation throat from one ear to the other.' While at a supper in a private house in Washington, he made a brief speech about not making a speech, which he said he was sure would earn him the gratitude of everyone in that most political of cities, when he was interrupted with the joyful news that the ship bearing their letters from England, having been feared sunk, had finally staggered in. 'Among them are certain scrawls from little beings across the ocean, of great interest to me,' he told his fellow guests, and he begged leave to be allowed to go home and read them. Showing superhuman restraint, Catherine had waited before opening them till he returned; they read them together in transports of emotion until two in the morning. From Washington, they went to Richmond in Virginia, with glum foreboding, Dickens being acutely conscious of heading towards one of the great centres of slave-owning.

His account of his time there is urgent and appalled. On arrival, he immediately spots a notice on a bridge detailing fines for fast driving: 'Penalty – for Whites, five dollars; for Blacks – fifteen stripes.' In Baltimore, though he tries to avoid it, he finds himself in heated dispute with someone who insists that 'it's all damned nonsense what you hear in England – it's not in a man's interest to use his slaves ill.' Dickens replies that it is not in a man's interest to get drunk or to steal or to game, 'but he *did* indulge in it for all that'. The man is a little taken aback and asks him if he believes in the Bible. Dickens says he does, but if any man could prove to him that it sanctioned slavery, he would place no further credence in it. 'By God, sir,' his adversary replies, 'the niggers must be kept down, and the whites have put down the coloured people wherever they have found them.' A sardonic fellow passenger tells Dickens that he knows something of the slaves' fondness for their masters – when absconding slaves are brought back, he informs Dickens, 'it is as common for a runaway slave, retaken, to draw his bowie knife and rip his owner's bowels open, as it is for you to see a drunken fight in London'. Dickens is everywhere fierce and implacable on the subject of slavery. He can just about tolerate people saying that slavery is an abomination but one impossible to get rid of; but to say that it is a blessing, a fine institution, part of God's order, one of the greatest blessings of mankind, and so on, renders him apoplectic. He describes with horror a slave being burned alive for resisting arrest, quoting the leader in a local newspaper: *The abominable and hellish doctrine of Abolition – repugnant alike to every law of God and Nature.*

On they stump, he, Putnam, Catherine and Anne Brown, Catherine's maid; travelling conditions are primitive. His obsession with order makes it particularly hard for him: he arranges everything in their cabin 'as if we were going to be here for a month, which, thank God, we are not'. On one steamer he is in the ladies' cabin: 'it exactly resembles the dwarf's private apartment in a caravan at a fair'. On another notable occasion, he shares a cabin with twenty-seven other men, who spit all through the night on his neatly folded overcoat. 'I put it on a stool beside me and there it lay under a cross fire from five men – three opposite; one above; and one below'. Spitting is absolutely universal; even in the President's office in Washington, where there are at least spittoons. He refrains from comment; keeps up a steady flow of jokes with his cabin-mates till everyone is asleep; leaps out of bed at five thirty to plunge his head into a bucket of icy water, narrowly avoids a breakfast consisting of tea, coffee, salmon, steak, liver, potatoes, pickle, ham, sausage, then leaps off the boat to walk for five or six miles along the tow-path. The dauntless quartet cross the mountains by railroad: 'there are some queer precipices close to the rails, certainly; but every precaution is taken, I am inclined to think'. From the train, they see the desolation of the new settlements, half-abandoned, and Charles and Catherine give way to little outbursts of nostalgia for Greenwich Fair and the Crown and Sceptre. And all the while he is observing, noting, absorbing. In his letters to Forster, he is ever the superb reporter, describing a new town so vividly in twenty sharp lines of methodical observation, that an accompanying illustration would be redundant.

The steamer to Pittsburgh provides them with pleasanter accommodation. He equips his party with Life Preservers which he inflates 'with great solemnity' whenever they get on any boat. He identifies a problem in American life: 'I do not believe there are, on the whole earth besides, so many intensified bores as in these United States. No man can form an adequate idea of the real meaning of the word without coming here.' At every town they are uproariously greeted, overwhelmed with eager citizens, expected to address the town. 'I really think my face has acquired a fixed expression of sadness for the constant and unmitigated boring I endure.' He is never, ever alone. 'I dine out, and I have to talk to everybody about everything. I go to church for quiet, and there is a violent rush to the neighbourhood of the pew I sit in, and the clergyman preaches *at* me …' He is outraged when, in Cleveland, Ohio, a party of men gather outside his room to watch him wash, while Kate is still in bed. The local newspapers, he finds, are urging war with Britain: within two years, said one paper, they will be whistling 'Yankee Doodle Dandy' in Hyde Park. After reading this, he refuses even to speak to the Mayor; bypassing the planned reception, they go directly from their hotel to get the boat to Niagara Falls. And at last his spirits begin to lift.

> I saw two great white clouds rising up from the depths of the earth – nothing more. They rose up slowly, gently, majestically into the air. I dragged Kate down a slippery path leading to the ferry boat; bullied Anne for not coming fast enough; perspired at every pore; and felt, it is impossible to say how, as the sound grew louder and louder in my ears, and yet nothing could be seen for the mist.

He was blinded by the spray, and drenched. But, after a change of clothes, he went straight back to the Horseshoe Fall, dragging Kate with him.

It would be hard for a man to stand nearer God than he does there. There was a bright rainbow at my feet; and from that I looked up to – great heaven! To *what* a fall of bright green water! The broad, deep, mighty stream seems to die in the act of falling; and from its unfathomable grave, arises that tremendous ghost of spray and mist which is never laid, and has been haunting this place with the same dread solemnity – perhaps from the creation of the world.

At last: a phenomenon to match him. 'I can only say that the first effect of this tremendous spectacle on me was peace of mind – tranquillity – great thoughts of eternal rest and happiness – nothing of terror.' Anne was not impressed. 'It's nothing but water,' she said, 'and there is too much of that.' Anne had been a great help with Catherine, who had been prey to what Dickens calls her 'propensity': 'she falls into or out of every coach or boat we enter; scrapes the skin off her legs; brings great sores or swellings on her feet; chips large fragments out of her ankle-bones; and makes herself blue with bruises'. He calculated that she had had 743 falls during the American trip. This apart, she earned his approval: 'she has made a *most admirable traveller* in every respect … [she has] pleased me very much and proved herself perfectly game.' Odd phrases to use of the woman you love. They do not seem to describe what Dickens wanted out of a woman. Catherine had a modern view of marriage; she wanted it to be companionate. Up to a point, he was prepared to give her that: they would sit together agreeably enough while he played 'Home Sweet Home' over and over on his accordion. But this was just filling in the time pleasantly. He wants someone to worship, not to *know*. For intimate acquaintance, he has his friends. From Niagara he writes to Forster, telling him that as he stands listening to the roar of the waterfall, he longs to share it with him and Maclise. 'And, I was about to add, what would I give if the dear girl whose ashes lie in Kensal Green had lived to come so far along with us. But she has been here many times, I doubt not, since her sweet face faded from my earthly sight.' Poor Catherine; how could she compete with someone who was immortal?

The final lap of the tour was approaching: it was not really part of the American tour at all. Just across Lake Ontario from Niagara Falls is Canada, then, of course, British territory, and proud of it. This detour was nothing to do with sight-seeing: there was serious work in hand. Dickens had promised Lord Mulgrave, whom he had met on the *Britannia* on the outward journey and who served with the Coldstream Guards, to direct and act in a triple bill with the Garrison Amateurs at the Montreal Barracks. Dickens had chosen three dependable comic stand-bys of the sort he adored: *A Roland for an Oliver; Past Two O'Clock in the Morning*, a staple of Charles Mathews's son, Charles Jr; and *Deaf as a Post*. En route, Catherine and Charles stayed in Toronto and Kingston, where – despite what he called the 'wild and rabid Toryism' of his hosts – he was delighted to be re-acquainted with 'English kindness'. Here, he said, when they arrange horses and a carriage for you, they don't exact as payment 'the right of being always under your nose'. Once in Montreal, he set to work in earnest. For his part of Snobbington in *Past Two O'Clock in the Morning*, he had already sent off to New York for a wig, 'which has arrived, and is brilliant'; he immediately got to work, tearing his coat off, and transforming himself into

> … the stage manager and universal director, urging impractica-
> ble ladies and impossible gentlemen on to the very confines of
> insanity, shouting and driving about, in my own person, to an
> extent that would justify any philanthropic stranger in clapping
> me into a strait-waistcoat without further inquiry, endeavouring
> to goad Putnam into some dim and faint understanding of a
> prompter's duties, and struggling in such a vortex of noise, dirt,

bustle, confusion, and inextricable entanglement of speech and
action as you would grow giddy in contemplating.

This was pure bliss for Dickens: making things happen by
throwing all his energies at them, performing the role of the
director – and indeed the role of the character in the play – to
the hilt, leading his band of players and prompters to the top
of the theatrical mountain. 'This kind of voluntary hard labour
used to be my great delight,' he wrote to Forster. 'The *furor* has
come strong on me again, and I begin to be once more of
opinion that nature intended me for the lessee of a national
theatre, and that pen, ink and paper have spoiled a manager.'
It would not be the last time that thought would cross his
mind. It is often said, and rightly said, that he had the essential temperament of an actor, but it may be that even more
central to his existence was the idea of being an actor-manager,
a 'universal director', controlling destinies, pulling the strings,
releasing energies, arranging outcomes. At his writing desk, he
felt like an emperor; in the theatre, he felt like a god.

Just how divine the entertainment at the Queen's Theatre
in Montreal (capacity a whopping 1,500) might have been on
those May nights in 1842, is hard to judge. It was, of course,
the most enormous success. 'It went', said Dickens, 'with a
roar.' He himself played a succession of roles in which he
aimed for total disguise – and succeeded triumphantly in the
eyes of General Bagot, who, though sitting in the stage-box,
simply had *no idea* that it was Dickens under Mr Snobbington's
wig. The local reviewer waxed eloquent:

> We are sure that there was not a dry eye in the house during the
> whole representation – from excessive laughter, however. The
> helpless hypochondriacal Cockney, fond of his little creature
> comforts: methodical as a Quaker, and regular as the Horse
> Guards clock … was performed to the life by Mr Dickens.

He had already excelled himself as Highflyer in the first play. 'I really do believe that I was very funny: at least I know that I laughed heartily at myself: and made the part a character.' For the rest, his cast consisted of various captains, a belted earl, an Honourable, and their several ladies, 'all of whom were Capital'. And up there with them was Kate, with a dozen lines in the last play. 'Only think of Kate playing!' he wrote to Forster, 'and playing devilishly well, I assure you!' She only ever acted once again.

The following night the whole thing was repeated for the general public, and the ladies were replaced with professional actresses from Mr Latham's local company, and a different play substituted for the third piece. Again, it 'went' splendidly. Something deep within him stirred, something he had put away from himself, something he thought he had grown out of. Before too long, it would assert itself more forcefully. For the time being, in Canada and in the theatre, Dickens was restored from the vexations of the American tour, and turned his focus on 'home-home-home-home-home-home-HOME!!!!!!!!' Dickens wrote yearningly of his reunion with 'our darlings': 'whether we shall be able to surprise them, or whether they will be too sharply looking out for us; and what our pets will say; and how they'll look, and who will be the first to come and shake hands.' He longed to know 'the very colour of the bow on the cook's cap'.

He and Catherine took their time making their way back to New York, despite being in 'such a state of excitement'. In their last few days in the United States, they went up river to Hudson, in New York State, spent a night at Lebanon Springs, also in the Hudson valley, and visited a Shaker village. On 7 June, with no particular fuss, and attended by no crowds, they boarded ship. After their storm-tossed outward journey they had decided to come home by packet-ship rather than steamer ('the George Washington – Hoo-ray-ay-ay-ay-ay-ay-ay-ay!!!!'), and at the delicious prospect of it, he broke into his idea of Yankee:

> and you may have a pretty considerable damned good sort of a
> feeble notion that it don't fit nohow; and that it ain't calculated
> to make you smart, overmuch; and that you don't feel special
> bright; and not at all tonguey …; and that however rowdy you
> may be by natur', it does use you up com-plete, and that's a fact;
> and makes you quake considerable and disposed toe damn the
> en-gine.

These high spirits never let up for a moment on the ship: with three other passengers, he formed a group called the United Vagabonds, who sat at one end of the table, separate from everyone else at meals, and then roamed the ship bearing enormous rolls of plaster and huge pairs of scissors, two of the Vagabonds dressed up as those high-spirited medical students from *Pickwick Papers*, Mr Bob Sawyer and Mr Ben Allen; when the ship's captain fell ill, Dickens claimed that he recovered him. When he wasn't participating in these high-jinks, he was playing the accordion for the perhaps not entirely grateful passengers; it must have been like having the Marx Brothers on board. To add to the mayhem, the Dickenses had with them a Havana Spaniel that they had named first Boz, then Snittle Timbery and finally Timber Doodle; it was the gift of a New York theatre manager and had done the whole American tour with them. The voyage quickly passed on a wave of joyful anticipation; they arrived in Liverpool and came straight on to London and 'our darlings'. Arriving home, they 'expended themselves', as Dickens graphically put it, on the children, after which Dickens leapt into a cab to find Macready: they fell into each other's arms, weeping. Then he found Forster, who was at supper – he wept too, and then they both went off in search of Maclise, which resulted in yet more tears.

Dickens was back. It was all too much for his first-born, Charley, who, saying he was 'too glad', fell into convulsions later that night. Dickens's friend John Elliotson, Professor of Medicine at London University, was summoned to treat him. His diagnosis was that the sudden joy had 'perfectly turned Charley's brain and overthrown his system'. Elliotson said that he had never seen the like in a child. Charley recovered almost immediately, but it is an interesting example of having the full force of Dickens's personality turned on you.

EIGHT

Sledge-Hammer Blow

Dickens set to work on putting his thoughts on America into publishable shape, asking all the friends to whom he had so copiously written to loan him the letters he had sent them. His mind was very clear about what he had to say; the delicate matter was to phrase it in a form that would be palatable to the many friends on the other side of the Atlantic with whom he had no quarrel. There was no question that the verdict was largely unfavourable. As early as March of 1842, when he had been in the United States for little more than a month, he had sent Macready – who had written to him to reproach him for coming to too hasty conclusions – a letter that stated with absolute precision and fiery eloquence his considered opinion: 'This is not the republic I came to see,' he wrote, 'this is not the republic of my imagination.' Nothing that happened subsequently encouraged him to change his mind. 'I infinitely prefer a liberal monarchy – even with its sickening accompaniment of court circulars – to such a government as this,' he told Macready.

> In everything of which it has made a boast – excepting its education of the people and its care for poor children – it sinks immeasurably below the level I had placed it upon; and England, even England, bad and faulty as the old land is, and miserable as millions of her people are, rises in comparison.

America, he said, had a press more mean, and paltry and silly, and disgraceful than any country he knew, and a total absence of freedom of opinion. Whenever he had opened his mouth, he had been advised to be silent: on Democrats, on International Copyright, on Harriet Martineau, whose magisterial *Society in America* had appeared five years earlier. 'But what has she done? Surely she praised America enough?' he asked. 'Yes, but she told us some of our faults,' was the reply, 'and Americans can't bear to be told of their faults. Don't split on that rock, Mr Dickens, don't write about America; we are so very suspicious.'

He had no quarrel with the people, whom he found open, friendly, courteous, though 'in respect of not being left alone, and of being horribly disgusted by New York tobacco chewing and tobacco spittle, I have suffered considerably'. The sight of slavery, the hatred of British feeling on the subject, and 'the miserable hints of the impotent indignation of the South', had pained him greatly. However much he might like some of the ingredients of the dish, he said, 'the dish itself goes against the grain with me'. Later, he wrote to Forster to say that he had discovered 'I am an Englishman after all' and that he yearned after 'our manners and our customs'. It was his first exposure to mass adulation on this scale, and, like many people who court popularity, he found the actual experience of it on a one-to-one basis displeasing. He was subjected to the sort of invasive enthusiasm experienced today by rock stars or royalty (but without the protection of minders or security men). It rattled him, and *American Notes*, besides its probing account of the country, is informed by keen resentment of his discomfort. It is a curious mixture of vivid reporting, hard analysis, and personal irritation.

He finished the book in October. He was convinced that it was essentially well-meaning and would not cause offence, and would be understood as the affectionately frank comment of a friend. But for all that, he was nervous about its possible impact. He duly wrote an emollient Introduction, which Forster strongly advised him against including: it was over-defensive, Forster said, which would have the opposite effect to the desired one. At the very last minute Dickens withdrew the Introduction, perhaps unwisely. The American response to the book was predictable: Dickens, said the *New York Herald* (which only six months earlier had merrily chortled at his after-dinner drolleries), had 'the most coarse, vulgar, impudent, and superficial mind that ever had the courage to write about … this original and remarkable country'; this was fairly representative of the transatlantic press response. His American friends, on the whole, took it in good part. Dickens professed to be indifferent to the furore, but he was biding his time. He was by no means finished with America yet; more fur would fly before long.

It was time to start the new novel he had agreed to write for Chapman and Hall. At first he was uncertain of where to set it, and with Forster, Maclise and the maritime painter Clarkson Stanfield, he went on a typically titanic reconnaissance trip to Cornwall, striding along the cliffs and braving the elements, thinking that the novel might open there. It turned out that he wanted to write something entirely different: nothing less than an exposé of selfishness in human affairs. It would be a more elaborate and considered book than he had ever attempted, and he took his time to work it through in his mind; it was not until December that he started writing the first instalments of what, after the usual struggle to find the hero's exact name (he toyed with Chuzzlewig, Chubblewig, Chuzzletoe, Chuzzlebog, Sweezledon, Sweezlewag), would be called: *'The Life and Adventures of Martin Chuzzlewit, his relatives, friends and enemies. Comprising all His Wills and Ways, With an Historical record of what he did, And what he didn't.*

Shewing moreover who Inherited the Family Plate; who came in for the Silver Spoons, And who for the wooden ladles. The whole forming a complete Key To the House of Chuzzlewit.' The blithe and free-wheeling tone of this, with Dickens doffing his hat again in the direction of his adored Smollett, quickly ceased to be appropriate; a tone of dark irony pervades the writing from the very beginning.

Meanwhile his domestic life, so longed for during the American sojourn, resumed. He was at his most playful and high-spirited with the children, whom he endowed with exotic and ever-changing nicknames. There was nothing condescending about the way Dickens played with his children: if anything he took their games more seriously than they did, throwing himself into them with every particle of his formidable energy. 'I have never met anyone who entered into games with as much spirit and boisterous glee,' said Eleanor Christian. At Christmas the parties were lavish, but the high point of the festive year for the Dickenses was 6 January, Charley's birthday, and Twelfth Night. In 1842, the first New Year after their return from America, as well as the usual games and dancing, Dickens made a dramatic appearance in the flowing garb and pointed hat of a magician. He performed a dazzling conjuring act, which made the children 'scream with laughter at the funny things he said and did'. The following year, he and Forster bought up the entire stock-in-trade of a retired conjuror, and the tricks became spectacular. By now, magic had become a full-scale obsession: he acquired ever more elaborate devices, studied the work of other magicians, and performed large-scale illusions, now as much for the adults – including Carlyle and the painter Landseer – as for the children.

He practised devotedly: 'a man becomes a magician only by patient labour,' he wrote. 'The tree from which the enchanter's wand is culled is no other than obstinate, persevering work.'

He invented a character for himself: blacked up, in flowing magical robes with a turban, as if he had stepped straight out of the *Arabian Nights*, he now appeared as the Unparalleled Necromancer, Rhia Rhama Roos, 'educated cabalistically in the Orange Groves of Salamanca and the Ocean Caves of Alum Bay', his placard proclaimed. Cards burst into flames, watches found themselves in the middle of loaves of bread, dolls appeared, disappeared and re-appeared all over the room, blazing plum-puddings emerged from perfectly ordinary hats. Then the conjuror himself suddenly vanished, and minutes later, the familiar figure of Daddy strolled into the room in his tails.

Such it was to be a child of Charles Dickens. He didn't spoil the children; indeed he was rather strict with them in matters of punctuality and tidiness and cleanliness. But he never failed to listen to them. 'He considered,' said Mamie (as little Mary was always known), 'that an intelligent child's observation was accurate and intense to a degree; that such a child should be kindly and gently reasoned with until all such childish terrors and fears should gradually melt away.'

There was a new recruit to the ménage: Catherine Dickens's youngest sister Georgina, now sixteen. Georgy, still almost a child herself, had, the year before, regularly come over to play with the Dickens children while their parents were in America; they adored her, and it seemed the most natural thing in the world for Aunty Georgy to move in with them. She was wonderfully skilful around the house; little by little she took over many of the responsibilities that Catherine, frequently unwell, was unable to perform. Dickens adored her; the feeling was entirely mutual. The echoes of the situation with Mary Hogarth were not lost on Dickens himself: 'when she and Kate and I are sitting together,' he wrote to her mother, 'I seem to think that what has happened is a melancholy dream from which I am just awakening.' It is as if Dickens could not bear to be alone with Catherine, who seemed profoundly to displease him, despite her 'game' efforts on the American trek, to say nothing of her devilishly good acting in Montreal. Her physical maladroitness led him to write to his American friend, Mrs Colden (with whom he lightly told Macready he was in love): 'It is more clear to me than ever that Kate is as near being a Donkey as one of that sex whose luminary and sun you are, *can* be,' a remark doubly shocking, in that it's addressed to a woman, a woman who is, moreover – unlike Donkey Kate – the sex's luminary and sun.

He had told Forster that nothing had been the same between him and Catherine since the birth of their second child, Mamie, which suggests some sexual complications. Catherine was a charming and an interested hostess; she deferred to Dickens in particular and to male guests generally. She partook of the Victorian addiction to dreadful and meaningless puns, which Dickens pretended to deprecate, though unable to prevent himself from collapsing in laughter at them. Nothing fascinated Catherine more than to read the announcements of who was engaged to whom, who married, and who – shock horror – divorced. She was in many ways a conventional Victorian wife, but a very amiable and well-liked one. Dickens's two best friends, Daniel Maclise and John Forster, were both immensely fond of her; Forster's birthday and Charles and Catherine's wedding anniversary were, as it happens, on the same day, 2 April, and the three of them always dined together then. But underneath all the joviality and domestic delight, something was brewing.

It is hard to know exactly what to make of the events of the night of 12 July 1842, when Dickens entertained his friends, among them Macready and Walter Savage Landor, to a display of Mesmerism, with Catherine and Georgina as his subjects. Mesmerist theory – otherwise known as Animal Magnetism

– proposed the existence of a field of magnetic electrical energy that could be brought under control and could influence the condition, both physical and mental, of the subject. It is hardly surprising that such a theory would find a ready response in Dickens, whose own field of electrical energy was so evident; but it also spoke to his fascination with the human mind and what it might or might not be capable of. This was what propelled him into the penitentiaries and lunatic asylums: the burning curiosity to explore the furthest reaches of human possibility, for good and ill. Macready already knew about Dickens's fascination with the Mesmerist craze, which in England had been largely managed by John Elliotson, the friend who had attended Charley after his recent alarming seizure when his parents had returned from America. Dickens had attended one of a series of lecture-demonstrations at University College given by Elliotson four years earlier; during the course of it, Elliotson had put two working-class women into a trance in which they performed feats of unnatural strength, becoming impervious to physical pain. Dickens was converted, there and then, profoundly struck by this demonstration of the power of suggestion. 'After what I have seen with my own senses, I should be untrue both to [Elliotson] and myself, if I should shrink for a moment from saying that I am a believer, and that I became so against all my preconceived opinions', which was true enough: Dickens was an implacable opponent of the table-rapping, ectoplasm-emitting Spiritualists, whom he considered cheap frauds. Elliotson's methods were highly controversial, but despite the *Lancet*'s pretty conclusive exposé of Elliotson's two subjects – and, by implication, the tenets of Mesmerism – Dickens remained, to the end of his life, 'a believer'.

Once he became intrigued by Mesmerism, he inevitably sought to master it. And he had a ready subject to hand. 'Poor Catherine', as he so often described her, proved to be perfectly compliant to his will; in Pittsburgh, en route for Cincinnati by steamboat, he made the appropriate passes over her head in front of a group of interested onlookers, and six minutes later, she became completely hysterical. Another two minutes, and she fell into a profound sleep, from which he was then able gently to awaken her. Dickens reported this to Macready as part of his attempt to persuade the great actor to undergo it himself for the elusive malady from which he was at the time suffering, and promised he would repeat the exercise 'many, many, many times' for him. And so, in July 1842, after dinner, in front of Macready, Dickens used his influence on Catherine and Georgina, with the same gratifying results. Was this simply a party-piece, designed to amuse? Hardly: he believed in it deeply as potentially of great benefit to mankind. Perhaps he thought he could cure Catherine of the host of ailments to which she was prey (though in fact she was essentially robust; she outlived Dickens by nine years). Perhaps he even thought he could cure her clumsiness? Macready refused to be hypnotized, as did Dickens himself, but he used mesmerism on his children when they were ill, and, as he believed, saved the life of his illustrator, John Leech. He had limitless faith in it and its powers: 'I could magnetize a frying-pan,' he said. But he could not mesmerize his marriage back into life; indeed, before long, mesmerism revealed quite how seriously troubled it was.

No doubt he would like to have cast a spell over his father's activities, or perhaps cause him to disappear. John Dickens had been running up debts again, to the extent that Dickens had taken an advertisement in all the main newspapers disavowing responsibility for any debts run up in his name. Now John was writing him threatening letters. 'That father of mine!' Dickens exclaimed. 'How long he is, growing up.' Nonetheless, he liberated his parents from their rustic exile in Alphington (rather touchingly, the village's current website lists them as 'some notable people from Alphington') and found them a house in Blackheath, much nearer London, though scarcely central; much thanks they showed him. 'I am amazed and confounded,' he wrote, 'by the audacity of his ingratitude.' His brother Fred, of whom he had been fond, now proved to be a spendthrift in his father's mould; Dickens had to bail him out, too. 'He, and all of them, look upon me as something to be plucked and torn to pieces for their advantage ... My soul sickens at the thought of them.'

He forged ahead with *Chuzzlewit*, with plentiful examples of its theme of selfishness ready to hand. He believed the book to be 'in a hundred points immeasurably the best of my stories'; in a sense, it was, finely composed and magnificently sustained, but despite a plethora of brilliantly imagined characters, Pecksniff, Tom Pinch and Jonas Chuzzlewit among them, there is an angry misanthropy about these opening chapters that is impressive but not involving, and sales were not good. Even the triumphant arrival of Mrs Gamp, one of the glories of the whole of English literature, failed to improve sales. Alarmed by this evidence of a cooling of his readers' affection for him, to say nothing of the dip in his finances, he decided to uproot Martin and send him to America, in a dazzling blaze of unrelenting satire that enraged his readers in the United States. 'Martin has made them all stark staring mad across the water,' he exulted. In a burlesque of *Macbeth* on a Boston stage, a copy of the novel was thrown into a witches' cauldron, to a hearty cheer.

All this controversy had a beneficial effect on sales, but not enough. One day, William Hall of Chapman and Hall was at the office at the same time as Dickens, and lightly remarked that he hoped that they would not have to invoke the clause in the contract, inserted as a formality at the last moment, that if sales were to fall below the amount needed to pay back the advance, Dickens would have to refund £50. Dickens took deep offence, and walked out of the office. He brooded deeply, so deeply that he stopped writing. 'I am so irritated, so rubbed in the tenderest part of my eyelids with bay-salt,' he wrote to Forster, 'that a wrong kind of a fire is burning in my head, and I don't think I *can* write.' That 'wrong kind of fire' was something he increasingly often experienced. Here he was again, exactly where he had been with Bentley only two years before, feeling exploited. The injustice! The ingratitude! He had made Chapman and Hall what they were – and here they were, clawing back £50 from him at the slightest reduction of sales. He brooded and brooded. Soon enough, he was 'working like a dragon' again, composing some of his finest and darkest writing so far, in the devastating pages about the new settlement of Eden – the embodiment of all doomed illusions, where Martin nearly loses his wits – and in the slow revelation of the blackness of Jonas Chuzzlewit's poisoned soul. Even the mad comedy of Mrs Gamp turns black, her exasperation with her patients verging on the homicidal. Sales remained disappointing, and Dickens ominously insisted on sending back the £50 to Chapman and Hall.

It was at this point – purely for money, initially, Forster tells us – that he conceived the idea of writing a Christmas story. But with Dickens, nothing was ever simple: there was always a multiplicity of motives and a convergence of imperatives. His friend the Unitarian minister Dr Southwood Smith had sent him the Second Report of the Children's Employment Commission, on which Smith had sat; Dickens was, he told his friend, 'perfectly stricken down' by what he read. 'The necessity of a mighty change, I see.' His rage against the 'sleek, slobbering, bow-paunched, overfed, apoplectic, snorting cattle' of the ruling class boiled up within him. 'I never saw such an illustration of the power of the purse, or felt so degraded and debased by its contemplation.' His first impulse was to write a pamphlet entitled, 'An Appeal to the People of

England, on behalf of the Poor Man's Child', but within days other plans had formed: 'when you know them, and see what I do, and where, and how,' he wrote Smith, 'you will certainly feel that a Sledge hammer has come down with twenty times the force – twenty thousand times the force – I could exert by following out my first idea.' He started writing *A Christmas Carol* on 3 October, still in the midst of *Chuzzlewit*, just at the point where Martin, sunk in despair at the ruin of his hopes for Eden, begins to will himself dead, and is drawn back from the brink by his self-elected servant, Mark Tapley.

The day after he started writing *A Christmas Carol*, he set off to make a speech at the first annual soirée of the Manchester Athenaeum, a very different organization from the swish club of the same name in London to which he had been elected at such an early age. The Mancunian version conducted its affairs under the nobly Pickwickian watchword 'For the advancement of Knowledge and Learning'. Dickens sat on the platform with Disraeli, now a Conservative MP and the author of three celebrated political novels, and Richard Cobden, the hero of the still-continuing struggle to repeal the oppressive Corn Laws. The speech Dickens delivered was on a subject that never ceased to be at the heart of his thinking: ignorance. The Athenaeum offered facilities for working men to read and learn. 'This I know,' he said in his speech,

> that the first unpurchaseable blessing earned by every man who makes an effort to improve himself in such a place as the Athenaeum is self-respect, an inward dignity of character that once acquired and righteously maintained, nothing, no, not the hardest drudgery, nor the direst poverty, can vanquish. Though he should find it hard for a season even to keep the wolf of hunger from his door, let him but once have chased the dragon of ignorance from his hearth, and self-respect and hope are left him … my own heart dies within me when I see thousands of immortal

creatures condemned without alternative or choice, not to what our great poet calls 'the primrose path to the everlasting bonfire', but one of jagged flints and stones, laid down by brutal ignorance.

The starting point of *A Christmas Carol* is neither Tiny Tim, nor Scrooge, nor the Fezziwigs' ball: it is Ignorance and Want, the root causes, Dickens believed, of all the world's malaise. The history of the twentieth and twenty-first centuries suggests that he was not wrong.

After the speech, rapturously received, he went back to London, blazing away simultaneously at *Chuzzlewit* and *A Christmas Carol*. He finished the *Carol* six weeks later, at the end of November, effusively underlined the words THE END three times and then 'broke out like a madman'. Having established for all time an ideal vision of Christmas, he hurled himself into the real one with inexhaustible enthusiasm. 'Such dinings, such dancings, such conjurings, such blind-man's-bluffings,' he wrote to Forster, 'such theatre-goings, such kissings-out of old years and kissing-in of new one'. The climax of the festivities was reached at a Boxing Day party at Macready's house; the great actor being on tour in America, Dickens and Forster determined to give Mrs Macready the best imaginable Christmas. They exerted themselves 'till the perspiration was pouring down and they seemed quite *drunk* with their efforts,' reported Jane Carlyle to Thomas. 'Only think of that excellent Dickens playing the *conjuror* for one whole hour – the *best* conjuror I ever saw – (and I have paid money for several).' Forster featured in the crucial role of the magician's assistant. After the ladies' pocket handkerchiefs had been turned into sugar-plums, and Christmas puddings created out of the raw ingredients, and boxes full of guinea-pigs magically produced, Dickens went down on his knees to Jane – fusty, uptight Jane – to beg her to waltz with him. 'In fact, the whole thing', she reported to Carlyle, not entirely disapprovingly, 'was turning into something not unlike the Rape of the Sabines.' Forster got her onto her feet. 'Oh for the love of heaven let me go!' she cried out. 'You are going to dash my brains out against the folding doors!' 'Your *brains*!!' Forster shouted. 'Who cares about their brains *here? Let them go!*' This is the man the thirty-something Dickens called his best friend. One sees why. After the party, the two young men and Catherine, plus massive, lumbering Thackeray, went back to Devonshire Terrace 'to *finish the night there,*' as Jane Carlyle underlined it, 'and a *royal* night they would have of it I fancy!' She liked people with a touch of blackguardism in them, she concluded: and Dickens, as far as she was concerned, certainly fell into that category.

Dickens's high spirits were not unconnected with the universal triumph of *A Christmas Carol*. The book – gold-edged, with coloured plates by John Leech, each page outlined in red – was an instant bestseller; on Christmas Day, 1843, alone, it sold 6,000 copies. 'It is the greatest success, as I am told, that this ruffian and rascal has ever achieved.' Though there were sniffy reactions – 'the book does little more than promote the immense spiritual power of the Christmas turkey' – even those who were not generally disposed to praise Dickens did so. Thackeray, a friend, but a rival, too, wrote:

> Who can listen to objections regarding such a book as this? It is a national benefit and to every man and woman who reads it a personal kindness. The last two people I heard speak of it were women, neither knew the other, or the author, and both said, by way of criticism, 'God bless him!'

Lord Jeffrey declared, in the *Edinburgh Review*, that Dickens had 'done more good, and not only fostered more kindly feelings, but prompted more positive acts of beneficence, by this little publication than can be traced to all the pulpits of Christendom since Christmas 1842.' In 1871, the year after Dickens's death, Margaret Oliphant recalled that '*A Christmas Carol* moved us all those days ago as if it had been a new gospel.' The effect was immediate and practical: even curmudgeonly old Carlyle, according to Jane, had gone out and bought himself a turkey. 'The vision of *Scrooge* has so worked on his nervous system,' reported Jane of her husband, 'that he has been seized with a perfect *convulsion* of hospitality, and has actually insisted on *improvising* two dinner parties with only a day between.'

With *A Christmas Carol*, Dickens's popularity, which already eclipsed that of any other writer of his time, changed in kind. He became the embodiment of the best of the national spirit, a spokesman, not just for the oppressed and the disadvantaged, but for the essential integrity of a nation in the throes of radical transformation. There was widespread unease at the way in which capitalism was evolving, at the loss of community and the inter-relatedness of the groups within it. The writing of the book sprang directly from his horror at the condition of children in employment in the mines. Christmas, Dickens insisted, was mocked unless the absolute dregs of society were rehabilitated and the root causes of their rejection and elimination by society addressed. At the same time, he was consciously reviving an early, more personal sort of Christmas: the very snowiness he immortalizes was not an early Victorian phenomenon – the thirties and forties had seen a series of particularly mild winters – but a deep and passionate reversion to the Christmases of his own childhood. It was the measure of his genius, and of the power of his relationship with his readers, that he forged all these disparate elements into one overwhelming symbol, making Christmas the point of intersection of the whole life of society, at which a huge effort of benevolence, of generosity and of integration could be harnessed to heal the running wound at the heart of his own times. And his art reached a new peak of assurance and originality. The action is phantasmagoric, perfectly adapted to its material and Dickens's purpose. It is highly theatrical in the manner of his ideal theatre, the remembered theatre of his youth. No theatre, of course, could ever fully realize Dickens's spectacle (though many tried, and continue to try); no cinema has achieved the freedom and fluidity of the ribbon of dream that Dickens unfolds; no cartoon has ever managed the density and detail, the texture and tone that belongs to this extraordinary book. It is an almost magical performance, in which Dickens conjures up the scenes he requires then extinguishes them. In *A Christmas Carol* he communicates with his readers with quite extraordinary directness: throughout the story he is present himself: our 'faithful friend and servant', as he signs himself in the Preface to the book. The tone of its famous opening is chatty, informal, discursive: the storyteller talks directly to his reader.

Marley was dead, to begin with. There is no doubt whatever about that. The register of his burial was signed by the clergy-man, the clerk, the undertaker, and the chief mourner. Scrooge signed it. And Scrooge's name was good upon 'Change, for anything he chose to put his hand to. Old Marley was as dead as a door-nail. Mind! I don't mean to say that I know, of my own knowledge, what there is particularly dead about a door-nail. I might have been inclined, myself, to regard a coffin-nail as the deadest piece of ironmongery in the trade. But the wisdom of our ancestors is in the simile; and my unhallowed hands shall not disturb it, or the Country's done for. You will therefore permit me to repeat, emphatically, that Marley was as dead as a door-nail.

This is Dickens the buttonholer: your friend, your intimate, your brother, your self. 'Scrooge found himself face to face with the unearthly visitor,' he writes, a little later, 'as close up to it as I am to you.'

His readers bought the book in their tens of thousands. And, perfectly reasonably, he had expected that he would reap a gratifying financial reward from it. When this turned out not to be the case, he was shocked and bewildered. He had printed the book at his own expense, and wanted to make it as beautiful as possible; when Chapman and Hall, who distributed it, gave him the interim accounts, he found that all he had made was £230. In fact, he had made more, as he soon discovered when he got the next set of accounts, but the apparently poor returns and the lukewarm reaction to *Martin Chuzzlewit* convinced him that he had to change his life – and indeed reconsider his approach to his writing. His immediate reaction was rage against Chapman and Hall. He wrote them a letter of curt instructions: 'Do this – Do that – Do the other – Keep away from me and be damned!' as he told Forster. He also turned his fury against the pirates, in particular a firm positively flaunting the name of Lee and Haddock, who had brought out a version of *A Christmas Carol*, 're-originated from the original … and analytically condensed expressly for this work.' He took them to court, and received judgement against them, despite their claim to have made great improvements, including a sixty-line song for Tiny Tim. 'The Pirates are beaten flat!' he exulted. 'They are bruised, bloody, battered, smashed, squelched and utterly undone!' But Lee and Haddock declared themselves bankrupt, and Dickens found himself mired in a chancery suit from which he could not get out without dropping all charges; which he did. It cost him £700, which he had to write off. 'It is better to suffer a great wrong,' he remarked, bitterly, 'than to have recourse to the much greater wrong of the law.' This is a fine example of the way in which Dickens is us: he too is baffled and foiled by the law. He, unlike the rest of us, then goes on to write *Bleak House*.

He was beginning to want to get out of England again, making it an excuse to extricate himself from Chapman and Hall. He would take a sabbatical – lease the house, then 'fade away from the public eye for a year, and enlarge my stock of description and observation by seeing countries new to me, which it is most necessary for me to see, and which with an increasing family I can scarcely hope to see at all, unless I see them now.' He planned to walk through Switzerland, across the Alps, then on through France and Italy, 'take Kate perhaps to Rome and Venice but not elsewhere; and in short see everything that is to be seen.' He would write travel books. Perhaps. He would turn over the next novel in his mind and then publish it (his italics) *first in Paris*. He will be committed and obligated to NO ONE: 'no book-seller, printer, money-lender, banker or patron whatever, and decidedly strengthen my position with my readers, instead of weakening it, drop by drop, as I otherwise must.' He told Forster that he thought the scheme good though he saw the 'prepossessions' the other way – 'as leaving England, home, friends, everything I am fond of' but it seemed to him 'at a critical time, *the* step to set me right'. In response to Forster's reasonable objections, he wrote, still smarting from the public coolness to *Chuzzlewit*, 'I *know*, if I have health, that I could sustain my place in the minds of thinking men, if fifty writers started up tomorrow. But how many readers do *not* think! How many take it on trust from knaves and idiots, that one writes too fast, that one runs a thing to death' – something for which he was regularly denounced in the literary press. He felt that rest would do him good. 'You say two or three months, because you are to see me for eight years never leaving off. But it is not rest enough. It is impossible to go on working the brain to that extent forever.' His financial situation was equally critical; he could live, he thought, much cheaper abroad. In April things were so bad that he had to arrange an urgent loan of £100; would his means be sufficient for the future? – especially in the light of the 'never-satisfied, constantly recurring ... unreasonable, unjust' demands from his father and his brothers.

There was, moreover, the question of his emotional life. A perfect storm was brewing within him. In February of 1844, he had gone to Liverpool to address the Mechanics' Institute: he spoke stirringly, as always:

> Beneath this roof we breed the men who, in time to come, must be found working for good or evil in every quarter of society. If mutual forbearance among various classes be not found here, where so many young men are trained up in so many grades to enter on so many roads of life, dating their entry from one common starting point, as they are all approaching, by various paths, one common end, where else can that great lesson be imbibed?

Then he handed over to a young woman who was to play the piano: 'I am requested to introduce you to a lady whom I have some difficulty and tenderness in announcing – Miss Weller.' Any reference to Sam Weller gave him a guaranteed laugh. But, an observer noted, 'he kept his eyes fixed on her every movement'. Later, now milking the Weller jokes, he introduced her again as 'that god-child of whom I am proud'. When his duties as chairman came to an end, he went over to find her and her father. 'There was an angel's message in her face,' he told his friend T. J. Thompson, who was with him in Liverpool, 'that smote me to the heart.' He can't joke about her, he says, 'for she is too good ... spiritual creature that she is, and destined to an early death' (she died, as it happens, in 1910, at the age of eighty-five). Thompson wrote back to Dickens, telling him that he had fallen in love with the girl himself. 'I felt the blood go from my face to I don't know where,' Dickens replied, 'and my very lips turn white.' Thompson wanted to know what he should do. 'If I had your independent means … I would not hesitate … but would win her if I could, by God.' He encouraged Thompson to woo her, despite the gap in their ages and the girl having other interests; he even wrote to her himself, supposedly on his friend's behalf: 'I had that amount of sympathy with his condition, which – but that I am beyond the reach – the lawful reach – of the Wings that fanned *his* fire, would have rendered it the greatest happiness and pleasure of my life to have run him through the body. In no poetical or tender sense, I assure you, but with good sharp steel …' An astonishing letter with its naked sexual imagery to write to a nineteen-year-old girl whom he hardly knew. He was chafing inside his sexual cage; time to uproot himself and go – somewhere – anywhere.

NINE

Animal Magnetism

After taking advice, he decided that the historic Italian coastal city of Genoa was the ideal place to go. He found someone to take the house in Devonshire Terrace for a whole year, and accordingly, the day after the last instalment of *Martin Chuzzlewit* appeared, he, Kate, Georgina, five children – another had been born at the beginning of the year: 'Kate is all right again, and so, they tell me, is the baby. But I decline (on principle) to look at the latter' – three servants and a dog, set off for Dover in the carriage Dickens had specially bought for the purpose. Once in France, they rattled on to Marseilles, continuing by boat to Genoa. They had hoped to stay in Byron's villa, but finding that it had become a wine-shop, they rented the Villa di Bagnerello, 'a mighty old, wandering, ghostly, echoing, grim, bare house' in which, nonetheless, and despite the grey skies and the oppressiveness of the *sirocco* and the omnipresence of vermin – 'I always expect to see the carriage going out bodily, with legions of industrious fleas harnessed to and drawing it off, on their own account' – they settled in for two agreeable months, avoiding their fellow English and going mildly native. They went to the local theatres; Dickens was especially charmed by the marionettes: 'The height to which they spring; the impossible and inhuman extent to which they pirouette; the revelation of their preposterous legs; the coming down with a pause, on the very tips of their toes, when the music requires it … I shall never see a real ballet with a composed countenance again.' They were charmed by Genoese social life: they dined with witty, appreciative, sophisticated people: marquises, consul-generals, bankers; Dickens and Catherine started to learn Italian.

In September, they moved to the enormously grand and historic Palazzo Peschiere, filled with frescoes, some designed by Michelangelo. Dickens set up his study, with a commanding view of the famous lighthouse, the Lanterna, with its state-of-the-art rotating Fresnel lens; but he missed London, above all his long traversals of it, by day and night. He fully understood for the first time how crucial for him external stimulation was: as he marched through the great metropolis, he drew energy from its energy, and his absorption of its life – its tragedy and its comedy – replenished him, nourished and sustained him; he would emerge from a five-hour walk glowing and renewed. No such possibilities in the sleepy suburbs of Genoa. However, the sound of the bells that swept up to him from the port below gave him the title and the metaphor for his next Christmas Story: *The Chimes*. He soon had his steam up, as he wrote to Forster: 'I get up at seven; have a cold bath before breakfast and blaze away, wrathful and red-hot, till 3 o'clock, when I usually knock off (unless it rains) for the day.' 'Knock off' is very good, as if he were doing a simple routine job of work, blazing away, nine to five. In fact, *The Chimes*, more directly than anything he ever wrote, is his plea for the dignity and respect of the working man. Perhaps too direct: at times it becomes a speech or a pamphlet. Forster observed that, since his American tour, Dickens had acquired 'the habit of more gravely regarding many things before passed lightly enough' and that reading Carlyle had convinced him of 'the hopelessness of any true solution of either political or social problems by the ordinary Downing Street methods'. He had lost all faith in Parliament's capacity to put down 'any serious evil'. It was down to him, then: he gladly accepted his responsibility. He wanted the whole of society to be converted, as Scrooge had been converted. After his first glimpse of the great historic buildings of Italy, he had been moved to say to Forster:

> When I saw those places, how I thought that to leave one's hand upon the time, lastingly upon the time, with one tender touch for the mass of toiling people that nothing could obliterate, would be to lift oneself above all the dust of all the Doges in their graves, and stand upon a giant's staircase that Samson couldn't overthrow!

He drew his strength from the people – his people; they made him strong, even as he toiled to make them strong.

The moment he finished writing *The Chimes*, he felt impelled to go back to London to read it out loud to his core circle; he duly leaped into the carriage with his sturdy guide and courier, Louis Roche, and together they took a two-week tour of the great cities of Northern Italy. In Milan he felt it cruel 'not to have brought Kate and Georgy', but it was Forster whom he longed to have by his side as he gaped at Venice. He left Roche and the carriage in Milan, proceeding alone through Switzerland, crossing the Simplon by sledge, utterly exhilarated by the life-threatening descent from the summit. He saw Basle and Strasbourg, and arrived in Paris on 28 November, having written letters all the way; they would form the basis of his book *Pictures from Italy*. Finally, triumphantly, he arrived in London a day early, and flung himself into the arms of Maclise and Forster. On 3 December, he read *The Chimes* at Forster's chambers to a small group of his closest friends, including Carlyle and Douglas Jerrold; Maclise, who was also there, made a drawing of the event, in which light seems to be streaming from Dickens's head, as his listeners sit in a sort of emotional trance. Two nights later, he read it again, to some of the same people, but this time including Macready; the great actor was prostrate with emotion, 'undisguisedly sobbing and crying on the sofa'. That was the tribute that meant most to him: the acknowledgement of the most admired performer of his day. 'What a thing it is,' Dickens wrote to his wife after the reading, 'to have power', crystallizing, in a sense, the theme of his life: his journey from the absolute and humiliating impotence of the blacking warehouse, to a position of increasing mastery and influence. This reading of *The Chimes* marks the beginning of a new phase in that journey, a desire to experience his power even more directly, to communicate even more personally, than he did in his writing. It was a desire that would grow and grow, until in the end, it killed him.

He left London on the ninth, staying in Paris for a few days, where he saw Macready, who was just beginning a short season there. He also met and was cordially received by the great names of Parisian literature of the mid-1840s: Alexandre Dumas, Victor Hugo, François-René de Chateaubriand, Théophile Gauthier, and the prodigiously successful author of *The Wandering Jew*, Eugène Sue. One night he went to the theatre with Macready to see Mlle St George: 'once Napoleon's mistress, now of an immense size, from dropsy, I suppose; and with little weak legs she can't stand upon. Her age withal somewhere between 80 and 90 … every stage conventionality she ever picked up (and she has them all) has got the dropsy too, and is swollen and bloated hideously.' His account of the players' shortcomings shows the sharpness and professionalism of his observation of the stage: 'The other actors never looked at one another, but delivered all their dialogues in the pit, in a manner so egregiously unnatural and preposterous that I couldn't make up my mind whether to take it as a joke or an outrage,' he wrote to Forster. 'You and I, Sir, will reform it utterly,' which points to another aspect of his life that would soon open up.

* * *

He was back in Genoa in time for Christmas 1844, to which he applied himself with all his characteristic ebullience and passion. But he managed to find time, amongst all the partying, the dancing and the conjuring, to help their neighbours at the Palazzo Rosso, M. and Mme de la Rue, with a problem. The Dickenses had dined with the de la Rues just before his trip to London. The husband, Émile, was a Swiss banker; the wife, Augusta, was English-born. This 'most affectionate and excellent little woman' suffered from *tic douloureux*, a set of debilitating nervous symptoms. Dickens was certain that Augusta's condition would be amenable to treatment by Mesmerism, so, just before Christmas, with Émile de la Rue's enthusiastic encouragement, he put Augusta in a trance. Little by little, he began to uncover the contents of her unconscious. He was astonished not only at what he found there, but also by his own power: the results were spectacular. These sessions were conducted in private, to the entire approval of Émile, and the deep disapproval of Catherine Dickens. But he brushed Catherine's objections aside: he had started on something that, given his nature, he was impelled to pursue to its conclusion. What he was doing was far from John Elliotson's somewhat boulevard demonstrations of freakish behaviour: using hypnotism, Dickens was in effect giving Augusta de la Rue a course of psychoanalysis, some forty years before Freud's experiments with the same technique led to the formal creation of the discipline. At first Dickens concentrated on relieving what Freud and his mentor Jean-Martin Charcot would describe as hysterical symptoms – extreme tension, violent spasms, facial contortions; often he would be at her side all night at the Palazzo Rosso. The experience sometimes left him so disturbed that in the early hours of the morning Catherine would find him pacing up and down in a room filled with lit candles.

He saw Augusta through many terrible anguished nights, providing her with the balm of deep and refreshing sleep.

Eventually, he got her to talk when she was in a trance. She spoke of hostile people talking about her, criticizing her; later she mentioned a brother, whom she pitied deeply; eventually she spoke of a terrifying Phantom that was haunting her. Dickens became feverish with excitement: the prospect of a total cure inspired him to prescribe ever more hypnosis sessions. He could think of little else. He was writing nothing; all his imaginative powers were focused on Augusta. Then, in mid-January 1845, it was time, to his great irritation, for him and Catherine to go on their long-planned tour across Italy. They were heading for Rome via La Spezia, Carrara, Pisa, Siena and Leghorn, then on to Naples where they would be joined by Georgina. Dickens was loath to leave his patient, as he now saw her: he was, he told Émile, 'Augusta's humble servant and physician'. Reluctantly, he set off with Catherine, leaving instructions that he should be kept informed of every development in her condition. As they rattled through the great Tuscan cities, letters giving minute-by-minute accounts of Augusta's situation chased them, and long replies full of detailed advice were raced back to Genoa. But this was not enough for Dickens. He surmised that it might be possible to exercise his Mesmeric powers at long distance. Augusta and he accordingly set aside an hour every day during which he trained his full mental force on her. It appeared to work; she improved. On one occasion, they happened to be travelling at the designated hour, Dickens on the box carriage and Catherine hoisted up beside him to take the air. Dickens nevertheless focused on 'his patient'. After a while, he was conscious of Catherine's muff falling onto the floor; he looked up and found her in a trance. He had accidentally hypnotized his wife.

At last they arrived in Rome, at the height of the Carnival, which predictably thrilled Dickens; he strode heroically about in the Campagna, but was obsessively drawn back again and again to the Coliseum, haunted by its ruined grandeur, the crumbling remains of the greatest power the world had ever known. On they went to Naples, which Dickens loathed for its shabbiness and ugliness; there they were joined by Georgina, then continued down the coast, down to Pompeii and Herculaneum. Dickens was duly awed by the cities stopped dead in their tracks. 'Next to the wonder of going up and down the streets,' he later wrote in *Pictures from Italy*,

> and in and out of the houses, and traversing the secret chambers of the temples of a religion that has vanished from the earth, and finding so many fresh traces of remote antiquity: as if the course of Time had been stopped after this desolation, and there had been no nights and days, months, years, and centuries, since: nothing is more impressive and terrible than the many evidences of the searching nature of the ashes, as bespeaking their irresistible power, and the impossibility of escaping them.

But the source of all this devastation, Vesuvius, was the great destination for Dickens; they set out to conquer it. 'By prodigious exertions, we passed the region of snow and came to that of fire – desolate and awful you may well suppose,' Dickens wrote to Forster.

> It was like working one's way through a dry waterfall, with every mass of stone burnt and charred into enormous cinders, and smoke and sulphur bursting out of every chink and crevice, so that it was difficult to breathe. High before us, bursting out of a hill at the top of the mountain … the fire was pouring out, reddening the night with flames, blackening it with smoke, and spotting it with red-hot stones and cinders that fell down again in showers.

On, on, Dickens strode, with the women struggling to keep up with him. At the base of the topmost cone, Georgy and Kate were finally obliged to stop. Dickens went inexorably on, with one other member of the party and the guide. 'The sensation of struggling up it, choked with fire and smoke, and feeling at every step as if the crust of the ground between one's feet and the gulf of fire would crumble in and swallow one up (which is the real danger), I shall remember for some little time.' The letter continued, 'we looked down into the flaming bowels of the mountain and came back again, alight in half a dozen places, and burnt from head to foot.' On the way down, two men and a boy from another party fell down the crevasse. One of the men died; the boy and other man were covered in blood.

Dickens was exultant: 'My clothes,' he cried, 'are burnt to pieces.' He had kind words for Georgy and Kate: 'My ladies are the wonder of Naples, and everybody is open-mouthed.' For clumsy, now rather more than pleasantly plump Catherine, the ascent of Vesuvius was little short of heroic. Obviously there were no lengths to which she would not go to fight for her man – all in vain, alas. The regular bulletins Dickens was receiving from the Palazzo Rosso now indicated a resumption of Augusta's old symptoms, so Dickens insisted that the de la Rues join them at Rome, where they would be staying for three weeks on the way back to Genoa. When Dickens's party at length arrived in the Holy City, which was, to Dickens's disgust, in the throes of Holy Week, Augusta was already installed in the hotel with her husband, and in urgent need of her 'humble servant and physician', who unhesitatingly offered her his usual twenty-four-hour service. Even he was shaken by exposure to her 'myriads of bloody phantoms of the most frightful aspect'; at one o'clock one morning, a terri-fied Émile de la Rue woke him up to deal with her. She was 'rolled into an apparently insensible ball, by tic on the brain'. Within half an hour Dickens had calmed her, and she fell asleep. He increasingly saw Augusta as a battleground on which he was locked in a mortal struggle with a Phantom; this

Phantom loomed larger and larger in his imagination, threatening, Dickens was sure, to expunge her very existence.

These titanic nights were followed by instructive days spent sightseeing with the de la Rues, unless Augusta needed his Mesmeric services, in which case Dickens would resume his treatment wherever they happened to be: 'sometimes under olive trees', he told a correspondent, 'sometimes in Vineyards, sometimes in the travelling carriage, sometimes at Wayside Inns during the midday halt'. When they left Rome, via Florence, the de la Rues, at Dickens's insistence, travelled back with them. Goaded beyond endurance, Catherine finally rebelled, increasingly convinced that Dickens was in love with Augusta, and – despite Émile de la Rue's apparent approval of their being constantly together – very possibly having an affair with her. This suggestion deeply outraged Dickens, but Catherine would not be mollified. She declared that she would no longer speak to the de la Rues, and when they got back to Genoa, he felt obliged to explain her behaviour to them. The knock to his pride was intense. The de la Rues were understanding; no further reference was made to the matter. Dickens continued to treat his patient, and to socialize alone with the de la Rues, and when the time came, some eight weeks later, for the Dickenses to leave Genoa, in a gesture of almost inconceivable insensitivity, Dickens elected to stay with the de la Rues at the Palazzo Rosso while Catherine and Georgina and the family got on with the tedious business of packing up.

The numerous Dickens entourage, with its multifarious bags and baggage, coachman, servants, women, children and dog, then headed back to London through Northern Italy and Switzerland, whose landscape of course roused Dickens's titanic inclinations: the precipitate descent from the summit on the newly opened Alpine route was thrillingly terrifying for him; what the rest of the family thought is another matter. On they went, through Germany and Belgium, where they met up with Forster, Maclise and Douglas Jerrold. They were back in London at the beginning of July.

Dickens's mental state during this Italian sojourn had been tumultuous even by his standards. The de la Rue episode drew from him his most self-dramatizing behaviour, casting himself in the role of protector, saviour, healer, thaumaturge. The fact that he was inspired to assume these roles by a young woman helpless in the grip of a malign power is clearly significant; it is hard to imagine him being so galvanized if the sufferer had been male. The way in which he dramatized his relationship to women is symptomatic of an apparent inability to be at ease with them; they always seem to occasion some disturbance of his soul. It was in Genoa, quite soon after his arrival, that Mary Hogarth, never, on his own admission, far from his waking thoughts, entered his dreams again, in spectacular fashion. He had been troubled with rheumatism, 'knotted round my waist like a girdle of pain', which stopped him from sleeping. When sleep did finally come, he had a peculiarly vivid dream – he called it a vision – in which, like Scrooge, he was visited by a spirit. He immediately knew that it was Mary's spirit, and that it was 'full of compassion and sorrow for me'. This realization, he said, 'cut me to the heart'. He sobbed, asking for a sign: would the spirit relieve Mrs Hogarth – Mary's mother, but he dared not use those words – of her distress? The spirit would. Then, 'in an agony of entreaty', he asked 'what is the True Religion?' He asked the spirit whether perhaps the form of religion was unimportant 'if we try to be good'. Not waiting for an answer, he then pressed it to say whether Roman Catholicism was best, because it made one think of God more often, and 'believe in him more steadily'. The spirit told him – 'full of such heavenly tenderness for me that I thought my heart would break' – that for *him* it was the best. When he woke, at dawn, tears were running down his face, and he woke Catherine, repeating the story over and over.

It is extraordinary that Dickens, with his settled loathing of the Roman Catholic Church, should, even in a dream, have come to such a favourable opinion of it. He believed profoundly in God and revered the figure of Christ (though denying his divinity), to the day he died, but he had little truck with organized religion, finally settling on that most secular of persuasions, Unitarianism; as it happens, Forster was a Unitarian before him. The core of the dream, though, is the compassion and the 'heavenly tenderness' which Mary Hogarth extended to him. This is what cut him to the heart. The desperate need for a healing, female presence that he had found in Mary but that had eluded him since, however famous and powerful and prosperous he had become, was a constant with him. Perhaps that was what his subconscious had led him to dream: Mary the Mother of God, so central to Catholicism, is the apotheosized version of Mary, his angel, extending understanding forgiveness, unquestioning kindness and consideration.

Clearly Catherine was entirely unable to furnish any of this, or indeed much of what he needed. Though capable of the occasional gesture of affection towards her, his tone with her was increasingly severe, even authoritarian. Early in their stay in Genoa, Macready's sister Susan Atkins had visited them for a month; neither Kate nor Georgy could endure her, and Dickens was obliged to exercise ingenious diplomacy to preserve the peace. When he went back to London to read *The Chimes* to his inner circle, leaving Susan with them, he wrote severely to Catherine that she must be nice to their visitor, because 'I could never forgive myself or you if the smallest drop of coldness or misunderstanding were created between me and Macready.' Dickens's attachment to his male friends was sacrosanct (until he fell out with them, at any rate), and Catherine needed to be clear about her significance in the scheme of things.

TEN

Every Man in His Humour

Forster, who studied Dickens very closely, wrote of the Italian sojourn that 'it was the turning-point of his career'. He was unquestionably right, but the changes were taking place several strata below the surface. In Italy, he had scarcely written anything apart from *The Chimes*. This was part of a deliberate policy of exposing himself to new stimuli and to re-charging the batteries of his imagination. It was understood that he would produce a Christmas Book every year; and of course he continued to write letters on his usual stupendous scale – the ones he wrote from Italy, especially those to Forster, were partly intended for future use. But of a new novel there was no stirring whatever. Despite the financial success of *The Chimes*, which had done well enough for him to have Devonshire Terrace lavishly redecorated during their time abroad, with new wallpaper in blue and gold, new hand rails, and liberal amounts of gold mouldings, he was turning over various ideas as to how to secure his income without the commitment of starting another novel. He started to ponder two old ventures, both of which in their different ways came to fruition; both were predicated on the premise that he would be in full control of them.

The first took longer to mature. It was the idea, so close to his heart, of the weekly magazine made up of a variety of smaller pieces – 'notices of books, notices of theatres, notices of all good things, notices of all bad things' – most of which he would write himself, but many of which would be written by others: the heart of the enterprise, however, its absolute purpose, would be to keep him in frequent and direct communication with his readers. 'I would at once sit down upon their very hobs; and take a personal and confidential position with them which should separate me, instantly, from all other periodicals periodically published,' he wrote. He had a name for the magazine that he felt 'people would readily and pleasantly connect with *me*'. That name was *The Cricket*: 'I would chirp, chirp, chirp away in every number till I chirped it up to – well, you shall say how many hundred thousands.' The aim was to promulgate what he called *Carol* philosophy: 'cheerful views, sharp anatomisation of humbug, jolly good temper … and a vein of glowing, heart, generous, mirthful, beaming reference in everything to Home and Friends and Fireside.' The magazine did not come about immediately, but this quintessentially Dickensian notion soon re-emerged in slightly modified form; it was very dear to his heart, representing, as it does, the Apollonian, the Pickwickian, the positive and affirmative aspect of Dickens's artistic impulse, leaving him to explore the darker byways of his inner life in the novels he would soon be writing.

The planned magazine's name survived in that year's Christmas Book, *The Cricket on the Hearth*, which soon rivalled *The Chimes* in sales. It is hard in the twenty-first century to respond warmly to the story's parable of the eponymous insect's resolution of a husband's unjust jealousy (though it may have had some complex resonance for Dickens in the light of his deteriorating domestic life), but John Peerybingle and his little wife Dot, Caleb Plummer and his blind daughter Bertha, enchanted Victorian England. As with its predecessor, and all his subsequent Christmas Books, it was dramatized – with Dickens's imprimatur – by the impresario-performer Albert Smith, who had contributed to *Bentley's Miscellany* during Dickens's editorship. The play was premiered at the Adelphi Theatre, just a week after the book's publication, to triumphant effect; within a month, seventeen unauthorized versions of it were playing across London.

In fact, a great deal of 1846 was dominated for Dickens by theatrical activity; his old itch to perform was asserting itself again. He and Forster, a keen amateur actor himself, had often spoken of putting on a play. Dickens was scarcely back from Genoa than he was asking him: 'ARE we to have that play??? I have often thought', he wrote to Forster, 'that I should have been as successful on the boards as I have been between them.' On stage in Montreal, he said, '(not having played for many years) I was as much astonished at the reality and ease, to myself, of what I did as if I had been another man'. The play they settled on, rather surprisingly, was Ben Jonson's *Every Man in His Humour*, which (heavily re-written) had been a big success of Garrick's, but it had latterly fallen out of favour; Macready had had a flop with it some years earlier. Forster says they were drawn to the play by Jonson's theory of Humours, though as it happens, and despite its title, the play is not an especially thorough-going example of the theory: *Martin Chuzzlewit*'s Pecksniff is a rather more complete example of being single-mindedly possessed by one quality than is Jonson's jealous Kitely. It is no surprise, on the other hand, that Dickens should have been drawn to Jonson's world of exaggerated characterization and exuberantly hard-edged language; the names of the dramatis personae alone, featuring Roger Formal, George Downright, Mr Wellbred and the servant Brainworm, are a small step away from Dickens's own cast lists. He and Forster used Garrick's version, 'smoothing it down' even more, with the result that it was, Dickens told Macready, 'not long', which could scarcely be said of the original. One way and another, they turned it into a most unlikely smash hit.

It was a large-scale operation, and it took some planning. Just as he had done in Montreal, Dickens seized the responsibilities of management with both hands. Even Forster was taken aback. 'I never seemed till then to know his business capabilities,' he writes. 'He adjusted scenes, assisted carpenters, invented costumes, devised playbills, wrote out calls and enforced as well as exhibited in his proper person everything of which he urged the necessity on others.' His intentions for the production were crystal clear: his instructions to scene-painters and tailors precise and detailed, accompanied by visual references from Elizabethan paintings. 'Supernatural exertions are being made,' he told his brother Alfred, rejoicing in the excellent work of the craftsmen. The actors, however, rather disappointed him – 'so far'. He expected nothing less than excellence: they might be amateurs, but Dickens made no concessions. The company was an astonishing one, not by thespian standards, but as a representative slice of early Victorian men of letters: Henry Mayhew, playwright and author of the articles that would before long become *London Labour and the London Poor*, Mark Lemon (editor of *Punch*), Douglas Jerrold, radical journalist and author of the classic melodrama, *Black-Eyed Susan*, John Leech, illustrator of all of Dickens's Christmas Books, Gilbert à Beckett, playwright, humorist and Poor Law Commissioner. This was Dickens's circle: radical, high-spirited, and most of them in some way connected to the stage; even Maclise, who was not in the play, but was very much part of his circle, was the son of an actor; so was Jerrold. Mayhew played Knowell, Forster took Garrick's old part of the obsessed jealous husband Kitely, and Dickens bagged the role of the swaggering soldier, boastful Bobadil. Like a Method actor, he started living the part, corresponding in Bobadilian mode: 'The player Mac hath bidden me to eat and likewise drink with him, thyself, and short-necked Fox tonight,' he wrote to Forster. 'An' I go not, I am a hog, and not a soldier.' He took extreme pains with the design of his costume, providing his own sword. He and Forster took the interpretation of the play very seriously, and when they fell out over a scene, Dickens appealed to the greatest living actor. He was rather miffed when Macready took Forster's side, but he abided by his verdict ('with the worst grace in the world,' he said jestingly). In fact, he was having the time of his life: 'I think of changing my present mode of life and am open to an engagement,' he told Macready, only half tongue-in-cheek.

They rehearsed solidly every evening for six weeks; at the performance, in September 1845, Miss Kelly's little theatre in Dean Street in Soho was heaving with a frightfully chic audience, dolled up to the nines; the press was liberally represented. Dickens was not temperamentally inclined to hide his light under a bushel, and his protestation to Augusta de la Rue that 'it had got into the papers despite all our protestations' was somewhat disingenuous. 'How I wish you could have been there!' he wrote to her. 'I have known nothing short of a Murder to make such a noise before.' The Duke of Devonshire had come a hundred miles in one direction, Tennyson a hundred miles in the other. Such was the success of the performance that there were immediate demands for repeat performances; even Dickens can scarcely have guessed that what had been planned as a bit of fun would be revived again and again over the next three years, twice by Royal Command – once for Prince Albert, the second time for the Queen herself. It was Dickens's night in every department: the production, the general standard of playing, above all his own acting. He had, said Forster, 'the title to be called a born comedian, the turn for it being in his very nature', though he noted, commenting on Dickens's adulation for Mathews, that 'his strength was rather in the vividness and variety of his assumptions, than in the completeness, finish or ideality he could give to any part of them'. This 'quickness and keenness of insight' enabled him to show first Bobadil's 'bombastical extravagance and comical exaltation' then his 'tragical humiliation'. A famous painting shows Dickens in the role – all flourish and fantasy.

His joy in acting – the sense of release it gave him – was palpable. 'Though he was always greater in quickness of assumption than in steadiness of delineation,' said Forster, 'there was no limit to his delight and enjoyment in the adventures of our theatrical holiday.' Jane Carlyle was not in holiday humour when she saw it: she rather despised the audience, and had nothing but contempt for the performers, including 'poor little Dickens, all painted in bland and red, and affecting the voice of a man of six feet'. The opinion Dickens really craved was that of Macready, who confided in his diary that he found him good, but not great. The reviewers had no such reservations: 'Mr Dickens assumed the swagger of the "Paul's Man" with an ease that belonged to a stage veteran rather than an amateur.' The *Morning Post* declared that 'Should it be this gentleman's fate to witness the ebb-tide of his popularity as a novelist, it is evident that there is another road to public favour open to him, in which he is not less likely to be successful than literature.' This would be said again and again over the years, to his great satisfaction. Forster was perhaps the first of many to notice how closely his writing and his acting were connected:

> He took up the higher calling, but it included the lower. There was no character created by him into which life and reality were thrown with such vividness, that to his readers the thing written did not seem the thing actually done, whether the form of disguise put on by the enchanter was Mrs Gamp, Tom Pinch, Mr Squeers, or Fagin the Jew. He had the power of projecting himself into shapes and suggestions of his fancy which is one of the marvels of the creative imagination, and what he desired to express he became.

Forster's suggestive last phrase describes the essential gift of an actor; supremely, Dickens is the writer as actor.

Despite his delight in performance, it was animating the entire enterprise that really inspired him. 'I have always had a misgiving in my inmost heart,' he told Mme de la Rue, 'that I was born to be the manager of a theatre.' The idea of running a theatre spoke to so many aspects of his nature: galvanizing a team, shaping destinies, serving the public, permitting the power he knew he had in him to be exercised in benevolent mode. His desire to create a daily newspaper partook of the same impulse – that, and his growing political frustration. Ever since he had come back from America three years earlier and learned of the failure of the only remaining Liberal news-paper, *The Courier*, he had been angling to launch a new one, but no one would back him, leaving readers, as he felt, with-out a paper that addressed the matters that touched people's 'business and bosoms most'. The idea now returned to him, even more strongly.

As always with Dickens, once he had conceived a notion, he rapidly moved forward to its completion, brooking no objection. Forster opposed the idea purely on practical grounds, but, with sweet reason, Dickens refused to budge. 'In all intellectual labour,' Forster noted, 'his will prevailed so strongly when he fixed it on any object of desire that what else its attainment might exact was never duly measured; and this led to frequent strain and unconscious waste of what no man could less afford to spare.' This time he had no difficulty in attracting support from investors of a broadly Radical persuasion: the gardener and architect Joseph Paxton; anti-Corn Laws supporters; railway magnates. His publishers, Bradbury and Evans, who at first were merely going to print the paper, now put themselves forward as backers. Another major investor, Sir Joshua Walmsley, was a proponent of reform based not on class conflict but, as he put it, on 'a joint concern for the welfare of the entire country', which became the basic political platform of the paper. Dickens set to work vigorously, offering large salaries to leading journalists, many of whom showed considerable interest in joining him, to the degree that established newspapers felt threatened. Dismayed by the standard of candidates for the editorship, Dickens now proposed himself for the job (at twice the advertised salary). Forster was strongly against it: it would, he said, do little to enhance his 'fame and genius', but Dickens, on the one hand convinced that he could do the job better than anyone else, and on the other still looking for a stable source of income, had already made his mind up. A deeper underlying motive was his constant craving for direct engagement with his readers: 'I have, sometimes, that possibility of failing health or fading popularity before me, which beckons to such a venture as this. At the worst, I have written to little purpose if I cannot *write myself right* in people's minds, in such a case as this.'

At that point, a leading City broker went under, which forced one of Dickens's most important backers to pull out. Dickens warned Bradbury and Evans that investing in the paper might ruin them, but they stood firm. As his assistant, he secured the sterling services of W. H. Wills, an established sub-editor whose work he had published in *Bentley's Miscellany*; and although many of the people he had approached changed their minds and stayed put, he assembled an excellent staff with many distinguished journalists, among them Forster as drama critic and leader writer, and Dickens's father-in-law George Hogarth as music critic; his father John he engaged as chief reporter, a sign of a thaw in their relationship. All through December 1845, Dickens toiled away on the new paper; the *Daily News*, as they named it, was announced on 27 December 1845, whereupon *The Times* launched a savage attack on *The Cricket on the Hearth*, that year's Christmas Book, which had appeared just two weeks earlier: Fleet Street was on the defensive.

The new paper hit the streets on 21 January 1846; despite the immense amount of planning and a number of trial runs, the front page was a mess, full of typos and poorly aligned, to the unconcealed delight of the competition. The rest of the paper was highly creditable, mixing news with stories and editorial matter, the first newspaper ever to do so. In the first edition, Dickens nailed the paper's principles to the mast: 'Progress and Improvement … a very healthy Education, Civil and Religious Liberty, and Equal Legislation'; he also contributed a 'Travelling Letter from Italy', a slightly re-written version of one of the letters he had sent Forster. A healthy 10,000 copies of the first edition were sold; but sales on subsequent editions rapidly declined. More proprietors were sought and found; but Dickens was utterly exhausted by the demands of editorship: his years as a reporter had done nothing to prepare him for it. Although his team were united on domestic issues, they diverged wildly on foreign affairs, and nothing he could do or say would bind them together. He began to realize that he had made an enormous mistake, and as usual in such situations, he picked a fight with his publisher. This time William Bradbury of Bradbury and Evans was the one who caught it in the neck.

As before, the issue was one of authority. Dickens accused him of 'interposition between me and almost every act of mine at the newspaper office', which he declared to be 'as disrespectful to me as injurious to the enterprise'. It appears that Bradbury had criticized John Dickens, and Dickens rose like a lion to defend him: there was, he said, 'no more zealous, disinterested or useful gentleman attached to the paper'. But despite these fusillades, he knew in his heart that he would not continue with the editorship; after seventeen editions, he handed in his notice, appointing Forster as his successor. He told Augusta de la Rue that his reason for doing so had been his dispute with the business managers (Bradbury and Evans) whom he believed 'would be the ruin of what would otherwise have been a very fine property'; there is no evidence whatever that this was the case. Nonetheless, Dickens told her, he 'walked bodily out of the enterprise.' He continued to write occasional pieces for the *News*, notably on capital punishment and crime and education, and a further eight 'Travelling Letters from Italy', but his relationship to it was peripheral. After nine months, Forster, who had taken on the editorship most reluctantly, relinquished it to Charles Wentworth Dilke. Dilke stabilized the paper financially and consolidated its liberal stance, making it a force to be reckoned with.

The entire episode of Dickens's editorship is extraordinary and highly characteristic, an example both of the force of his willpower and of its limitations. Insofar as what he wanted to achieve was dependent on him, he was unstoppable. But an enterprise like creating a major national daily paper, dependent on so many factors and so many individuals, proved to be beyond his reach. Forster, who had from the beginning opposed Dickens's assumption of the editorship, nonetheless noted that the *News* (which survived until 1930, when it merged with the *News Chronicle*) remained loyal to the programme Dickens set out for it: 'The paper would be kept free from personal influence or party bias; and would be devoted to the advocacy of all rational and honest means by which wrong might be redressed, just rights maintained, and the happiness and welfare of society promoted.'

Immediately after leaving the *News*, Dickens called in the letters he had written to friends from Italy, put them together with the 'Travelling Letters' from the *Daily News* and in due course offered them to the public, with great success, as *Pictures from Italy*. In the preface to that book, he confessed to his readers – in one of those periodic bulletins by which he maintained his personal relationship with them – that it had been 'a mistake, in so departing from his old pursuits, to have disturbed the old relations between himself and his readers'. The *Daily News* episode was an attempt to re-define himself; it was as if he wanted to be anything other than a novelist. Around the same time he offered himself as a London magistrate. He was, very sensibly, turned down (although the thought of Dickens on the bench is a delectable one). Despite the huge success of the Christmas Books, he felt he was not speaking, as only he could, for his fellow countrymen, articulating their anxieties, celebrating their oddities, affirming their values. Somehow he was not fully living up to his own conception of himself as the Tribune of the People. And then, at last, the relative failure of *Chuzzlewit* now three years behind him, he felt within him the stirrings of a new novel. 'Vague thoughts of a new book are rife within me,' he wrote to Lady Blessington. 'I go wandering about at night into the strangest places.' He was ready again to surrender to his genius.

But not in England. The failure of his editorship of the *News* was too present. He found he could not 'shut out the paper, here, sufficiently to write well', and determined to leave the country again. Bradbury and Evans, who, despite his contretemps with Bradbury on the *News*, he retained as his publishers, announced A NEW ENGLISH STORY by Charles Dickens in twenty parts. So once again his sizeable entourage, including, as ever, the dog, was uprooted and set off, on 31 May 1846, via Ostend – partly by steamboat, partly by rail, partly by coach – for Switzerland, ending up in Rosemont, a villa by the lake in Lausanne, 'whence' he told Augusta de la Rue, 'I should run over to Genoa immediately'. He would have preferred to have stayed in Genoa, he confided in her, but Catherine – 'though I have beset her in all kinds of ways' – would not contemplate it. But Lausanne proved a productive environment: soon after settling in, and the books, the ink, and the bronze ornaments without which he could not write, had arrived, he was able to make the exuberant upper-case announcement to Forster:

BEGAN *DOMBEY*!

He had planned the new book carefully, outlining the essential course of the plot – what he called 'the stock of the soup' – then written (not without difficulty) the first instalment. But having done that, he needed to focus quickly on the Christmas Book, to which end he decided – naturally – that he would 'run and look for it' in the glaciers of the French part of Mont Blanc, in nearby Chamonix. He took his womenfolk with him. 'We went by a mountain pass not often crossed by ladies, called the Col de Balme, where your imagination may picture Kate and Georgy on mules *for ten hours at a stretch*, riding up and down the most frightful precipices.' He did the tough stuff on his own. 'I went into all sorts of places; armed with a great pole with a spike at the end of it, like a leaping-pole, and with pointed arms buckled on to my shoes; and am all but knocked up.' The elemental inspiration worked its usual charm on him; the impact on his nervous system of such exposure stirred his creativity in ways entirely separate from the subject matter of whatever he might be writing. The central figures and the great underlying themes of his work come not from what he has seen and heard, but from deep mysterious places within him. Here in France he pushed himself with reckless intensity. He was determined to get to a green spot covered with wild flowers lying 'among the most awful mountains' across the Mer de Glace, but 'I could find no Englishman at the hotels who was similarly disposed'. Even Louis Roche, his intrepid courier, whom he had nicknamed The Brave, *'wouldn't go. No sir!'* So he went alone. Dickens boasted that he was 'the admiration of Chamonix'. He may not have been able to conquer the *Daily News*, but he was more than a match for Mont Blanc.

Back in Lausanne, he went on his usual rounds of the criminal and medical institutions: at the Asylum for the Blind he was shown the work they did not just with the blind but with the deaf and the dumb as well. He met a little blind girl, one of the inmates, who constantly laughed ('good God! Conceive what at!'), and a youth with whom he made some sort of contact by giving him cigars. '*M. Dickens m'a donné des cigares,*' the boy said, over and over. Elsewhere, he met a prison doctor who rejected the American model of solitary confinement, instead, to Dickens's heartfelt approval, putting them to work plaiting straw, weaving, and making shoes. Altogether, he liked Lausanne in particular and Switzerland in general. To some extent, he was simply glad to be away from England; when he did run into fellow countrymen they were 'always Tory, hang 'em!' But his enthusiasm for the Swiss was not simply by default. He greatly admired their political system:

> 36,000 in this small canton, petitioned against the Jesuits – God knows with good reason. The Government chose to called them 'a mob'. So, to prove that they were not, they turned the government out. I honour them for that. They are a genuine people, these Swiss. There is a better metal in them than in all the stars and stripes of all the fustian banners of the so-called and falsely-called United States.

He discerned the baleful influence of Catholicism in two adjoining cantons: 'On the Protestant side, neatness; cheerfulness; industry; education; continual aspiration, at least, after better things. On the Catholic side, dirt, disease, ignorance, squalor and misery.' He saw its workings closer to home: 'I have a sad misgiving that the religion of Ireland lies as deep at the root of all its sorrows ... as English misgovernment and Tory villainy.' Despite his political furore, these letters from

Lausanne bubble with gossip, anecdote, and opinion, teeming with character sketches. He was even tempted to get a show on: 'There is not a bad little theatre here; and by way of an artificial crowd, I should certainly have got it open with an amateur company, if we were not so few that the only thing we want is an audience ...'

Since arriving in Switzerland, he had written a number of papers on the subject, dear to his heart, of the Ragged Schools, for the incumbent Whig Prime Minister, Lord John Russell, who had become an increasingly close friend; he had written half of *The Life of Our Lord*, an account of the Gospels for his children, not intended for publication; and several instalments of *Dombey and Son*. The latter was now coming easily, after a difficult start, so much so that he actually overwrote some instalments: 'Invention, thank God, seems to be the easiest thing in the world: and I seem to have such a preposterous sense of the ridiculous after this long rest ... as to be constantly requiring to restrain myself from launching into extravagances in the height of my enjoyment.' Nonetheless, he found it hard to work at speed in Lausanne or indeed Geneva because of

> ... the absence of streets and numbers of figures. I can't express how much I want these. It seems as if they supplied something to my brain, which it cannot bear, when busy, to lose. For a week or a fortnight I can write prodigiously in a retired place (as at Broadstairs) and a day in London sets me up again and starts me. But the toil and labour of writing, day after day, without that magic lantern, is IMMENSE!!! ... I mention it as a curious fact, which I have never had an opportunity of finding out before.

The book was an immense success from the beginning – '*Dombey* sale BRILLIANT!' – and marked a return to critical favour after the perceived feebleness of the Christmas Stories.

The splendid sales ensured Dickens's financial security, which is not without mild irony in that it is the first of a cycle of novels in which he puts capitalism, in this instance Business, in the dock: the novel's full title when it was published in book form was *Dealings with the Firm of Dombey and Son: Wholesale, Retail and for Exportation.*

During *Dombey*'s composition, he had frequent recourse to elemental stimulation. In September, he and Kate and Georgy went up the Great St Bernard. Eventually, they reached the famous convent:

> No vegetation of any sort. Nothing growing, nothing stirring. Everything iron-bound and frozen up. Beside the convent, in a little outhouse with a grated iron door which you may unbolt for yourself, are the bodies of people found in the snow who have never been claimed and who are withering away – not laid down, or stretched out, but standing up, in corners and against walls; some erect and horribly human, with distinct expressions on their faces; some sunk down on their knees; some dropping over on one side; some tumbled down altogether, and presenting a heap of skulls and fibrous dust. There is no other decay in that atmosphere; and there they remain during the short days and the long nights; withering away by grains, and holding ghastly possession of the mountain where they died.

This in a letter: it would be a highlight of any other man's novel.

Despite regular exposure to Nature and the Sublime, he was finding the current Christmas Story, *The Battle of Life*, a struggle. He was very pleased with the title, but found it hard to get much further; indeed, he was tempted to give it up altogether, the first time he had ever given up something he had started, he said. In his early days, he had made a habit of being engaged on writing two books at the same time, but had never started two together. 'I am constantly haunted by the idea that I am wasting the marrow of the larger book, and ought to be at rest,' asking himself the question we all ask of him – where did it come from, the energy, the invention, the passion? In the event, he steeled himself to the task: he was very loath to lose the money 'and still more to leave any gap at Christmas firesides which I ought to fill'. The little book was finished by the end of October; the riotously sentimental story, concerning a father's conversion from cynicism when one daughter gives up her lover in favour of another daughter, was not critically admired. Dickens, said *The Times*, was responsible for the 'deluge of trash' that 'inundates the Christmas book market'; 'Exaggerated, absurd, impossible sentimentality,' observed the *Morning Chronicle*. It has not subsequently done much better in critical report, but it sold very handsomely at the time; the stage version, by Albert Smith for the Dickens theatrical veterans Robert and Mary Keeley, was equally successful, and the servant Clemency provided a notable role for Mrs K, earlier an acclaimed Mrs Gamp.

In mid-November, driven by Dickens's restlessness, the family had taken leave of Lausanne and established itself in Paris. Dickens himself returned to London briefly to oversee the stage production of *The Battle of Life*, then went back to Paris, where, in January 1847, in the fifth number of *Dombey and Son*, he put an end to the short unhappy life of Paul Dombey. 'Between ourselves,' he wrote to his friend Angela Burdett-Coutts, 'Paul is dead. He died on Friday night at about 10 o'clock; and as I had no hope of getting to sleep afterwards, I went out, and walked Paris until breakfast-time next morning.' He always felt that way when he had killed a character, even though, as in the case of Paul, the death was long premeditated, planned from the very beginning. Paul's demise caused an immense sensation, even in Paris (in England, it was said to have stopped the nation in its tracks). In general, though, Dickens was restless in the French capital, which he found to be in a bad way: the widely reported death of the *grande horizontale* Marie Duplessis, the model for the eponymous *Dame aux camélias* in the smash-hit play by Alexandre Dumas *fils*, a year later, exercised Dickens greatly: he was appalled by what it said about French society during the last days of the reign of Louis-Philippe (though, paradoxically, he was deeply shaken by the play when he saw it). He concluded that 'the disease of satiety, which only less often than hunger passes for a broken heart, had killed'.

On a more mundane level he was exasperated by the workmen working outside the apartment, and unable to find anywhere to write comfortably. He walked the city incessantly, day and night, satisfying his need to keep applying savage stimuli to his imagination, to his nervous system, to prevent creative or physical lethargy setting in; maintaining his *élan vital*, which had once been so effortless to him, became, even when he was in his mid-thirties, more difficult. He was compulsively drawn to the morgue; one visit there disturbed him so much that he had to keep away for a while, but he recovered sufficiently to drop by on New Year's Eve, 1846. There he came upon the corpse of an old man who had been murdered:

> It seemed the strangest thing in the world that it should have been necessary to take any trouble to stop such a feeble, spent, exhausted morsel of life. It was just dusk when I went in; the place was empty; and he lay there alone, like an impersonation of the year eighteen hundred and forty six.

Even as he moodily and metaphorically contemplated the dead old man, his sense of humour, which rarely deserted him entirely, however wretched and restless he might be, asserted itself: 'I find I'm getting Inimitable, so I'll stop.'

Later, Forster arrived, and they did the rounds together – plays, cabarets, operas, galleries – and visited the great: the poet-politician Lamartine, the prolific melodramatist Scribe, and Victor Hugo, again, 'by whom Dickens was received with infinite courtesy and grace'. Dickens spoke French poorly, according to Forster, 'his accent being somehow defective', but he 'practised himself into writing it with remarkable ease and fluency'. All the while, he continued writing *Dombey*. At a certain point, finding that the next number of the novel was short by two pages, he had to rush back to London to make up the shortfall while the printers waited, then returned to Paris, but almost immediately went home again because of Charley Dickens's having succumbed to scarlet fever. Back in London, work on *Dombey* was slow. He slithered into a despairing lethargy. His wretchedness, he told Georgy, was 'inconceivable'; writing was agonizing. But the public response to the story was phenomenal; Macready confided to his diary that after reading the seventh number, he had been unable to speak to Dickens for sobs. Thackeray, at the time a serious rival, burst into his publisher's brandishing the offending edition and crying: 'There is no writing against such power as this – One has no chance! – it is unsurpassed – stupendous!' The spectre of *Chuzzlewit*'s relative failure had been at last laid to rest. But the success did nothing to assuage Dickens's restlessness. His already tense state was rendered worse by an unprovoked attack on him by one of his horses, 'under the impression that I had gone into his stall to steal his corn, which upon my honour I had no intention of doing'. The attack left him feeling a 'low dull nervousness of a most distressing kind' for some time.

Catherine, meanwhile, gave birth to their seventh child, Sydney. She suffered excruciatingly: the specialist said he had never seen anything like it. Dickens was appalled – 'my dear Kate suffered terribly' – but there seems to have been no thought in his mind to avoid the cause of the suffering. During this period he was, as it happens, much preoccupied with the situation of women, specifically those then referred to, without inverted commas, as 'fallen'. The work of rehabilitating them was a passion of Angela Burdett-Coutts, the formidable daughter of the noted Radical MP, Sir Francis Burdett; her grandfather on her mother's side was a distinguished banker, whose fortune of £3 million she inherited at the age of twenty-three, at which point, she incorporated his name into hers. At a stroke, she became the richest woman in England; by the time of her death, in 1906, she had distributed in philanthropic gifts the exact amount of her original inheritance. She met Dickens in 1839, two years after she came into her inheritance; she was immediately drawn to what she called his 'restlessness, vivacity, impetuosity, generous impulses, earnestness and frank sincerity', a description of great particularity, testifying to her own sharpness of mind and precision of observation. She was indeed one of the most brilliant women of her time – the future Edward VII referred to her as 'after my mother, the most remarkable woman in England'. She was rather forbidding in appearance, a fact that a steady succession of aspiring husbands was more than willing to overlook; she turned them all down, instead proposing to the then seventy-five-year-old Duke of Wellington, who gently demurred. Dickens was drawn to her for quite other reasons; and she became his closest female friend, a relationship that – no doubt because of her lack of physical allure – caused no anxiety to Catherine.

Burdett-Coutts and Dickens were united in their determination to address the enormities of the age; she had the money to do it, and Dickens guided her on how it might be achieved. Their first great joint cause was the Ragged Schools for the free education of destitute children, to which Burdett-Coutts gave large sums of money; but despite Dickens's friendship with the Prime Minister, Lord John Russell, they were between them unable to activate the political will to establish the schools on a permanent and widespread basis. Their next venture, in 1847, was more under their control: the establishment of a Home for Homeless Women. Dickens found the premises in Lime Grove, in Shepherd's Bush in West London, and personally arranged the lease. It was called Urania Cottage, the name a fortuitous reference to the transformation of the women from votaries of the sexual Venus to followers of the celestial one. Once involved, Dickens took his responsibilities with deep seriousness. A year before the opening, only a couple of months before embarking on *Dombey and Son*, he wrote a remarkable and comprehensive 2,000-word letter to Burdett-Coutts, outlining a practical plan for the establishment of an asylum or institution; in all its essentials, his plan was implemented.

Dickens was particularly clear about the attitude they should adopt towards the women. To begin with, Dickens wrote, there must be no humiliation of a girl or woman arriving at the asylum: 'it is explained to her that she has come there for *useful* repentance and reform, and because her past way of life has been dreadful in its nature and consequences, and full of affliction, misery and despair *to herself*. Never mind Society, he wrote, when she is at that pass. 'Society has used her ill and turned away from her and she cannot be expected to take much heed of its rights and wrongs.' The destructiveness 'to *herself*' of the life she had led must be explained to her 'and there is no hope in it, or in her, as long as she pursues it'. She needed to be told that she was 'degraded and fallen, but not lost,' having this shelter; and that – most importantly – 'the means of Return to Happiness are about to be put into her own hands, and entrusted to her own keeping'. He proposed that the women should be motivated by a system of marks for good conduct and that the establishment should be in close contact with prison governors, familiar as they were with the women's histories. Numbers, he said, should not exceed thirty; and the final objective of the women's stay at Urania should be the creation of their own happy homes. If the women were to run away, they should always be allowed to return. It was, he said, important that they should be allowed to re-build their self-respect by being trusted with money – 'putting some temptation within their reach'. It was above all essential that the atmosphere should be 'cheerful and hopeful'.

And he offered to run the place himself. 'I don't know,' he wrote to Burdett-Coutts,

> whether you would be disposed to entrust me with any share in the supervision and direction of the institution. But I need not say that I should enter on such a task with my whole heart and soul; and that in this respect as in all others, I have but one task, as in all others, I have but one sincere and zealous wish to assist you, by any humble means in my power, in carrying out your benevolent intentions.

This is the greatest novelist of his age, at the height of his powers, offering himself for a task that would be a full-time job for any other man. Even more astonishingly, he actually did it, supervising and directing what he proposed should be called, not an asylum, or an institution, but a 'Home'; this seems to have been a coinage of Dickens's, the first use of the word in this context. Prior to the opening of Urania Cottage, Dickens took the trouble to meet and learn something of the lives of each of the first batch of inmates; he vetted the chaplain and chose the bedsteads, the dresses and the linen. 'You must not see the house until it is quite ready,' he wrote to Angela Coutts, with boyish excitement. With the letter, he enclosed a four-page leaflet intended for distribution to women in prison. It is an extraordinary document, written in Dickens's most personal and direct manner:

> You will see, on beginning to read this letter, that it is not addressed to you by name. But I address it to a woman – a very young woman still – who was born to be happy and has lived miserably; who has no prospect before her but sorrow, or behind her but a wasted youth; who, if she has ever been a mother, has felt shame instead of pride in her own unhappy child. You are such a person, or this letter would not be put into your hands. If you have ever wished (I know you must have done so some time) for a chance of rising out of your sad life, and having friends, a quiet home, means of being useful to yourself and others, peace of mind, self-respect, everything you have lost, pray read it attentively and reflect upon it afterwards. I am going to offer you, not the chance but the *certainty* of all these blessings, if you will exert yourself to deserve them. And do not think that I write to you as if I felt myself very much above you, or wished to hurt your feelings by reminding you of the situation in which you are placed. GOD forbid! I mean nothing but kindness to you, and I write as if you were my sister.

He writes of their lives from close personal observation:

> You know what the streets are; you know how cruel the companions that you find there are; you know the vices practised there, and to what wretched consequences they bring you, even while you are young. Shunned by decent people, marked out from all other kinds of women as you walk along, avoided by the very children, hunted by the police, imprisoned, and only set free to be imprisoned over and over again – reading this very letter in a common jail you have already dismal experience of the truth. But to grow old in such a way of life, and among such company

– to escape an early death from terrible disease, or your own maddened hand, and arrive at old age in such a course – will be an aggravation of every misery that you know now, which words cannot describe. Imagine for yourself the bed on which you, then an object terrible to look at, will lie down to die. Imagine all the long, long years of shame, want, crime, and ruin that will arise before you. And by that dreadful day, and by the judgment that will follow it, and by the recollection that you are certain to have then, when it is too late, of the offer that is made to you now, when it is NOT too late, I implore you to think of it and weigh it well.

He urges them, whether they accept or reject the offer, at least to consider it.

If you awake in the silence and solitude of the night, think of it then. If any remembrance ever comes into your mind of any time when you were innocent and very different, think of it then. If you should be softened by a moment's recollection of any tenderness or affection you have ever felt, or that has ever been shown to you, or of any kind word that has ever been spoken to you, think of it then. If ever your poor heart is moved to feel truly, what you might have been, and what you are, oh think of it then, and consider what you may yet become.

'Believe me,' he ends, in terms not unlike those in which he addressed his readers, 'that I am indeed, YOUR FRIEND.'

Notions of self-transformation and self-respect, quite independent of any religious association, were central to Dickens's thinking, and were deeply radical in a world where virtually all eleemosynary activity was based on explicitly Christian notions of repentance and acknowledgement of the Gospels. Dickens was closely involved in Urania Cottage for nearly ten years, implementing the principles he had formulated with considerable firmness, ejecting girls when necessary, speaking to them sternly if he thought that was required. It was, in fact, another of his benevolent dictatorships. But the fundamental compassion that underscored it, the fellow feeling with the women – the same empathy that underlies all of Dickens's charitable work – is highly original and unique in his own time, and came from a deep place within himself. 'The very poor and unprosperous were not his clients whose cause he pleaded,' as Forster said, 'but in some sort his very self.' In his prison pamphlet, Dickens urged, '[D]o not think that I write as if I felt myself very much above you … GOD forbid!' He put himself into their minds: he identified with them. In the 1846 letter to Angela Coutts, he wrote of the women they would be admitting to Urania Cottage:

> There is no doubt that many of them would go on well for some time, and would then be seized by a violent fit of the most extraordinary passion, apparently quite motiveless, and insist on going away. There seems to be something inherent in their course of life, which engenders and awakens a sudden restlessness and recklessness which may be long suppressed but which breaks out like Madness.

He knew whereof he spoke.

In the build-up to the opening of Urania Cottage, during the month of July, he had given free rein to his own personal form of restlessness and recklessness: the theatre. At the beginning of 1846, he and Forster had done a couple of benefit performances of *The Elder Brother*, a remarkably obscure Jacobean play by Philip Massinger and John Fletcher, notable chiefly for its ripe invective ('a flat dull piece of phlegm, shap'd like a man', growls one character of another; 'gaudy glow-worm', snaps someone else), which no doubt they revelled in, and now they revived *Every Man in His*

Humour, with two new after-pieces, visiting Manchester and Liverpool in the highest of spirits. The occasion – or frankly, the excuse – for reviving the play was the perennial impecuniosity of Leigh Hunt, the much-loved *littérateur* and fantastical survivor of the generation of Byron and Shelley, now in danger of complete financial collapse. This excuse disappeared when Lord John Russell secured a pension for him; the proposed London performances, much to Dickens's chagrin, were cancelled and he retreated to Broadstairs. 'I am at a great loss for blowing my superfluous steam off, now that the play is over – but that is always my misfortune – and find myself compelled to tear up and down, between this and London, by express trains.' This is almost too crude a metaphor for the sexual frustration that often seems to be driving him. Before, of course, his writing had given him the release he craved, but now that was uphill work: 'Deep slowness in the Inimitable's brain.' He speaks of being in 'a dreadful state of mental imbecility'.

The following year, after finishing *Dombey*, he was back in theatrical harness, this time with a new production of *The Merry Wives of Windsor*, the proceeds to go towards endowing a curatorship at Shakespeare's birthplace in Stratford-upon-Avon. They added an after-piece: *Animal Magnetism*, a satire on Mesmerism by Mrs Inchbald; it was one of the farces in Dickens's father's library at Portsmouth that he had read over and over again as a boy. The piece, according to Dickens, was so funny that they could scarcely carry on – 'I have seen people laugh at the piece till they hung over the front of the boxes like ripe fruit' – which is surprising, if true, because the text is a rather feeble and formulaic little comedy; what is remarkable is that it remorselessly sends up something that Dickens took very seriously indeed. They completed their repertoire with *Every Man in His Humour*, always much in demand; after two performances in London at the Haymarket Theatre, one of them in the presence of Victoria and Albert, they took themselves to Birmingham, Bristol, Manchester, Liverpool, Edinburgh and Glasgow, where they were joyously acclaimed. In *The Merry Wives*, Dickens played Justice Shallow and Master Slender, Anne Page's gormless suitor. Dickens's Shallow was particularly admired: he adopted 'a senile stoop and feeble step' for the part, into which he infused 'a certain attempted smartness of carriage'. When he spoke it was with 'a kind of impeded sibillation of utterance, as if through loss of teeth'. He was all but unrecognizable, and there was 'a Storm of plaudits' when the audience realized who he was. His Slender had a 'vacant, loutish air' and was 'full of sheepish naïveté', and as always he made sure that he got his laughs. 'In the enjoyment as in the labour,' wrote Forster,

> he was first. His animal spirits, unresting and supreme, were the attraction of rehearsal at morning, and of the stage at night. At the quiet early dinner, and the more jovial unrestrained supper, where all engaged were assembled nightly, his was the brightest face, the lightest step, the pleasantest word. There seemed to be no need for rest to that wonderful vitality.

They made the sizeable sum of £2,500 which they handed over to the Scottish playwright John Sheridan Knowles, whom they had proposed for the curatorship of the Shakespeare house. Knowles, now fallen on hard times, was, as it happens, the author of *The Hunchback*, the play whose original production had delayed Dickens's audition for the Covent Garden Theatre and stopped him from pursuing a stage career and pushed him towards writing, so we owe Knowles, at several removes, a sizeable debt. At the end of the tour, Dickens had his usual slump: 'I have no energy whatsoever, I am very miserable. I loathe domestic hearths. I yearn to be a vagabond,' he wrote to his fellow player on the tour, Mary Cowden

Clarke, from Devonshire Terrace. 'Why have I seven children – not engaged at sixpence-night-apiece, and dismissable for ever if they tumble down, not taken on for an indefinite time at vast expense and never – no, never, never – wearing lighted candles round their heads?' (like the fairies in *Merry Wives* presumably). 'A real house like this is unsupportable after that canvas farm wherein I was so happy. What a humdrum dinner at half-past five, with nobody … to see me eat it, compared with *that* soup, and the hundreds of pairs of eyes that watched its disappearance.' He wrote with tongue only half in cheek. He firmly believed that his passion for the stage was shared by the rest of humanity. At the Annual Dinner of the General Theatrical Fund, of which he was a trustee, and whom he addressed regularly, he declared:

> The Drama is founded on an eternal principle in human nature … in this room, in Windsor Castle, in an African hut, in a North American wigwam, there is the same inborn delight and interest in a living representation of the actions, passions, joys and sorrows of mankind. In England, of all countries on the earth, this interest is purified and exalted by the loftiest masterpieces of human fancy, and the proudest monuments of human wit. Such an art I hold to be imperishable; reverses it may suffer … but nothing, to my thinking, can root it out.

In December of 1848, the dramatization of his latest Christmas Book, *The Haunted Man* (not, perhaps, one of the loftiest masterpieces of human fancy), appeared at the Adelphi; the book itself, trounced critically, sold splendidly, and Twelfth Night was celebrated by Dickens and friends with the usual orgy of conjuring, acting and dancing, all of it extremely well rehearsed. He had been taught the polka by his little daughters Katey and Mamie. 'My father was as much in earnest about learning to take that wonderful step correctly, as though there were nothing of greater importance in the world,' recollected Mamie.

> Often he would practise gravely in a corner, without either partner or music, and I remember one cold winter's night his awakening with the fear that he had forgotten the step so strong upon him that, jumping out of bed, by the scant illumination of an old-fashioned rushlight, and to his own whistling, he diligently rehearsed its 'one, two, three, one, two, three' until he was once more secure in his knowledge.

He partnered Mamie and six-foot-two John Leech partnered Katey, who was all of nine years old, and they were greeted with 'hearty applause'. Dickens then swept up Mrs Macready into his arms: 'For two mortal hours', he told her husband, they 'danced without ceasing ... reducing to "tarnal smash" (as we say in our country) all the other couples one by one.'

The family was to be enlarged yet again ten days later; Henry Fielding Dickens was born on 16 January 1849. A little over a year earlier, Catherine had had a miscarriage on a train en route for Glasgow, and was attended by Joseph Simpson, the pioneer of the use of chloroform as a surgical anaesthetic; the year before he had first, highly controversially, used it for delivering a child. Dickens had thoroughly acquainted himself, as only he could, 'with the *facts* of chloroform – in contradistinction to the talk about it'. When Catherine's labour began, and the child did not come easily, Dickens immediately sent for the extremely experienced anaesthetist from Bart's Hospital. The doctors, he said, 'were dead against it': contemporary medical theory indicated that mother or child would be rendered idiotic, that natural labour would be impeded, and – most worrying of all – that the woman would be excited to 'improper sexual feelings and expressions'. Despite these risks, Dickens stood his ground '(thank God, triumphantly)'. 'It spared her all pain,' he said, 'and saved the child all mutilation. It enabled the doctors to do, as they very readily said, in ten minutes what might otherwise have taken them an hour and a half. She was, to all intents and purposes, *well* the next day.' This was a huge breakthrough: Catherine had suffered long periods of post-natal discomfort and depression. This episode reveals not only Dickens's compassion, but also his undeviating faith in scientific progress. His criticism of capitalism contained no element of nostalgia, as we have seen, for the fine old Tory days; in Venice, he gave vent to his loathing of people who protested against the construction of a railroad across the water, 'instead of going down on their knees, the drivellers, and thanking heaven that they live in a time when iron makes roads, instead of … engines for driving screws into the skulls of innocent men.' His only demand of capitalism was that social progress should keep pace with its scientific counterpart. His embrace of chloroform was typical, and ahead of his times: its use in childbirth only gained widespread acceptance when, some five years later, Queen Victoria – just as prolific as Catherine – used it during the delivery of Prince Leopold in 1853, memorably dismissing her physicians' advice against it with the words '*we* are having the baby'.

Despite the morbidity about natural processes that sometimes descends upon the novels, in life Dickens was unsentimental and clear-eyed about them; when, in 1848, his eldest sister Fanny (who had always been frail) fell seriously ill with tuberculosis he did everything he could to be of practical help. He had become somewhat estranged from her on account of her extreme Evangelism: she and her husband, the tenor Henry Burnett, whom she had met at the Royal Academy, had both worked in the theatre and in concert halls; they also sang at Dickens's soirées, but they both came to feel that they were leading ungodly lives, so they went to Manchester to join a congregation of Dissenters, where they sang in the choir.

When those committed pleasure-lovers John and Elizabeth Dickens visited them, they were excused neither morning or evening prayers; Dickens did *not* visit. Fanny's only complaint in life was that the Sabbath and its Sacred Services never seemed long enough to her. Despite this huge temperamental and philosophical gulf between them, Dickens was deeply fond of her, and he visited her every day during the four months of her illness, at Hornsey in North London, where she and Henry had moved to be nearer medical attention. Her condition got worse and worse; on 1 September, Dickens saw her being seized by shocking paroxysms: 'the terrible aspect of suffering and suffocation – the appalling noise in her throat – and the agonized look around, which lasted I should think a quarter of an hour'. He forced himself to stay with her: as on his visits to the prisons, the hospitals, the morgues, the madhouses, he had to know, he had to see. The next day, 2 September 1848, Fanny was dead. She left behind her two sons, one of them, in Dickens's word, 'deformed'. Four months after his mother's death, this child, Henry, died – only two weeks after Dickens's son Henry was born. Dickens's letter of consolation to Fanny's husband, though properly compassionate, is astonishingly objective for the creator of Tiny Tim: 'I cannot but believe that the mercy of God has removed your poor dear boy.' A child afflicted as Henry was, he continues, 'must, if he lived, be inevitably doomed to great mental anguish, to a weary struggle with the difficulties of life, to many years of secret comparison in his own breast between himself and more healthy and fortunate children'. As Fanny's little boy was dying, Kate was yet again in what Dickens drily referred to as an 'anti-Malthusian state'; the baby, her ninth, was born in August 1850 and would be named Dora.

The year 1849 had begun with a celebration of the success of *The Haunted Man*. This unsatisfactory work, narratively feeble and lacking in descriptive power, might have been, had

Dickens engaged more deeply with it, one of his most power-ful stories. It is a Balzacian tale, whose central theme has a deep resonance in Dickens's own life: the brilliant chemist Redlaw has known 'wrongs and sufferings from under the burden of which he cannot escape'. A Ghost – his Double – appears; Redlaw asks to be allowed 'to forget my sorrow and wrong'. This wish is granted; gradually he realizes that memo-ries, however oppressive, are part of what it is to be human. At the end of the story, he has come to understand the precise meaning of the prayer, 'Lord, keep my memory green.' Dickens, now thirty-seven, after more than a decade of stupendous productivity, and despite having created a large family and established himself as one of the leading men of his age, was unable to find any rest within himself. His novels, though now more effortfully achieved, were getting deeper and darker; what he had lost in sheer exuberant inventiveness he had made up in intensity of thought. He now felt the need, for the sake of his work, but also for his sanity, to dig into the part of his life that he had deliberately repressed – his 'sorrow and wrong'. It seems to have been either in 1845 or 1846 that he wrote the autobiographical fragment of his early life that he handed to Forster at the beginning of 1849; by February of that year he was, he told Angela Coutts, 'in the first agonies of a new book'. The agonies were as much personal as literary. By March he knew what it was the book was to be called: *David Copperfield*.

ELEVEN

The Great Fight and Strife of Life

Dickens had struggled, as he often did, with names and titles. The field was narrowed by his decision that the initials of the central character must be an inversion of his own: he knew that autobiography was what he was about. David came easily enough; but the surname went through many transmogrifications: Copperboy, Copperstone, finally Copperfield. As for the title, he toyed with *Mag's Diversion* for some time, then *The Copperfield Disclosures*, *The Copperfield Records*, and *The Copperfield Survey of the World as It Rolled*. Forster, to whom each of these titles was submitted for comment, favoured the last; finally, for the serial version, Dickens settled on the cumbersome but complexly interesting *The Personal History, Adventures, Experience and Observation of David Copperfield the Younger of Blunderstone Rookery*, qualified by a final parenthetic phrase *[Which He never meant on any account to be published]*. This is Dickens's coming-out novel. The early part of it is essentially a lightly modified transcription of the autobiographical fragment, which, after he had shown it to Forster, he destroyed. The fragment had abruptly ended at the point at which he fell in love with Maria Beadnell; he could not bring himself at the time to relive that particular pain. It is telling that he was able to confront the trauma of the blacking warehouse, but not that of disappointed first love. Now he was ready to look at it: that catastrophic relationship and what it did to him runs through the whole of the latter part of *David Copperfield*.

It was Forster who had suggested that he should write the novel in the first person, a technique of which Dickens immediately became an absolute master. Forster's influence on his friend was, within clearly prescribed limits, immense and on the whole benevolent; Forster was that rare person, the friend as editor, a difficult position to sustain. Unexpectedly, Dickens welcomed, even actively encouraged, Forster's suggestions. It seemed to assuage the monthly agony of delivery, during which he lived with the fear that he could no longer do it, or that he would never get it right. He took no pleasure in the loneliness of creation. 'I have received your letter today and am overjoyed to find that you think so well of the number,' he wrote to Forster on one occasion. 'I thought well of it myself … but I did not know how far I might be stimulated by paternal affection.' Forster's suggestions were sometimes small and sometimes large; Dickens was perfectly willing on his advice to shift a whole character out of one novel into another. He even trusted him to cut text. 'I received your letter today. A decided facer to me! But I have no doubt you are right … in case more cutting is needed, I must ask you to try your hand. I shall agree to whatever you propose.' Though no one had anything like the influence over him that Forster did, there were other advisers, among them the distinguished Scottish advocate and literary critic, Judge Jeffrey, whom Dickens revered, and who had been one of his earliest champions; he had sometimes taken his advice. Forster was jealous of this, and with ill-concealed triumph quotes a letter of Dickens's concerning Jeffrey's input: 'I do not, at heart, lay much real stress on his opinion, though one is naturally proud of awakening such sincere interest in the breast of an old man …' Forster's position as Dickens's Critic-Laureate was secure, until, that is, Dickens's life was upended, and nothing was as it had been.

The first instalment of *Copperfield* was a decided hit – sales not quite as good as those of *Dombey and Son*, but the critical response was extremely warm. Dickens threw a splendid dinner in May 1849 to celebrate the successful launch. Guests included the Carlyles and Mrs Gaskell and Jerrold as well as Forster and Hablôt Browne, the illustrator; Thackeray came on after. There were always parties to celebrate the launch of a book and parties to celebrate its completion; there were even parties to celebrate its continuing success. Conviviality of this order was as essential to Dickens's life as the epic solitary walks that continued to take him across the city, especially at night. But there were walks with comrades, as well: the 'Walking Club', comprising Mark Lemon and John Leech (whose colour illustrations had so memorably adorned *A Christmas Carol*), the portraitist Frank Stone (responsible for the drawings for *The Haunted Man*) and Dickens, would meet weekly, take a train to Slough and go for long rambles, punctuated with laughter and refreshments.

The writing of *Copperfield* went on vigorously, though Dickens was assailed by a mysterious condition while on holiday with the family at Bonchurch on the Isle of Wight. 'The patient,' he said of himself, had an

> extraordinary disposition to sleep … extreme depression of mind, and a disposition to shed tears from morning to night … dull stupid languor … he has no purpose, power or object in existence whatever. When he brushes his hair in the morning, he is so weak that he is obliged to sit on a chair to do it.

He attributed it to the place; or was it perhaps *Copperfield*, the experience of re-living what he had hoped to put away from him for ever, the wound that he had re-opened? At any rate it passed. While he was still in Bonchurch, he invited John Leech to stay; Leech fell and split his head on a rock, becoming dangerously ill. Recovery was slow because he was unable to sleep, so Dickens hypnotized him, whereupon he fell into a deep slumber for ninety-five minutes. The following day he was markedly better, with full recovery shortly after. 'What do you think of my setting up in the magnetic line with a large brass plate?' he wrote to Forster. 'Terms, twenty-five guineas per nap.'

They stayed in Bonchurch for nearly three months, by which time he had written the first twenty chapters of *Copperfield*. It is interesting to note Dickens's reading during this holiday. It is a typically eclectic selection: all the minor tales and all the plays of Voltaire; Paul de Kock's racy novels of Parisian life; any number of travel books on exotic places, including several about Africa 'for which', says Forster, 'he had insatiable relish'. Dickens's reading was avid, unsystematic and idiosyncratic, which was part of what made him such an original. He knew Shakespeare virtually by heart, likewise Fielding, Smollett, Defoe and Goldsmith, to say nothing of *The Arabian Nights*, but he knew neither Marlowe, Milton nor Pope. Comparing a newly composed scene in *Dombey and Son* to Jane Austen, Forster had been astonished to find that Dickens had never read a word she had written. He read voraciously and at high speed, thought nothing of reading a book twice in a row, and was readily moved by the sentimental and the grandiloquent. He was fully abreast of the work of his contemporaries. His taste in literature is surprisingly undiscriminating; his analysis of individual writers is precise, betraying the eye, not of a critic, but of an editor: 'it seems to me', Forster reports him saying of an unnamed popular novel, 'as if it were written by somebody who lived next door to the people, instead of inside 'em'.

His hankering after editorship had not abated since his reluctant abandonment of *The Cricket*. He was as keen as ever to establish a direct communication with his public. There was a general, if vague, presumption among his readers that *Copperfield* was in some measure confessional; in the Preface to the printed edition he had said that he was 'in danger of wearying the reader whom I love, with personal confidences, and private emotions'. He felt, he said, as if he were 'dismissing some portion of himself into the shadowy world', and that 'no one can ever believe this Narrative, in the reading, more than I have believed it in the writing'. No one would know, till Forster let them know in the *Life of Dickens*, published two years after his death, why it was that Dickens believed in it quite so fervently. In 1869, in a revised Preface to *Copperfield*, he bashfully confessed that it was his 'favourite child'. But despite this new level of intimacy with his readers, he still felt the need of a regular forum in which he could address them directly. There was one example of direct contact with them that he might have wished to have avoided: Mrs Jane Seymour Hill, a person of restricted growth who practised as a chiropodist near Dickens's house in Devonshire Terrace, recognized herself in *David Copperfield*'s malevolently ogling dwarf Miss Mowcher, with her alarming catchphrase 'Ain't I volatile?' Mrs Hill wrote to him: 'I have suffered long and so much from my personal deformities, but never before at the hands of so gifted a man as Charles Dickens. Now you have made my nights sleepless and my daily work tearfull.' Dickens was mortified, and promised to alter the course he had plotted for the character so that the Reader would 'hold it in a pleasant remembrance'; this he did, having Mowcher help Peggotty to find Emily, rather than assist Steerforth in his seduction of her. His ability and willingness to respond either to advice or, as in this case, personal hurt – not unlike that of a writer on a weekly soap opera – suggests an uncommon degree of flexibility, almost post-modern, in his sense of the overall plan of his novels: within the world he has created, all sorts of outcomes are possible.

In July 1849, a third of the way through the serialization of *Copperfield*, he announced to Bradbury and Evans that he remained keen to create a periodical magazine. He needed to find a formula for it that satisfied him, though, and, as it had with *The Cricket*, his imagination took fantastical form: the controlling conception, he told a polite but mystified Forster, was to be a kind of semi-omniscient, omnipresent, intangible creature,

> a cheerful, a useful, and always welcome SHADOW, which may go into any place … and be in all homes and all nooks and corners, and be supposed to be cognisant of everything, and go everywhere, without the least difficulty. Which may be in the Theatre, the Palace, the House of Commons, the Prisons, the Unions, the Churches, on the Railroad, on the Sea, abroad and at home.

All correspondence from readers would be addressed to the Shadow. 'I want him to loom as a fanciful thing all over London.' People would ask, he said, 'What will the Shadow say about this?' or 'Is the Shadow here?' 'It is The Thing that is at everybody's elbow, and in everybody's footsteps. At the window, by the fire, in the street, in the house, from infancy to old age, everybody's inseparable companion.' In other words, it is Dickens as he would wish to be perceived: indispensable and omnipresent.

It is one of the oddest ideas to have come out of a mind that was, as he himself often observed, very odd indeed. Even in an age before Jung's identification of the Shadow with weaknesses, shortcomings, and base instincts, 'a reservoir for human darkness' (to say nothing of Orson Welles: 'the Shadow knows what Evil lurks in the heart of man'), shadows have rarely been seen as benevolent figures. Forster could make neither head nor tail of it, and told him diplomatically that, though he was charmed by it, he was unable to conclude anything out of it that had 'a quite feasible look'. Dickens was dreaming a periodical, not seriously planning one. Practical and brilliantly effective though he could be in action, when he applied his imagination to something it ran riot. 'As his fancies grew and gathered round it, they had given it too much of the range and scope of his own exhaustless land of invention and marvel.' The tension in Dickens between his absolute commitment to realism and 'practical power', and his recurrent longing for 'a wildness, a strangeness', is nowhere more in evidence than here: 'hardly any more characteristic idea survives him', noted Forster, even as he quietly killed it.

Sober sense soon prevailed. Almost without pausing, Dickens now outlined a 'feasible' format for the magazine. He carried over from his earlier shadowy effusions 'particular notions' upon the selected materials: there should always be a subject – Piracy, the history of Knight-Errantry, the Holy Grail, 'A History of Savages, showing the singular respects in which all savages are like each other; and those in which civilised men, under circumstances of difficulty, soonest become like savages.' It was not to be merely utilitarian in spirit: 'with all familiar things, but especially those repellent on the surface, something was to be connected that should be fanciful or kindly.' All the reviews, essays, criticism should 'distinctly and boldly (go) into what in one's own view ought to be the spirit of the people and the time'. There would be poetry, and short stories, both by Dickens and others. All these things were agreed between Dickens and Bradbury and Evans. Then there was the usual agonizing over a title: should it be called *Mankind*? Or *Everything*? *The Rolling Years*? *The Microscope*? Or, coming right out with it, *Charles Dickens/Conducted by Himself*? Finally, with a typical nod to the stage, a Shakespearean title was chosen. The allusion is to Henry V's great St Crispian speech before Agincourt:

> then shall our names
> Familiar in his mouth as household words
> Harry the king, Bedford and Exeter
> Warwick and Talbot, Salisbury and Gloucester
> Be in their flowing cups freshly remember'd.

The theatrical association was confirmed by the office's location, opposite the Lyceum Theatre; the front door was actually next to the stage door of the Gaiety. The first issue of *Household Words* appeared in March 1850, and one of Dickens's earliest dreams was finally realized. 'We aspire,' he wrote in the first edition,

> to live in the Household Affections, and to be numbered among the Household thoughts, of our readers. We hope to be the comrade and friend of many thousands of people, of both sexes, and of all ages and conditions, on whose faces we may never look. We seek to bring into innumerable homes, from the stirring world around us, the knowledge of many social wonders, good and evil, that are not calculated to render any of us less ardently persevering in ourselves, less tolerant of one another, less faithful in the progress of mankind, less thankful for the privilege of living in this summer-dawn of time.

At last he had a direct line to his readers; and for the first time he was master of his own destiny, with freedom of action. In fact it would turn out that he was more bound than ever, obliged to step in (like an actor-manager taking over a part when one of the actors is ill or drops out), to say nothing of the demands of day-to-day business. But the crucial thing was that, as well as giving houseroom to many excellent writers –

the first number began the serialization of Mrs Gaskell's powerful social document, *Lizzie Leigh* – the magazine was a perfect outlet for various aspects of Dickens's own preoccupations, both political and personal.

He had had a sort of dry run at crusading journalism when he wrote nine political articles for *The Examiner*, the influential magazine edited by Forster. Among them were three detailed and passionate articles under the title *Paradise in Tooting* about the nefarious practice of child-farming. These and the other six articles range wide over the enormities of the day, especially judicial; ignorance was a particular enemy. In a sense, he was establishing the platform not only of *Household Words* but of his remaining five novels. He had, of course, spoken frequently of social conditions in the speeches he was increasingly called upon to give. These were always stirring events, both for himself and for his audience. He spoke to the Mechanics' Institution, the United Law Clerks' Society, the Newsvendors' Benevolent Institution, the Metropolitan Sanitary Association, the Gardeners' Benevolent Institution; he spoke at the Mansion House in London and the opening of the Free Library in Manchester and at the meeting for the Removal of Trade Restrictions on Literature. To each he gave the impression that their institution or society held a special place in his heart and in the national life; he revealed detailed knowledge of their histories and their activities; he made graceful and self-deprecating references to his own books and characters, which were always warmly received; he made jokes pertinent to the organization that set the room on a roar; and he invariably ended with a roof-raising peroration that sent the audience out into the night, ready for the fray. His two most regular engagements of this kind were the Royal Literary Fund and the Royal Theatrical Benevolent Fund; these two passions were combined in a venture into which he plunged himself with his usual passion in the autumn of 1850, while he was wrestling, as he put it, with the last chapters of *Copperfield*. To an almost superhuman degree, Dickens was able to juggle his activities simultaneously, but there were limits: declining an invitation to attend a meeting of the Metropolitan Sanitary Association's committee on interments, he wrote, 'If I get fierce and antagonistic about burials, I can't go back to *Copperfield* for months and months. This is really the sort of condition on which I hold my inventive powers; and I can't get rid of it.'

Putting on plays, on the other hand, evidently did not inhibit his inventive powers. Throughout October he was busy with the arrangements for yet another revival of *Every Man in His Humour*, this time under the aegis of Sir Edward Bulwer-Lytton, at Lytton's country house at Knebworth in Hertfordshire. Dickens and Lytton (ten years Dickens's senior) had met as part of William Harrison Ainsworth's circle in the late 1830s; in terms of popularity, the older man rivalled Dickens in his novels on Ancient Roman and occult themes, and he was a successful dramatist to boot, one of his plays, *Money*, being a rather brilliant comedy that holds its own in the twenty-first century. Dickens was a great admirer of the novels, especially *Zanoni* and *The Last of the Barons*, and though they were on opposite wings politically, they were united in their desire to improve the standing of the profession of letters. Together they 'embarked on a design', as Dickens put it,

> to smooth the rugged way of young labourers, both in literature and the fine arts, and to soften, but by no eleemosynary means, the declining years of meritorious age. And if that project prospers, as I hope it will, and as I know it ought, it will one day be an honour in England where now it is a reproach.

Acknowledging Lytton's initiative in giving birth to the project, he described it as 'originating in his sympathies, being brought into operation by his activity, and endowed from the very cradle by his generosity'. Dickens's feelings for Lytton were warm, and coloured by the romance he felt towards the better sort of aristocrat, a sentiment that co-existed with his loathing of the whole principle of the peerage:

> In the path we both tread, I have uniformly found him from the first the most generous of men; quick to encourage, slow to disparage; ever anxious to assert the order of which he is so great an ornament; never condescending to shuffle it off, and leave it outside state rooms, as a Mussulman might leave his slippers outside a mosque.

Lytton's feelings for Dickens were slightly more complex. A year before Dickens's death, he jotted down, to be attached to his collection of letters from Dickens, an account of his friend and colleague: it contains a number of sharp insights.

> He has been fortunate in escaping the envy of fellow writers – & has aided this good fortune by a very skilful care of his own fame – watching every occasion to refresh it – he understands the practical part of authorship better than any writer – his nature is good & genial – but from his study of popularity – he a little over-parades his goodness.

He concludes that Dickens 'hit on that which he can do better than any other man and is only less than himself when he deviates from it – certainly, on the whole, one of the greatest geniuses in fiction the World has produced'. *En passant*, Lytton notes: 'An admirable actor, he is not without theatrical arts off the stage – he can even be insincere, though unconsciously so.'

There was no doubting the strength and authenticity of Dickens's feelings about the position of the writer. From the moment he started to make his living by writing, Dickens had fought for fair treatment, including proper emolument, for work done. His copyright battles continued to the very end; and though he fought fiercely for this aspect of 'the practical part of authorship', his concern was as much for the dignity of the job as for professional reward. He and Lytton were agreed that what was needed was not charity, which to some extent the Royal Literary Fund could offer, but an incentive to self-respect for writers. The performances of *Every Man in His Humour* at Knebworth – to largely aristocratic audiences (Lytton's neighbours, for the most part) – were to raise money to fund a Guild of Literature and Art. The visionary plan was to build a writers' colony on the estate; they would be given money to allow them time to write: established writers would receive £200, younger ones £100, not insubstantial sums for the time. But the scheme never caught on: writers, young and old, resented it, feeling patronized. The Guild slogged on for some years before finally failing; Dickens and Lytton were simply a century ahead of their time. Financially struggling Victorian writers preferred cash in hand. For the present, the three performances, in November of 1850, went off, as they always did, 'in a whirl of triumph', with Dickens in superb form as Bobadil, Leech, Lemon, Jerrold and Stone taking other roles; Georgy took part, having substituted for Catherine who, as if in fulfilment of Dickens's description of her as a donkey, had had the misfortune to fall through a trap-door at rehearsals in London.

Lytton had meanwhile written a play, *Not So Bad as We Seem*, a light eighteenth-century pastiche, with a leading part for Dickens in it, for performance the following year, both in London and on the road; Dickens thought the play 'most admirable', though in truth it is only mildly amusing. But it was a big play with lots of parts for all the splendid strollers, as they dubbed themselves. Before that, in January 1851, the theatrically insatiable Dickens rushed up to Rockingham Castle in Leicestershire, the seat of Richard and Lavinia Watson, whom he had met in Lausanne, and who had quickly become very important to him: *David Copperfield* is 'affectionately inscribed' to them. The Watsons had specially built a theatre for him. This was serious stuff: Dickens's theatremania was catching. After demonically rehearsing, as only he could, for six days, he put on three farces – *A Day After the Wedding*, *Used-up* and *Animal Magnetism* – and acted in them all. In *Used-up* he played a gentleman who disguises himself as a plough-boy, and had a triumph; Catherine, having avoided falling down any traps, appeared in the same play in the small role of the disgruntled widow, Lady Maria Clutterbuck, which thenceforth became her nickname in the family. The evening was crowned by the infallibly uproarious *Animal Magnetism*. After the final performance, they all danced until the small hours of the morning; and then the Dickenses travelled straight back to London. That night, after a railway journey of some hundred and twenty miles, he dined with the Prime Minister, Lord John Russell.

In February 1851 it was theatre all the way in London. He went to see Macready, first as King Lear ('it was the mind of Lear on which we looked,' Dickens wrote in a review of the performance in *The Examiner*. 'The heart, soul and brain of the ruined piece of nature, in all the stages of its ruining, were bare before us'), then, later that month, as Macbeth. This was the great actor's Farewell Performance; he was only fifty-eight. Dickens was deeply moved by the event: as 'a mere boy', he wrote to Macready the following day, he had been one of his faithful adherents in the pit, and 'no light portion of my life arose before me when the great vision to which I am beholden … faded so nobly from my bodily eyes last night'. It is an intensely emotional, almost overwrought, letter, a letter that as much laments the transformation of the mere boy into his present incarnation as it does the departure of Macready from the stage:

> If I were to try to tell you what I felt, I should only blot this paper with some drops that would certainly not be of ink, and give very faint expression to very strong emotion. What is all this in writing? It is only some sort of relief to my full heart, and shows very little of it to you; but that's something, so I let it go.

He and Forster had been busy arranging a farewell dinner for the great man, and as usual had over-ridden the desires of the person being honoured: Macready had wanted a sonnet Tennyson had written for him to be read at the end of the evening, but Dickens firmly told him that he was 'perfectly certain that it would not do at that time'; Dickens of course prevailed. The arrangements all went wrong to begin with, but came right in the end, providing a rousing farewell for the actor.

The demand for places at the banquet, on 1 March 1851, was immense. A young actor called John Coleman failed to get one, so he enterprisingly wrote to Dickens, who by return of post sent him 'a characteristically courteous autograph letter enclosing a ticket'; the unknown young actor found himself seated between the Prussian Ambassador and Thackeray. Coleman observed Dickens closely: 'his speech was as florid as his costume,' he noted. 'He wore a blue dress-coat faced with silk and aflame with gorgeous brass buttons, a vest of black satin, with a white satin collar, and a wonderfully embroidered shirt.' He commented on Dickens's appearance to his neighbour. 'Yes,' drawled Thackeray, 'the beggar is as beautiful as a butterfly, especially about the shirt-front.' Even at nearly forty, world-famous, and a national institution, he was still not quite a gentleman. Dickens's speech was not about Macready (Bulwer-Lytton did that, rather dully and partially inaudibly); his job was to propose the toast to Lytton, which he did with characteristic generosity. He did, however, briefly but powerfully evoke the Farewell performance itself:

> When I looked round on that vast assemblage, and observed the huge pit hushed into silence on the rising of the curtain, and that mighty surging gallery where men in their shirt sleeves had been striking out like strong swimmers – when I saw that boisterous human flood become still water in a moment …

Dickens's writing about actors and about the theatre is not especially memorable, but his writing about the audience, and the effect of a performance on an audience, is incomparable. For all his flair as an actor, and his disciplined brilliance as a director, he remained, at heart, a fan.

Meanwhile, things were difficult on the domestic front. He was not finding it easy to locate a new, larger house to accommodate his apparently ever-swelling family; and that March, Catherine appeared to be in the grip of some sort of nervous disorder – 'an alarming disposition of blood to the head, attended with giddiness and dimness of sight'; it was, says Dickens, 'not at all a new disorder with her'. The condition was no doubt exacerbated by the alarmingly poor health of her most recent baby, her ninth: seven-month-old Dora. Dickens, ever eager to pursue the latest scientific methods, dispatched her to the spa of Great Malvern, in Worcestershire, where Dr James Wilson was pursuing his somewhat controversial Hydropathic treatments, in which the patient was frequently immersed in freezing spring water. Catherine was to be placed, Dickens said, with some firmness, 'under a vigorous discipline of exercise, air and cold water'. He and Georgina and Catherine's faithful maid Anne Brown would accompany her, which they duly did, but in practice once Dickens had escorted her to Malvern, he was there only for short spells: his duties on *Household Words*, his rehearsals for the premiere of Bulwer-Lytton's *Not So Bad as We Seem* – with a Royal Command performance of it looming – and the suddenly deteriorating state of his father's health all demanded his attention.

John Dickens was in the incapacitating grip of the urethral condition that had dogged him for over twenty years; it had indeed been the reason for his departure from the Navy Pay Office (giving the phrase an honourable discharge a whole new meaning). John had concealed his worsening condition from even his closest family; a crisis was abruptly reached towards the end of March 1851, when he was informed by his doctors that without surgical intervention 'mortification and delirium, terminating in speedy death' were inevitable. They then performed 'the most terrible operation known in surgery', in Dickens's words, presumably a direct incision from the frenum to the scrotum, without the aid of the chloroform that had so helped Catherine in her recent confinements, or any other anaesthetic. Dickens came into the room immediately after the operation; it was, he said, 'a slaughter house of blood'. John Dickens was 'wonderfully cheerful and strong-hearted', and bore it with astonishing fortitude. Dickens himself was reeling; it provoked his old blacking warehouse malady: 'all this goes to my side directly, and I feel as if I had been struck there by a leaden bludgeon'. He continued with his editorial duties (he was currently sleeping on the floor at the *Household Words* offices); made tactful suggestions to Lytton about the new play; issued instructions to the scene-painters; dealt with equerries at Buckingham Palace concerning the royal visit, and with the Duke of Devonshire, at whose

London house the play was to be performed; spent as much time with the children, especially little Dora, as he could; and went endlessly back and forth to Malvern, a four-hour train journey in those days, to monitor Catherine's progress and generally cheer her up.

Whenever he was in London, he visited his father, finding him 'as well as anyone in such a state, so cut and slashed, can be'. The end was not far off; John Dickens died on 31 March, at the age of sixty-six, 'O so quietly,' Dickens wrote poignantly of a man who in his lifetime had been a veritable fountain of verbosity and noisy bonhomie. By good chance, Dickens happened to be there when his father died. He was numbed by the event. 'I hardly know what to do.' He held his mother for a long time, and they wept bitterly together. He told her, without irony, that she must rely on him for the future – as if she had ever relied on anyone else – and that he would pay whatever debts his father had run up. Next day, he went to Highgate Cemetery to secure the ground for his father's grave. 'The longer he lived, the better man I thought him,' he said to Forster; he wrote the inscription on the tombstone that immortalized his 'zealous, useful, cheerful spirit'. John's peccadilloes were forgotten, as Dickens recollected with affection his father's characteristic Micawberisms: noting the retirement of a doctor friend, Dickens remarks that they will be sorry to lose his advice 'or, as my father would say, to be deprived, to a certain extent, of the concomitant advantages, whatever they may be, resulting from his medical skill, such as it is, and his professional attendance, in so far as it may be so considered'. On another occasion, Dickens reported, John had rather magnificently remarked to a Nonconformist, 'The Supreme Being must be an entirely different individual from what I have every reason to believe Him to be, if He would care in the least for the society of your relations.' Dickens was not unaware what a boon it had been for him as a writer to be brought up by a father given to such utterances, to say nothing of his industriousness and his sunny temperament.

Dickens was somewhat winded by John's death. In a letter to Catherine, he expresses a rare moment of loss of will: 'I have sometimes felt, myself, as if I could have given up, and let the whole battle ride on over me.' He tried to put off an engagement to chair the Annual Dinner of the General Theatrical Fund, but they could find no one to replace him, so on 14 April 1851, he came up specially from Malvern to do it. He dropped by at Devonshire Terrace and played for a while with little Dora, who seemed much improved, and then set off for the Lords' Tavern. When he entered he was hugely acclaimed and, despite his low spirits, experienced his usual exhilaration in front of an audience, performing his chairmanly duties with customary aplomb. Forster was there, as ever, and so was Mark Lemon. Just before Dickens rose to make his main speech, one of Dickens's servants appeared and urgently took Forster aside. He had come direct from Devonshire Terrace: little Dora had suddenly died. Dickens, oblivious of what had happened, rose, and a transfixed Forster heard him say:

> Let any of us look back upon his past life and say whether he owes no gratitude to the actor's art! Not just because it is often exercised in the midst of sickness, poverty and misfortune – other arts, God knows, are liable to like distresses! Not just because the actor sometimes comes from scenes of affliction and misfortune – even from death itself – to play his part before us; all men must do that violence to their feelings, in passing on to the fulfilment of their duties in the great strife and fight of life.

Forster consulted with Lemon; they decided that there was nothing to be gained from telling Dickens what had happened. On he went:

> But because in the relief afforded us by the actor's art, we always find some reflection, humorous or pathetic, sombre or grotesque, of all the best things that we feel and know. If any man were to tell me that he owed no great acknowledgement to the stage, I would only ask him the one question, whether he remembered his first play? Oh, gentlemen, if you can but carry your thoughts back to that night, and think a little of the bright and harmless world it opened to your view, full well assured am I that we shall hear of it expressively from Mr Culliford [the treasurer].

It was one of his very best speeches, heartfelt, wide-ranging, funny, a comprehensive tribute to the theatre but particularly to actors of all degrees and abilities. He made toasts, he introduced speakers, one of whom was Forster, who, knowing what he knew, had somehow to propose Dickens's health. Alluding to the death of John Dickens, only a fortnight before, he noted that Dickens was present 'at great personal sacrifice, which few men would have ventured to have made'; the words must have had unbearable extra significance for him. Dickens replied graciously, raising further cheers and laughs. There were more toasts, more replies, more cheers, more laughter. Eventually, he made the traditional last toast, ending, 'The Drama was full of beautiful specimens of woman's love and woman's wit, but without stopping to draw comparisons between the characters of Desdemona, Juliet or other interesting creatures of the poet's brain, he would conclude by giving them, "The Ladies".' As he stood down amid thunderous applause, Forster and Lemon broke the terrible news to him, and he immediately returned to Devonshire Terrace. He spent the night at the side of his dead child, and then wrote a letter to Catherine, which Forster took down to Malvern, while Dickens made the arrangements for the funeral and burial of his child. In effect, he staged a scene, carefully scripted.

> My Dearest Kate
>
> Now observe. You must read this letter very slowly and carefully. If you have hurried on this far without quite understanding (apprehending some bad news), I rely on your turning back and reading again. Little Dora, without being in the least pain, is suddenly stricken ill. She woke out of a sleep, and was seen, in one moment, to be very ill. Mind! I will not deceive you. I think her *very* ill. There is nothing in her appearance but perfect rest. You would suppose her quietly asleep. But I am sure she is very ill, and I cannot encourage myself with much hope of her recovery. I do not – why should I say I do, to you my dear! – I do not think her recovery at all likely.

He is sure, he says, that Catherine will want to return home immediately but he enjoins her 'to come home with perfect composure' and to remember, as he has often told her before, that they cannot expect (having as many children as they do) to be exempt from the afflictions of other parents.

> If – *if* – when you come, I should even have to say to you 'our little baby is dead', you are to do your duty to the rest, and then shew yourself worthy of the great trust you hold in them.

Having delivered the letter to Catherine in Malvern, Forster, still obliged to maintain the fiction that Dora was alive, accompanied her back to London; a nightmarish journey it must have been. Back in London, Catherine would finally

have heard the words Dickens had so carefully prepared her
to hear.

TWELVE

Not So Bad as We Seem

Catherine behaved impeccably. She was, Dickens wrote, 'quite resigned to what has happened and can speak of it tranquilly. She is so good and amiable that I hope it may not hurt her.' In fact, her reaction to Dora's death was simply delayed. Dickens himself behaved with absolute self-control, until one day, for no discernible cause, he broke down and sobbed for an hour in the presence of his daughters. But then it was on, on, dealing with the pressing business of staging the Royal premiere of Lytton's play *Not So Bad as We Seem*. When both Catherine and Dora were ill, Dickens had asked permission of the Palace for the performance to be deferred; this was immediately and without demur agreed to, and a later date fixed. This date now loomed. There was no question of it being put off again, so, despite what had just happened, Dickens plunged ahead with determined vigour. The play needed alterations; the cast needed constant attention; the decor was nothing but trouble. 'My legs swell so, with standing on the stage for hours together, that my stockings won't come off,' he wrote.

> I get so covered with sawdust among the carpenters, that my Infants don't know me. I am so astonishingly familiar with everybody else's part, that I forget my own. I roar to the Troupe in general to that extent that the excellent Duke (who is deaf) thinks in the remoteness of his own little library that the wind is blowing hard.

The performances were taking place at Devonshire House, the Duke of Devonshire's London home, at his particular request. The Duke had taken a great shine to Dickens, shyly asking him whether he might be allowed to know him better; Dickens liked the Duke, another example of the better sort of aristocrat. The Duke was enchanted to be surrounded by all this life and activity, and was able to dispense detailed advice on Ducal protocol (there being a Duke in the play). He was also involved in dealing with the unusual problem of Lytton's estranged wife Rosina. This demented and embittered woman announced that she intended to sabotage the performance, threatening to appear disguised as an orange girl. This immensely excited Dickens's sense of drama, and he arranged for his friend Inspector Field of the Detective Police to be present in plain clothes. Dickens's nocturnal prowlings of the city in the company of the police had continued unabated, with the result that 'any of the detective men will do anything for me'. In the event, no disgruntled orange girls were found to be present.

The show went with some élan, though it was generally felt to be too long and not quite funny enough. The cast was – for a benefit to raise money for a Guild of Writers and Artists – an appropriate mix of writers and painters: Jerrold, Forster, Lemon, Dudley Costello for literature, for the fine arts the portraitist Frank Stone, the allegorist Augustus Egg and John Tenniel (later to be Lewis Carroll's illustrator for *Alice in Wonderland*). Dickens's Lord Wilmot – a young man at the head of the Mode more than a century earlier – was not among his most inspired assumptions, aristocratic nonchalance not being his forte as an actor; Macready thought the whole event dull. Dickens had his big moment ten days later when they added *Mr Nightingale's Diary*, a farce written for the occasion by Mark Lemon, and then substantially re-written by Dickens. He had attempted to write a farce himself, but failed, for the interesting reason that 'I am constantly striving for my reputation's sake to get into it a meaning that is impossible in farce; constantly thinking of it, therefore against the grain, and constantly impressed with a conviction that I could never act in it with the wild abandonment which can alone carry a farce off.' He had his full measure of wild abandonment in *Mr Nightingale's Diary*. His character, the lawyer Gabblewit, disguises himself (for no especially good reason) as various different characters. It is an *hommage* to – or a direct steal from, depending on how you look at it – Charles Mathews; Dickens seized the opportunity to play each of Gabblewit's assumed characters as one of his own creations: Sam Weller, Mrs Gamp, Jingle, and so on. These sections, obviously written by him, contain some droll Wellerisms, and, especially, some vintage Gampery:

> Arter his own parential father, as never (otherwise than through being bad in liquor) lost a day's work in the wheelwright's business, which it was but limited, Mr Nightingale, being wheels of donkey shays and goats, and one was even drawed by geese for a wager, and went right into the centre of the parish church on a Sunday morning on account of the obstinacy of the animals, as can be certified by Mr Wigs the beadle afore he died drawing on his Wellington boots, to which he was not accustomed, arter a hearty meal of beef and walnuts, to which he was too parshal, and in the marble fountain of that church, this preciousest of infants was made Absalom, which never can be unmade no more, I am proud to say, to please or give offence to no one, nowheres and nohows.

By all accounts it was outrageously funny, bliss for his readers in the audience (in other words, the entire audience) to see the characters they knew and loved brought to life by the man himself. A seed was no doubt sown in his mind.

The fact that he had flung himself into these activities with such joy so soon after his double bereavement did not go unremarked: 'Oh, yes,' said the ever-vinegary Jane Carlyle, 'Mr Dickens is always in the habit of acting with a dead father in one pocket and a dead child in the other.'

Playing the landlord Lithers in *Nightingale* and the valet Smart in *Not So Bad* was the twenty-seven-year-old Wilkie Collins, who was a friend of Augustus Egg and just at the beginning of what was clearly going to be a notable career as a novelist. He and Dickens took to each other immediately. Indeed, Dickens's friendship with him marks a sea change in his own life; it was also the beginning of the end of his intense closeness with John Forster, who in the biography calmly notes that Collins 'became, for all the rest of the life of Dickens, one of his dearest and most valued friends'. Forster found himself slowly edged out of the very special place he occupied in Dickens's heart: Dickens now needed another other self. Forster, for all his high spirits as a young man, was to a large extent a stabilizing figure in Dickens's life, full of shrewd advice both financially and artistically, a pillar of rectitude and deep religious conviction. Collins was his exact opposite, a destabilizing figure, bohemian, morally lax, permissive in the extreme. Even physically, he presented an extreme contrast to the burly, assertive Forster: five foot six, bespectacled, with tiny hands and feet but broad shoulders, his large head made even larger in appearance by a bulge on the right side of his forehead. He had a soft, dreamy quality, which may partially have derived from the laudanum that he took in ever greater quantities to relieve the pain from the arthritis that plagued him throughout his life.

The contrast with Forster, who was becoming more and more assertive – 'in tip top state of amiability', Dickens found him on one occasion, 'but I think I never heard him *half so loud*!

He so disordered me that by no process I could possibly try, could I get to sleep again' – could hardly have been greater; nor could the contrast with Dickens himself, with his driven brilliance. The relationship between the two men grew rapidly despite their thirteen-year age difference, and the great gap in their achievements; Collins quickly found himself at the heart of, and to some extent the facilitator of, profound developments in the older man.

At the beginning, it was Collins's whole-hearted support for the Guild that had endeared him to Dickens, who was determined to make a large amount of money for it from *Not So Bad as We Seem* and *Mr Nightingale's Diary*; they later took them on a riotous tour round the country. But before that happened, Dickens had a more pressing concern: he needed to find a new house. After her initial fortitude at the time of Dora's death, Catherine had not rallied well, so Dickens sublet Devonshire Terrace and took a cottage in Broadstairs where she and the family went to stay for the summer; no sooner had they arrived there, than Dickens's friend Frank Stone announced that he was going to sell the lease of his huge gloomy house in Tavistock Square in Bloomsbury. Dickens immediately saw its possibilities. The sale was effected in July 1851; it took some months to implement his ambitious plans for the house, during which time he slept mostly at the *Household Words* offices when he was in London.

While he was attending to its affairs, he totally gave himself over to the magazine: he was to be glimpsed pacing up and down in his office at all hours, urgently cogitating, constantly combing his hair. From the beginning he firmly shaped it according to his original brief; as well as encouraging new fiction (novellas to start with), he launched campaigns, vigorously promoting, among other causes, sanitation and housing reform. The pieces were not simply polemical: they were seriously researched and properly backed with statistics. The

219

range of articles was enormous; among them was one proposing a Channel tunnel. But he made sure that a balance was
struck between political pieces and purely entertaining ones.
As well as commissioning work from established writers –
Bulwer-Lytton, Charles Reade, Trollope – he encouraged
young men like George Meredith, Coventry Patmore, and his
new friend Collins. Not that any of them were credited, which
stopped Dickens's chum Douglas Jerrold from writing for the
magazine. The banner clearly proclaimed that *Household
Words* was 'Conducted by Charles Dickens', which meant,
Jerrold said, that the writing was not so much anonymous as
mononymous. And it is true: Dickens's hand was on everything: re-naming, trimming, sharpening articles for maximum
impact. He was in effect co-writer of virtually every piece that
appeared in the magazine, though he took pains to reflect the
writer's own tone, and carefully massaged their egos.

In the midst of all this home-building, editorial and actor-
managerial activity, the deep springs of his creativity were
welling up again, heralded by the usual symptoms. 'I begin to
be pondering, afar off, a new book,' he wrote to Angela
Burdett-Coutts, who had become the closest confidante of the
intimate details of his artistic life, 'and, as it begins to grow,
such a torment of desire to be anywhere, but where I am,
violent restlessness and vague ideas of going I don't know
where, I don't know why, takes hold of me, that it is like *being
driven away*.' He went no further than Broadstairs, but by
November he was writing the book that at first he thought to
call *Tom All-Alone's* or *The East Wind*, but which almost as soon
as he hit his stride became *Bleak House*. The work proceeded
vigorously and fluently, apparently unaffected by the
Dickenses' move to their majestic new house in Bloomsbury.
They installed themselves even before the work was completed.
Moving is turmoil under any circumstances; Dickens of course

directed the move personally, supervising every detail of the enormous changes he had decided on: though it was merely rented, he determined to put his stamp on it. Massive alterations were needed: a new kitchen range, a new entrance, ventilators, bells. He insisted that the shower – with which he began every day – was self-contained. Having satisfied himself that the workmen knew what they were doing, he would retire to his study, which he had lined with dummy bookcases whose jokey spines he had devised himself – *Hansard's Guide to Refreshing Sleep*, for example, and *Cats' Lives* (in nine volumes) – arrange the bibelots on his desk (duelling green-bronze frogs, a man with squirming puppies overflowing out of his pockets, an ivory knife) and then settle down to write the book that increasingly looks like his supreme masterpiece, in which his prodigious metaphorical inventiveness is tightly allied to an intricately powerful narrative, to overwhelming effect; the highly original device of splitting the story between tenses and narrators – its heroine, in the past, its narrator in the present – is one of Dickens's most startling innovations.

It was an immediate success, with gratifyingly high sales: 32,000 in monthly sales, compared to *Copperfield*'s 26,000. It was not without hostile responses: John Stuart Mill despised Dickens's mockery of Women's Rights in the book, and G. H. Lewes derided the death by spontaneous combustion of the novel's Krook: Dickens, partly basing his defence on a paper by his scientifically suspect Mesmerist friend Dr Elliotson, stoutly maintained its biological feasibility, just as, more credibly, he insisted that Gridley's interminable law case at the centre of the book was entirely factual. There were those who disparaged the darkness of his vision, among them Forster, who rejected the book largely on the grounds that all the characters are simply too unpleasant; he gives no background to Dickens's work on it, and certainly suggests no input of his own, apart from persuading Dickens to tone down the satirical portrait of Leigh Hunt, upon whom Jarndyce's dilettante friend Harold Skimpole is so patently based. In fact – and this is one of the frustrations of Forster's *Life of Dickens* – for him, *David Copperfield* (with whose form and much of its content he had been so intimately involved) was the zenith of Dickens's achievement, and all the later novels, apart from a last-gasp recovery with *The Mystery of Edwin Drood*, representative of a decline in his powers. His relationship with Dickens had now changed fundamentally, though they remained intimate; to nobody did Dickens write more eloquently about his life than to Forster, and this continued to the end.

On 7 February 1852, Dickens had celebrated his fortieth birthday, with no great fanfare: 'My dear Beard,' he wrote to his old friend from journalistic days, 'next Saturday as ever is, is the Inimitable's birthday. Will you come and dine with us, and drink that noble creature's health, at 6?' He seems not to have been inclined to take stock of himself, but it is perhaps worth doing so on his behalf. The still youthful-looking, as yet unbearded, author was the most famous man in England; his literary powers were at their height, in full flood with the new book, the first episode of which would appear the following month; he had a splendid new mansion to accommodate his large and thriving family; he was actively engaged, through *Household Words*, in influencing the pressing social issues of the day; he had a uniquely personal relationship with his readers; he was prosperous. And yet, as Forster reports, he was still in the grip of what his alter ego David Copperfield calls 'a vague, unhappy want or loss of something'. The antidote, though not the remedy, was furious activity. As well as continuing to write the monthly episodes of *Bleak House*, and produce the weekly edition of *Household Words* (in which he was serializing his fiercely compressed *Child's History of England*), and give speeches, and supervise the activities of

Urania Cottage, and visit prisons, and stalk the city at night in the company of the constabulary, in November 1851 he and his band of literary and painterly amateur actors took to the road again, on a massive and extended tour of the country with the double bill of *Not So Bad as We Seem* and *Mr Nightingale's Diary*.

They went to Bath, Clifton, Manchester, Liverpool, Shrewsbury, Birmingham, Nottingham, Derby, Newcastle, Sunderland, Sheffield, Manchester again and Liverpool again. The logistics of all this were very challenging: it was no mere one-off gala, but a serious tour, which might have daunted a professional theatre management. As well as the acting company, there were carpenters, gasmen, hairdressers, tailors, dressers, servants. They all lunched together, dined together and supped together, in the highest of animal high spirits, leap-frogging and larking about. It was not without its anxious moments, either: in Sunderland, Dickens was tipped off that the building, newly erected, was unsafe and might collapse at any moment. At that point there were a thousand people in it. Dickens talked to the builder, whom he found he trusted, and took a gamble that it was safe. Throughout the performance he was terrified that at every laugh, every round of applause, every cheer (and there were many), the whole thing might come tumbling down. But no: it was a glorious triumph. The tour was another titanic achievement; titanic was Dickens's default mode. Much money was raised for the Guild; too bad that it went to waste.

As ever, when all the excitement of the tour was over, Dickens fell into depression. He started struggling with *Bleak House*, and was tormented with dreams of leaving the country; nonetheless he took the time to make 'a good-natured' journey to Walworth (near Southwark) to see an allegedly gifted youth rehearse in a play. Dickens concluded that the boy had talent, and told him so. 'I remember what I once myself wanted in that way, and I should like to serve him.' He gave his more or less annual speech to the Royal Theatrical Fund, and in May of 1853 he entertained the French actor François Régnier and his wife; he and Dickens had something in common, beyond the theatre: they had both lost daughters. Told how openly distraught Régnier had been at the little girl's funeral, Dickens said, in a letter to Forster, 'How one loves him for it.' And then he added one of his most penetrating observations about acting: 'But is it not always true, in comedy and in tragedy, that the more real the man, the more genuine the actor?' In June, Dickens had a most uncharacteristic bout of illness, a recurrence of a childhood kidney complaint, and it kept him – 'for the first time in my life' – in bed for a week. The previous December he had noted that his energy was not quite what it had been: 'Hypochondriacal whisperings tell me that I am rather overworked. The spring does not seem to fly back again directly as it always did when I put my own work aside, and had nothing else to do.' Quite when he ever had nothing to do is unclear, but it is striking that for the first time he acknowledged his mortal limitations.

Within days of the kidney attack, the spring anyway flew back, and he was restored to full blazing health, and vigorously attacking the seventeenth episode of *Bleak House*. He and the family then went to Boulogne, staying in a modest villa with a small wood attached. The villa was owned by a certain M. Beaucourt-Mutuel who was deeply proud of it, especially the large garden with its prodigious rose bushes, closely modelled by its owner on 'the English Garden'. 'There is a guidance to any room in the house,' wrote Dickens, 'as if it were a place on that stupendous scale that without such a clue you must infallibly lose your way, and perhaps perish of starvation between bedroom and bedroom.' The villa came with its own cow, which provided their milk; fresh garden produce was available too. He was enchanted and diverted by the locals, and ploughed on happily with the novel, which was now coming to its conclusion. In readiness for an end-of-novel walking tour, he rapidly polished off his *Child's History of England*, which ends with the Glorious Revolution of 1688, the triumph of Protestantism and the final ousting of Catholicism, in the form of King James II. It had been appearing in *Household Words* over the previous two years. He dictated some of the book to Georgina, who now added the role of amanuensis to her already bulging portfolio within the Dickens household. She now occupied the curious position of co-mother with Catherine, teaching the children to read, attending their various needs and helping to maintain the clockwork regularity and efficiency that Dickens demanded of his domestic life. Catherine's principal, exhausting, activity was giving birth, which she had done again, a year before, in March of 1852, when their tenth child, Edward Bulwer Lytton Dickens, was born, 'a brilliant boy of unheard-of dimensions'. Plorn, as he was quickly nicknamed, proved to be the last child. Whether this betokens a slackening of their intimate relations, or a conversion to the use of birth-control methods, we do not know; the boy was the apple of Dickens's eye.

In September 1853, returning briefly to London from Boulogne, Dickens polished off a little editorial work on *Household Words* and then, the following month, he was off on a tour with his new best friend Wilkie Collins and the mutual friend who had introduced them, the painter Augustus Egg; the family returned to London under their own steam. The walking trip, which started in Switzerland, was on an epic scale; neither Collins nor Egg were ever in the best of health, and the pace must have been severely daunting to them. Dickens, needless to say, was renewed and exhilarated by the challenge. At the beginning of the tour, they all grew beards, or tried to, as if to indicate that they were rugged men of nature; but the outcrop of hair was disappointingly exiguous, so Dickens shaved his off, *pour encourager les autres*. They stubbornly maintained theirs, both eventually sporting superb bushes of quintessentially Victorian fullness. Dickens took time off from striding across glaciers and surveying the world from mountaintops to visit Haldimand's Institution in Lausanne, seeking out the blind boy to whom he had once given cigars. The boy evinced no recognition of him, though Dickens thought that if he had given him a cigar, there might have been; the little girl who had laughed so merrily ('at what, for God's sake?') had been discharged as mentally defective.

The trio went on to Genoa, with Dickens making a beeline for the de la Rues, with whom he was happily reunited; Augusta was still invaded by her hallucinations, but Dickens seems not to have attempted to mesmerize her. Both de la Rues sent warm greetings to Catherine. This reunion stirred up all Dickens's old resentment of Catherine's behaviour eight years earlier. He wrote to her to remind her of his having been obliged to tell the de la Rues about her suspicions, and wondered whether she didn't now agree that she was making a mountain out of a molehill. 'Your position beside these people is not a good one, is not an amiable one, not a generous one – is not worthy of you at all.' Then, somewhat chillingly, he instructed her to write a letter saying that she had heard of Augusta's sufferings and 'that you couldn't receive her messages of remembrance without a desire to respond to them – and that if you should ever be thrown together again … you hope it will be for a friendly association without any sort of shadow upon it.' She meekly obeyed. Dickens's tone is that of Murdstone in *Copperfield*, taming a too-lively wife. He tells Catherine what she should do, tells her what she should say – gives her a script, in fact, which she obediently performs. This is Dickens again treating people in life as he treats his characters: he arranges their destinies, uses them for his purposes. It would not be the last time that he behaved towards Catherine in this way.

Equally typically, once he had got what he wanted by the ruthless exercise of his will, he then plunged back into life with renewed joyous abandon. The trio toured Italy, Dickens revisiting the cities he had discovered on his first Italian journey, once again finding Naples 'one of the most odious places on earth', and falling in love with the *marionetti* in Rome, as he had done in Genoa. Rome was then in the grip of malaria, which had virtually decimated the Roman population. Dickens, brilliantly informed as he was on matters sanitary, accurately diagnosed the problem. On they went: after Rome, Florence, thence to Padua, Venice and Turin. These were epic journeys, involving long days of travel, but the three of them were enchanted with each others' company. Dickens was fascinated by the free-thinking Wilkie, who, he told Catherine in a letter,

> occasionally expounds a code of morals taken from modern French novels, which I instantly and with becoming gravity smash. But the best of it is, that he tells us about the enormous quantities of Monte Pulciano that he has drunk and what not, that he used to drink when he was last there, and what distinguished people said to him in the way of taking his opinion, and what advice he gave them and so forth being then exactly thirteen years of age ...

The affectionate, teasing, sneakingly admiring, words of an older man contemplating a younger, freer one. Dickens felt enclosed, confined, shackled; he was not sufficiently affirmed by the ever-grudging critics. Catherine, valetudinarian, heavy, unarousing, offered no stimulation; he felt himself oppressed both by managing *Household Words* and having to keep writing, writing, writing. He wanted freedom, fun, the sensual life.

Wilkie suggested an altogether different way of life from his – sexy, shame-free, exploratory, improper. Dickens, always in crisis of one sort or another, was now rapidly approaching his mid-life crisis. And like everything else in his life, it would be the mid-life crisis to end all mid-life crises.

The travellers arrived back in England on the eleventh; after celebrating the usual sumptuous Christmas in the new house, Dickens made good the promise he had given to the Birmingham Literary and Scientific Institute the previous year to read 'something' for them. For every possible reason, *A Christmas Carol* was the choice for the twenty-seventh of December, with the only slightly less popular *Cricket on the Hearth* on the twenty-ninth. The *Carol* was so successful that he had to do a repeat performance on the thirtieth, specifying that it must be for working people, at reduced prices. It was an overwhelming experience both for the audience and for Dickens, one that in time would become addictive. He had finally found a way of uniting his two primary drives, to write and to perform, and in doing so he would take his all-important relationship with his public to an even more intense and personal level. 'They lost nothing, misinterpreted nothing, followed everything closely, laughed and cried with the most delightful earnestness,' Dickens wrote, 'and animated me to that extent that I felt as if we were all bodily going up into the clouds together.' The new venture began slowly, but before very long its momentum became unstoppable.

THIRTEEN

The Ice-Bound Soul

Despite inclement weather, Birmingham Town Hall was packed on 27 December: 1,700 people fought their way through a heavy snowstorm to attend the reading. What better preparation for *A Christmas Carol*? Dickens had been a little apprehensive of performing to such an enormous audience. His previous readings had been confined to his domestic circle – he had read *The Chimes* to his friends in Forster's rooms, *Dombey* to the expatriates in Genoa, *Bleak House* to his family; their reactions had been most gratifying. But direct contact with his public, and on such a scale, was a new thing. He need not have worried. From the beginning, it was 'as if we had been sitting round the fire' At the repeat performance on 30 December, when he appeared 'they all rose up and cheered most enthusiastically', said the Birmingham *Telegraph*, 'and then became quiet again, and then went at it afresh'. As he started to speak, at the very first word there was 'a perfect hurricane of applause'. When that subsided, he spoke to praise the projected Birmingham and Midland Working Men's Institute, for which his performances were fund-raisers. As always, he urged his audience of working men and their families to 'have a share in the management of the institution'. It must not be a charitable organization, he said, but one based on self-help and self-determination, leading in the end to self-respect.

> Erect in Birmingham a great Educational Institution, properly
> educational; educational of the feelings as well as of the reason;
> to which all orders of Birmingham men can contribute; in which

> all orders of Birmingham men can meet; wherein all orders of
> Birmingham men are faithfully represented; and you will erect
> a temple of Concord here which will be a model edifice to the
> whole of England.

When the cheers had died down he proceeded, as he said, to 'the pleasant task to which I assure you I have long looked forward.'

The reading lasted three hours, with a ten-minute break. That would change, as would many other things. He immediately sensed the extraordinary potential of this form of acting. It was in fact an extension of his procedure as a writer. With Dickens, the reader is always conscious of his presence: the author is performing his characters. His daughter Mamie reported that when he was writing, he would leap up to the mirror to observe the expression on his face as the character's words passed through his mind. Their utterances are brilliantly constructed performances, brilliantly shaped with a view to the reader's reactions. Even the descriptive passages have the quality of arias, often, tellingly, falling into blank verse. And indeed, the books, as they appeared in their instalments, were frequently read aloud within family groups. Given Dickens's very particular gift as an actor, his incomparable mimicry and his fascination with transformation, performing his own texts in public was a perfect fusion of the narrator's voice, delivered with unique authority, with Mathewsian monopolyloguing. Despite the relative lightness of his voice and the lisp that in the end, after long and arduous work, he almost completely eliminated, there has never been another author-reader even remotely as well-equipped to perform his own work. His experience with amateur productions in huge halls across the country had strengthened his vocal instrument and taught him how to fill the spaces with vocal energy, not simply relying on volume. His palpable joy in responding to the audience set the place on fire: it was genuine interaction, with real give and take. His listeners were not passive auditors of the master's voice: they were participants. A year after these first readings, he told an audience in Bradford that if they felt disposed 'as we go along to give expression to any emotion, whether grave or gay, you will do so with perfect freedom from restraint, and without the least apprehension of disturbing me'. He asked them to imagine the event as 'a small social party assembled to hear a tale told round the Christmas fire'. What he wanted, he said, 'was the establishment among us, from the very beginning, of a perfectly unfettered, cordial, friendly sentiment.' And that is what he got – plus, to his great gratification, a great deal more. The fervour of his audiences, their passionate approval of him and everything he stood for, were mother's milk to him.

Immediately after the Birmingham readings he was inundated with requests for more from all over the country; some of the requests came with offers of money. This was a bit of a shocker: the idea of being paid to perform was by no means consonant with the Victorian notion of how a literary gentleman was expected to conduct himself. As far back as Genoa, when Dickens had read from *Dombey* with, as he put it, 'unrelatable success', he had toyed with the idea of going professional with the readings, and had teased Forster, who was violently opposed to the idea, about the London theatres he might hire for him: 'shall I take the St James's? ... I don't think you have exercised your usual judgement in taking Covent Garden for me. I doubt it is too large for my purpose.' Forster was not at all amused, because he knew that Dickens was less than half joking. He viewed the success of the readings in Birmingham with dark suspicion: 'to become publicly a reader,' wrote Forster, 'must alter without improving his position publicly as a writer, and that too was a change to be justified only when the higher calling should have failed of the old success.' This tight-lipped argument, so rapidly advanced just at the moment when Dickens had identified his overwhelming need for contact with his public, would cause Dickens to dig his heels in ever more, and further cooled their former intimacy. Dickens wanted purer contact with his readers, wanted to be directly hooked up to his life-blood, wanted to feel more fully alive. Forster's view was postulated on the way the writer is perceived: 'it raised a question of his own self-respect for himself as a gentleman'. He even wheeled in Shakespeare as having a poor opinion of a profession 'which, in the jealous self-watchfulness of his noble nature, he feared might hurt his mind.' Dickens would, he felt, inevitably lose dignity and respect by becoming, in effect, a paid entertainer. Forster's bewilderment was understandable, since such a thing was without precedent: no great writer had ever *performed* in this way. He further thought that the energy released by this venture would in itself become addictive and prove a drain on what Dickens himself called the marrow of his genius; and in this he was not necessarily wrong.

But all of this was in the future; for the next four years Dickens confined himself to pro bono activities as a reader, to the gratification and considerable financial benefit of many worthy organizations. Immediately after the Birmingham readings, he turned to yet another form of theatre: his Twelfth Night entertainments, coinciding with Charley's birthday. These were becoming more and more ambitious, having expanded to fit the much larger spaces of Tavistock House. In 1854, it was Henry Fielding's *Tom Thumb*. Dickens was the Ghost of Gaffer Thumb; Mark Lemon, 'a very mountain of child-pleasing fun in himself,' said Forster, was Glumdalca, captive Queen of the Giants. Five-year-old Henry Dickens was the eponymous star of the show: 'the small helmeted hero' went through the comic songs and the tragic exploits 'without a wrong note or a victim unslain'. As usual, the Unparalleled Necromancer Rhia Rhama Roos conjured.

Shortly after *Tom Thumb*, Dickens's purely writerly skills were in urgent demand: the novel being serialized in *Household Words* was failing, with a consequent decline in circulation, and he was persuaded by Bradbury and Evans that 'a story of me, continued from week to week, would make some unheard of effect', as he told Angela Burdett-Coutts. This meant writing in weekly instalments, which he described as 'CRUSHING' work; the resulting novel, *Hard Times*, is his shortest and in some ways his most severe, lacking his characteristic exuberance of language and without an overarching metaphor. For these qualities, it has been in equal measure disparaged and admired. He had been pondering the iniquities of Industrialization for some time, and used the book to raise political issues in a fairly unmediated form; Utilitarianism, and the sort of education that addressed only reason and not the feelings, came under fire, too. He did a certain amount of quick field research, but was rather disappointed by the strike he visited in Preston: nothing seemed to be happening. He quizzed Mark Lemon about circus slang for the representatives of cheer among all the grimness, the performers in Sleary's Equestrian Circus: 'People mutht be amuthed,' their boss regularly lisps, a view with which, of course, his author concurred, but which he chose not particularly to promote in this novel. The title was virtually descriptive of the process of composition. Working on it, Dickens felt exhausted, 'used up' – hardly surprising, given that it was a mere six months after he had finished writing *Bleak House*.

To restore him, he and the family went back to Boulogne, to a different château also owned by the ever-ebullient M. Beaucourt-Mutuel. While he was there, Prince Albert and the self-crowned Napoleon III had an official meeting concerning the Crimean War, which had begun the year before;

Beaucourt-Mutuel danced and squealed with excitement. Dickens was less thrilled: he had once had supper in London with the Emperor when, as Louis-Napoléon, he was about to stand for election as President; his imperial self-transformation filled Dickens with disgust. Dickens went off for his usual walk, in the opposite direction to where the meeting was taking place; coming back he passed the Royal personages, who were accompanied by about fifty soldiers. He doffed his hat; the Prince and the Emperor followed suit, a rare nod of government to art. Inquiring among the French soldiers, he discovered a lack of enthusiasm for the war that he found grimly satisfying. He was planning to include a series in *Household Words* called 'Member from Nowhere' about the widely unpopular war: 'I gave it up reluctantly and with it my hope to have made every man in England feel something of the contempt for the House of Commons I have. We shall never begin to do anything till the sentiment is universal.'

In the military camp, by way of consolation, he saw the best conjuror he had ever seen, performing mind-boggling feats of mentalism. His name was Giovanni Bartolomeo Bosco, he was corpulent and sleazy in appearance, and he was, according to Dickens, 'So far as I know, a totally original genius, and that puts any sort of knowledge of legerdemain, such as I supposed that I possessed, at utter defiance.' He assessed him with professional discrimination: 'I never saw anything in the least like this; or at all approaching to the absolute certainty, the familiarity, quickness, absence of all machinery, and actual face-to-face, hand-to-hand fairness between the conjuror and his audience, with which it was done. I have not the slightest idea of the secret.' The climax of Bosco's act was mind-reading: the audience secretly agreed upon a date, then the magician was blindfolded with table-napkins and covered with a great cloth 'so that his voice sounded as if were under a bed'. After a while, the figure was seized with agitation and burst out,

> What is this I see? A great city, but of narrow streets and old-fashioned houses, many of which are of wood, resolving itself into ruins. How is it falling into ruins? Hark, I hear the crackling of a great conflagration, and, looking up, I behold a vast cloud of smoke and flame! The ground is covered with hot cinders, too, and people are flying into the fields and endeavouring to save their goods. This great fire, this wind, this roaring noise!

When the blindfolds were removed from Bosco, it was revealed that the year chosen was 1666, the year of the Great Fire of London. Catherine was co-opted into the proceedings, too, and Bosco was unerringly able to write down in advance whatever might come into her head. This of course was pure enchantment for Dickens, and a source of some competitive interest.

Then he was back to the churning toil of writing *Hard Times*. He was, he said, 'stunned with work'. To Forster he described himself as 'three parts mad, and the fourth delirious'. Finally he finished the last instalment just six months after starting it, writing to Wilkie Collins that they should have five days of 'amiable dissipation and unbounded licence in the metropolis'. When he came back to London with the manuscript they did exactly that: 'I have been in a blaze of dissipation and have succeeded (I think) in knocking the remembrance of my work out.' Back in Boulogne, he was, he told Mrs Gaskell, 'so dreadfully lazy (after finishing *Hard Times*), and lie so much on the grass, reading books and going to sleep,' though he was in fact heavily preoccupied with *Household Words* business, on account, as it happens, of Mrs Gaskell: after the fillip *Hard Times* had given sales, her *North and South* serial was dragging the circulation down again. 'I am not surprised. It is wearisome to a degree,' he wrote to Henry Wills, his sub-editor on *Household Words*. 'Never mind! I am ready to come up to the scratch on my return, and to shoulder the wheel.' Underlying all this was his endemic discontent, which partly betokened the germination of a new novel, partly his deeper sense of unfulfilment. Responses to *Hard Times*, with a few notable exceptions – Ruskin's, for example – were negative, even the circus sequences were thought to be half-hearted, and the rest doctrinaire and rather dull ('sullen socialism', said Macaulay). 'I have visions of living for half a year or so, in all sorts of inaccessible places, and opening a new book therein,' he told Forster. 'A floating idea of going up above the snow-line in Switzerland, and living in some astonishing convent hovers above me,' adding, *'restlessness*, you will say. Whatever it is, it is always driving me, and I cannot help it.' He had rested, he said, for ten weeks; sometimes he felt as if it had been a year. 'Though I had the strangest nervous miseries before I stopped. If I couldn't walk fast and far, I should just explode and perish.'

Back in London, some of this disturbing energy was channelled into political protest: he raged against Britain's involvement in the Crimea, while at the same time determined that 'Russia MUST be stopped.' Disorders at home in Britain concerned him even more deeply: in the face of 20,000 deaths that summer from cholera, he launched a passionate demand for improvements in the living conditions of the poor, calling for the workers to fight for themselves, and to join with the middle classes to achieve their simple rights. He was as ever frank in his utter contempt for both government and Parliament. He no longer thought that securing the vote for working men was a priority; what mattered far more was improving living conditions: sanitation, proper housing, decent wages. But he despaired of a favourable outcome. 'I do reluctantly believe,' he wrote to Macready, 'that the English people are habitually consenting parties to the miserable imbecility into which we have fallen, *and never will help themselves out of it*. Whoever is to do it, if anybody is, God knows.' Lord Aberdeen's feeble government had fallen because of their mismanagement of the Crimean War; Lord Palmerston's, which succeeded it, was profoundly indifferent to the situation of the people. Dickens implacably lampooned 'the noble lord', but his politics were never merely argumentative: they were grounded in the reality of what he saw.

He continued his noctambulistic researches into the condition of the people: he was known all over London, and treated with respect as a friend and partisan. One night, Forster reported, he found himself in Whitechapel outside the door of the workhouse. Up against the doorway of the house were leaning, in the pouring rain and storm, what seemed to Dickens to be seven heaps of rags: 'dumb, wet, silent horrors' he described them, 'sphinxes set up against that dead wall, and no one likely to be at the pains of rescuing them till the General Overthrow.' He sent in his card to the Master, who gave it his prompt personal attention, but he could do nothing: the casual ward was full. The rag-heaps were all girls; Dickens gave a shilling to each of them. One girl, 'twenty or so', had been without food day and night. 'Look at me,' she said, as she clutched the shilling and, without thanks, shuffled off. So with the rest. There was not a single 'thank you'. A crowd, meanwhile, only slightly better than these objects of misery, had gathered round the scene; though they saw the seven shillings given away, they asked for nothing for themselves, recognizing, 'in their sad, wild way the other greater wretchedness', and made room in silence for Dickens to move on. This eerie apparition is typical of Dickens's nocturnal experience: was he in their dream or were they in his? His presence there is ambiguous: he is neither voyeur nor social worker. He is a witness of, and in some measure a participant in, the girls' distress: he absorbs it into his soul, and this fuels him, not only to rage against their condition, but to take it on himself.

By day, his walks were of a different order. He strode out vigorously, bluffly. 'His appearance in walking dress in the streets, during his later years,' wrote his colleague at *Household Words*, George Augustus Sala, 'was distinctly "odd", and almost eccentric, being marked by strongly-pronounced colours, and a fashioning of the garments which had somewhat of a sporting and somewhat of a theatrical guise.' He was everywhere: 'A hansom cab whirled you by the Bell and Horns at Brompton, and there was Charles Dickens striding, with seven league boots, seemingly in the direction of North-End Fulham. The Metropolitan Railway disgorged you at Lisson Grove, and you met Charles Dickens plodding sturdily towards the Yorkshire Stingo ...' Otherwise his energies went into speeches, readings, and Twelfth Night theatricals at home in Tavistock Square – rehearsed on a daily basis with his accustomed passionate seriousness. In January 1855, even this supposedly festive show was imbued with Dickens's political fury. The play was a lightly adapted version of Planché's *Fortunio and His Seven Gifted Servants*. In it, Dickens played first Mr Measly Servile ('the expectant cousin of the Nobility in General'), and then a testy old Baron, singing a comic anti-Russian song, Gilbert and Sullivan *avant la lettre*:

> A despot I am of the regular kind
> I'm in a fierce mood and I'm out of my mind
> And man was created to swallow the pill
> Of my wrong-headed, Bull-headed absolute will.

This number, as performed by Dickens, made Thackeray fall off his seat laughing. There were banners announcing the acts, mostly featuring the kids: 'Return of Mr Charles Dickens junior from his German engagements'; 'Engagement of Miss Kate, who declined the munificent offer of the management last year'; 'First appearance on any stage of Mr Plornishmaroontigoonter (who has been kept out of bed at a vast expense)'; characters were announced: Mr Passé, Mr Mudperiod, Mr Measly Servile, and Mr Wilkini Collini. Interestingly, as well as Measly Servile, Dickens was Mr Passé. Passé or not, he spared no effort or expense in staging an ideal childhood for his children – and himself.

Shortly after his birthday in early February 1855, Dickens was plunged back into his own childhood. He had gone to Gravesend for a celebratory dinner; afterwards walking to Rochester 'between walls of snow varying from three to six feet high through which a road had been hewn out by men', and through the snow drifts he caught a glimpse of Gad's Hill, the house he and his father had walked to and marvelled at in those long distant Chatham days, idyllic in memory, before the catastrophic, life-changing months of internal exile at Warren's Blacking. He saw that the house – 'literally,' he told Henry Wills, 'a dream of childhood' – was for sale. 'I used to look at it as a wonderful Mansion (which God knows it is not), when I was a very odd little child with the first faint shadow of all my books in my head – I suppose.' In the fairy-tale way in which so much of Dickens's life unfolded, a day or so later Wills found himself at supper sitting next to the woman who owned it, and, since the recent death of her father, wanted to sell. Wills set the wheels in motion to effect its purchase.

Then, just two days later, another, less idyllic, part of Dickens's past suddenly loomed up. The eve of his departure for a Parisian jaunt with Wilkie Collins ('it was a year of much unsettled discontent with him,' Forster remarks, tartly), he noticed a vaguely familiar hand on an envelope among a pile of letters. 'Suddenly the remembrance of your hand came upon me with an influence that I cannot express to you.' It was from Maria Beadnell, the lost great love of his early life, now in her forties, married with two children of her own. 'Three or four and twenty years vanished like a dream, and I opened it with the touch of my young friend David Copperfield when he was in love.' His reply to her bubbles and surges with almost skittish ardour, re-living moments from their past together, of the 'State of Spring in which I was either much more wise or much more foolish than I am now – I never know which to think it'. Oscillating between extreme vulner-ability and a due regard for the proprieties – throughout the letter he addresses her as 'Mrs Winter' – he quickly fills in family news and proposes a meeting, with their respective spouses, at Tavistock House. 'In the strife and struggle of this great world where most of us lose each other so strangely,' he writes, 'it is impossible to be spoken to out of the old times without a softened emotion. You so belong to the days when the qualities that have done me most good since, were grow-ing in my boyish heart, that I cannot end my answer to you lightly.' Palpably in the grip of deep emotion, he ends: 'we are all sailing away to the sea, and have a pleasure in thinking of the river we are upon, when it was very narrow and little. – Faithfully your friend.'

The letter, received on the eve of a trip to Paris in which we can only presume he was to achieve some kind of release from the frustrations of his existence, immediately put him in touch with his youthful self. His heart was overwhelmed all over again with the love he felt then and had since forbidden himself to feel. This sudden access of an emotion frozen or numbed or anaesthetized – a heady, shattering intimation of some kind of escaped perfection, a glimpse of an Eden whose existence he once knew of but to which life had not admitted him – shook him to the core of his being. 'These are things,' he wrote in his next letter to her, 'that I have locked up in my own breast and that I never thought to bring out any more.' In her reply, she told him, coquettishly, that she was toothless, fat, old and ugly: he didn't believe her. But when they finally met, she was all of those things, and worse. She was banal, prosaic, ordinary, tedious. The dream of the past suddenly turned nightmare. This 'grotesque revival', as he called it, was like an attempt 'to resuscitate an old play when the stage was dusty, when the scenery was faded, when the youthful actors were dead, when the orchestra was empty, when the lights were out'. Maria made innumerable attempts to meet him again, but he evaded her. 'Whoever is devoted to an Art must be content to deliver himself up wholly to it, and to find his recompense in it,' he wrote to her loftily (and not entirely accurately). He had given himself up entirely to his Art, and to the five hundred other things he managed to find time for every day. 'I am going off, I don't know where or how far, to ponder about I don't know what.' She replied, as people always do in these situations, that he had changed: 'Once upon a time I didn't do such things, you say. No, but I have done them through a good many years now, and they have become myself and my life.' The whole episode was hideous, a grotesque mockery of his youthful feelings, feelings to which he was desperately loyal, desperately indulgent; they were, he felt, the best of him. His momentary vulnerability had made a fool of him. He found himself baulked again in the realm of idealized emotion, trying to control and will the life of the heart. How dare plump, unlovely, boring Mrs Winter betray the Maria of his dreams and memories! It upset him deeply: he wrote to Leigh Hunt that he felt 'as infirm of purpose as Macbeth, as errant as Mad Tom, and as ragged as Timon'. Stage imagery was never far away with Dickens.

All this threw him into 'a state of restlessness impossible to be described', a restlessness redoubled by the burgeoning of a new book within him, a book to which he at first gave the richly suggestive title of *Nobody's Fault*. In time this would be replaced by the less expressive *Little Dorrit*, and would expand into a massive panorama of life in the mid-nineteenth century, organized around the central idea of incarceration. But for the while it was still germinating, and he was fulminating in *Household Words* against the catastrophic state of the nation:

> A country which is discovered to be in this tremendous condition as to its war affairs; with an enormous black cloud of poverty in every town which is spreading and deepening every hour, and not one man in two thousand knowing anything about, or even believing in, its existence; with a non-working aristocracy, and a silent parliament, and everybody for himself and nobody for the rest; this is the prospect, and I think it is a very deplorable one.

A few months later he roundly declared that 'representative government is become altogether a failure with us'. He had thrown his full weight behind the Radical MP, Austen Layard, whose attempt to introduce a Bill of Administrative Reform abjectly failed. Dickens, in apocalyptic vein, compared the mood in the country with the mood of pre-Revolutionary France: 'Any of a thousand accidents – a bad harvest – the last strain too much of aristocratic insolence or incapacity – a defeat abroad – a mere chance at home could precipitate such a devil of a conflagration as never has been beheld since.'

He was frequently asked to stand for Parliament, but he meant what he said: he held it in contempt. 'The House of Parler and Mentir', he called it: the House of Talk and Lies. He preferred direct influence: up and down the country he spoke again and again to gatherings, large and small, which were overwhelmed by his eloquence. 'His speeches,' wrote Forster, 'derived singular charm from his perfect self-possession, and to this he added the advantages of a person and a manner which had become as familiar and as popular as his books. The most miscellaneous assemblages listened to him as to a personal friend.' Dickens was by temperament a populist and a demagogue; argument and debate were not his medium at all. Government by plebiscite, as in Switzerland, was what he really admired. In his speeches and articles, he addressed specific malaises: his real platform was the abolition of class differences and the establishment of decency and benevolence in human affairs, a programme that was never going to find its place on any party political manifesto.

His political gloom seems to have influenced his next choice of theatrical venture: not a farce or a classic, as before, but *The Lighthouse*, a new play by Wilkie Collins loosely based on his 1853 short story 'Gabriel's Marriage' which had appeared in *Household Words*. It concerned three lighthouse men, cut off from the mainland for a month by storms: Dickens played Aaron Gurnock, the oldest of them, haunted by a murder to which he may have been party, and to which he finally confesses. The play was, as usual, done to the highest standards; the children's school-room at Tavistock House was converted into a highly professional theatre. Stanfield painted a front cloth for the show; he and Dickens realized the Eddystone lighthouse, in which the action was set, in slavish detail. As usual with Dickens, this private family undertaking took place in front of an audience of the great and the good, and the press was invited to comment on the event; half of literary London was there. He sent out invitations in suitably florid style: 'Tavistock House Theatre (Lessee and Manager Mr Crummles) presents *The Lighthouse*, by Wilkie Collins, designed by Clarkson Stanfield, R.A.' The leading role, the invitation said, was to be played by Vincent Crummles: it was a play within a play within a life. The drama depended, said Henry Morley, reviewing for *The Examiner*, on the acting of the part of Aaron, 'and it is in the hands of a master'. Possessed, as Morley put it, with a wild horror at all he recollects, he confesses to his son, who is the second of the lighthouse men. 'By innumerable master-touches on the part of the actor, we are shown what his rugged ways have been hiding up of the knowledge that stirs actively within his conscience.' Aaron finally frees himself of his burden of guilt: 'to the last that piece of truest acting was watched with minute attention by the company assembled; and rarely has acting on a public stage better rewarded scrutiny.' Dickens's lighthouse-keeper, Carlyle said, was like Poussin's Bacchanalia, *The Triumph of Pan*, at the National Gallery. Mary Cowden Clarke was over-whelmed: 'a wonderful impersonation, very imaginative, very original, very striking; his grandly intelligent eyes were made to assume a wandering look – a sad, scared, lost gaze, as one whose spirit was away from present objects.' All this is the more extraordinary in that the play is the stiffest fustian, conventional and overwrought.

The play was followed by a farce, as usual (*Mr Nightingale's Diary*, on this occasion), but it is clear that in *The Lighthouse* Dickens wanted to express something more in his acting than the mere comic abandon in which he so excelled. As Aaron Gurnock he revealed something of his inner discontent: it may perhaps have afforded him some relief to do so. The show was given again, with the now more or less obligatory Royal attendance, at Campden House in Kensington in aid of the Bournemouth Sanatorium for Consumptives. Then he went off on holiday with the family to Folkestone in Kent, applying himself assiduously to *Little Dorrit*. After early strug-gles, this was now coming much more easily; its success with the public eclipsed *Bleak House*, which in its turn had outstripped *David Copperfield*. He would never again know the sales of *The Old Curiosity Shop*, but to have reached as many people as he did with work as sombre, complex and demanding as *Little Dorrit*, with its series of anti-heroes and its encroaching sense of illness, is astonishing, though Dickens's great invention of the Circumlocution Office spoke particularly vividly to a country that was only just emerging from the bureaucratic catastrophe that was the Crimean War, Victorian Britain's Vietnam. On a private level, Dickens used the figure of Flora Finching to give vent to his feelings about Mrs Winter, née Beadnell: 'Flora, whom he had left a lily, had become a peony; that was not much. Flora, who had seemed enchanting in all she had said and thought, was diffuse and silly. That was much. Flora, who had been spoiled and artless long ago, was determined to be spoiled and artless now. That was a fatal blow.' His publishers, Bradbury and Evans, were partly responsible for the great success of the novel: their saturation marketing for it included 4,000 posters and 310,000 handbills. The critical response was mixed: many reviewers felt that he had written himself out. Dickens never read reviews, but he chanced upon one in *Blackwood's Magazine* that described the work as 'twaddle'.

Small wonder he preferred to spend as much time as possible out of the country. By the time *Little Dorrit* started to appear he had been with the family in Paris for some months, on the avenue des Champs-Elysées, making many visits to London, to Dover and to various Northern cities for charity readings and speeches; he was also editing *Household Words* and dealing with Urania Cottage business. But Paris was his base; they lived in a splendid rented house there. The city was dominated by financial life: vast fortunes were made and lost on the Bourse; failed investors were killing themselves at regular intervals. Materialism ruled, unabashed, culminating that year of 1855 in the Exposition Universelle. Some of this atmosphere found its way into *Little Dorrit*. Writing furiously, he became, he said, 'a Monster to my family, a dread Phenomenon to myself'. He felt impelled to 'plunge out into some of the strange places I glide into of nights in these strange latitudes'. With Wilkie, now also in Paris, he dashed off 'on some Haroun Al-raschid expedition'. Haroun Al-Raschid is, of course, the Caliph in *The Arabian Nights* whose wife Scheherazade narrowly escapes the beheading to which all his other wives have been condemned by telling him bewitching stories. The evening Collins and Dickens had in mind was one 'of a bachelor perspective of theatrical and other-lounging evenings'. What on earth did poor Catherine think he was up to, prowling around in Paris at the height of its Second Empire hedonism, the city of Offenbach and of sin? What did *he* think he was up to? It is hard to imagine him actually consummating his wild desires in these circum-stances, but he was certainly not doing anything to cool them.

'In Paris,' said Forster, 'Dickens's life was passed among artists, and in the exercise of his own art.' This was also true. If Wilkie was his companion in the *boîtes*, Forster accompanied him to the salons. He was a regular visitor to the theatre, where, whenever he could, he saw the actor he admired above all others, even above Macready: Frédérick Lemaître, immor-talized by Pierre Brasseur in Marcel Carné's great film *Les Enfants du Paradis*. 'Incomparably the finest acting I ever saw,' Dickens said of Lemaître in the melodrama *Thirty Years of a Gambler's Life*. 'Two or three times a great cry of horror went round the entire house: the manner in which the crime came into his head – and his eyes – was as truthful as it was terrific.' Dickens notes one of Lemaître's great 'points', as Victorian critics called them: crystallizing gestures:

> such an extraordinary guilty wicked thing he made of a knotted
> branch of a tree which was his walking stick … he sat at a little
> table in the inn-yard, drinking with the traveller; and this horri-
> ble stick got between them like the Devil, while he counted on
> his fingers the uses he could put the money to.

This could be a passage from one of his own novels, describing a Bill Sikes or a Jonas Chuzzlewit. It is a kind of acting for which we no longer have any use, but which was exactly what Dickens sought to do in *The Lighthouse*, and later in *The Frozen Deep*. Later still, and in a different form, he attempted it in the public readings from his own work that dominated his last years. He and most of his contemporaries saw it as an essential part of the actor's job to be memorable, and these 'points' were what people remembered: not their *interpretations* of roles, a word that would have seemed bewildering to a Victorian theatre-goer, if not actually impertinent. Acting, Dickens and his contemporaries believed, was the art of gesture, no more and no less. In general, Lemaître apart, he found the French theatre pompous, dull, overlong, but he enjoyed his time there: in Paris, Forster said, Dickens was fêted 'on an Oriental scale'. He was painted (very slowly and not very well) by the acclaimed portraitist Ary Scheffer; during the long hours of this tedious process, he managed to compose in his mind the current instalment (number five) of *Little Dorrit*. This torment apart, he felt entirely at ease in Parisian literary society; the poet (and failed Presidential candidate) Lamartine, introducing Dickens at a reception, told the assembled company that he had never heard a foreigner speak French so effortlessly, whereupon, according to Dickens's own report, he choked for ten minutes.

Back in London in May 1856, he was given permission to take three chums up to the top of St Paul's Cathedral to watch the festive firework displays celebrating the end of the Crimean War – a perfect Dickensian snapshot, the urban ecclesiastical equivalent of his ascent of Vesuvius. Soon afterwards, he took the family back to Beaucourt-Mutuel's villa at Boulogne. There was a constant trickle of visitors. Dickens was an enthusiastic and knowledgeable gardener, and he applied himself to the villa's garden for a few days – in character, needless to say: French farming garb of blue blouse, leather belt, and military cap that he described as 'the only (costume) for complete comfort'. Then he got back to work on *Little Dorrit*. At night, he liked to walk to the pier, where there were young holiday-making English couples: 'They are really, in their insolence and vulgarity, quite disheartening. One is so fearfully ashamed of them, and they contrast so very unfavourably with the natives.' *Il y avait des limites*, evidently, to the amusements of the people. At the villa, the family was terrorized by two cats who had their eyes on the resident canary (called, with Dickens's usual self-projection, Dick); French, the servant, managed to shoot one cat, but the other continued its war of attrition against the bird. In describing this incident, Dickens's admiration was all for the cat.

While thus amused by domestic and rustic diversions, and steadily working on *Little Dorrit*, he was stopped dead in his tracks by the arrival of Wilkie Collins's latest play, *The Frozen Deep*. It had been inspired by a recent scandal surrounding Sir John Franklin's doomed exploratory expedition to find the fabled Northwest Passage, the supposed sea route across North America; there were suggestions that some of the partic-ipants had resorted to cannibalism, although ultimately Franklin and the crew had died. Dickens had been electrified by the story and wrote several articles about it for *Household Words*. Collins's play was less concerned with the expedition than with a darkly troubled central character who, given every opportunity to kill a rival in love, instead saves the man's life. Collins knew exactly what Dickens wanted from the play: as with *The Lighthouse*, they actively collaborated in shaping and indeed to some extent in writing the piece. Dickens was again drawn to playing a nobly anguished central character: a self-destructive, Byronic figure, who goes to Africa to win a high place in his profession, to be worthy of the hand of the woman he loves. 'I braved danger and I faced death. I staked my life in the Fever-swamps of Africa to gain the promotion I only desired for her sake – and gained it. I came back to give her all … and her own lips, the lips I had kissed at parting – told me that another man had robbed me of her.' His parting words to her, he tells a friend, were: 'The man who has robbed me of you shall rue the day when you and he first met.' It is the highest piffle.

Dickens himself wrote the prologue to the play, every word of which seems to carry autobiographical overtones, hoping, as it does, that

> The secrets of the vast Profound
> Within us, an exploring hand may sound
> Testing the region of the ice-bound soul,
> Seeking the passage at its northern pole,
> Soft'ning the horrors of its wintry sleep,
> Melting the surface of the Frozen Deep.

As literature, the play is worthless, derivative, stale, clumsy. But Dickens scarcely saw it as a play at all: it was, in Jean Cocteau's formula, not so much a text as a pretext, an opportunity to create an atmosphere and to reveal character. In Boulogne, alongside his work on the beginning of the second Book of *Little Dorrit*, he planned in minute detail what turned out to be his last – and most ambitious – production. The holiday was cut short by an outbreak of typhus, so they took up residence at Tavistock House, where they had hardly been for two years, and Dickens immediately set about converting the house into a state-of-the-art theatre.

They returned to London in September 1856; from then until the following January, when *The Frozen Deep* was to be performed as that year's Twelfth Night entertainment, Dickens worked on it obsessively, four solid months of planning and preparation, while *Little Dorrit* flowed majestically from within. He and Collins spent many hours on re-working the script to accommodate the effects Dickens was planning; Collins was now part of the permanent staff of *Household Words*, which meant that their contact was more or less continuous. They collaborated closely on that year's Christmas Story, *The Wreck of the Golden Mary*, of which other members of the team wrote self-contained episodes. The tale is relatively straightforward: *The Golden Mary*, after a propitious start to the voyage to California, runs into ice floes, and is eventually capsized; after many weeks adrift, the ship's two lifeboats are sighted and rescued by another ship. In order to preserve order and sanity, the captain has his passengers and crew tell stories; another very familiar *Christmas Story* format. The story is divided between two narrators, the Captain of *The Golden Mary*, Ravender, and its Chief Mate, the reassuringly named John Steadiman. In a letter enclosing the story, Dickens wrote to Angela Burdett-Coutts: 'I am the Captain of the Golden Mary; Mr Collins is the Mate'; they wrote their own parts, as it were. There is a distinct difference of tone between the two voices, though the narrators share an essential sobriety of character: 'a person might suppose', says Ravender, 'that I am used to holding forth about number one. That is not the case', while Steadiman, who takes up the story once Ravender has succumbed to almost fatal fatigue, tells us that he has made up his mind to tell us 'the truth, the whole truth and nothing but the truth'. There is a thoroughly Dickensian cast of passengers and crew – a young mother and her angelic child (quickly nicknamed the Golden Lucy), a girl whose fiancé has gone to the bad in the gold mines, an elderly would-be prospector, selfish and haughty, with a name like the cry of a vulture (Rarx), who is consumed with avarice; there is also, though he merits only a line in the story, Ravender's charmingly named black servant, Tom Snow. Throughout there are remarkable passages in the writing, including a quite unforgettable Coleridgean vision of the half-dead mariners on the lifeboats orchestrating their feeble cries with every surge of the waves in the vain hope of being heard through the starless night by a passing ship.

The subject matter inhabits that territory in Dickens's writing which stands in such contrast to his teeming metropolitan landscapes: the elemental, and especially the element of water. The boy born in Portsmouth and brought up in Chatham had brine in his blood, and the sea voyage is described with precision: the blackness of the sky – 'like looking, without a ray of light, into a black bandage put as close to the eyes as it could be without touching them' – the moods of the sea – 'all was snug, and nothing complained. There was a pretty sea running, but not a very high sea neither, nor at all a confused one' – graphically evoked. The wreck itself is shockingly and memorably realized, breaking into Ravender's dream, with all of Dickens's characteristic personal violence. The most striking aspect of the story is Dickens's evocation of the clear-sighted heroism of his two narrators, both of whom – like Richard Wardour in *The Frozen Deep* – perform prodigies of stoical leadership in impossible conditions. Dickens, riven by guilt about his growing revulsion for his wife, longed for the self-respect that is Ravender's and Steadiman's birthright. All this fed into his work on *The Frozen Deep*, which sat in the forefront of his brain, even as *Little Dorrit* fomented in his subconscious. In October, Dickens wrote to Collins that he had just gone for a twenty-mile walk during which – 'to the great terror of Finchley, Neasden, Willesden, and the adjacent country' – he had learned the role of the existentially moody Richard Wardour. He and Collins (who was to play Aldersley, the man whose life Wardour refrains from taking) both grew beards: Dickens finally began to look like Dickens. His intense investment in the character of Wardour turned him, indeed, into a sort of alter ego. Bobby-dazzling Boz was a thing of the past; something much graver and more intense was settling on the brow of the forty-five-year-old Dickens.

Nevertheless, he plunged into the work with the highest of spirits and with even more alarming energy than usual. Because of the difficulty of finding rehearsal rooms, it was sometimes necessary to rehearse from midnight to 4 a.m. but this seemed to inconvenience no one, least of all Dickens himself. He gloried in it. He gives Macready a vivid glimpse of what it was to be Charles Dickens in the throes of his almost unimaginable productivity and creativity:

You may faintly imagine, my venerable friend, the occupation of these also grey hairs, between Golden Marys, Little Dorrits, Household Wordses, four stage-carpenters entirely boarding on the premises, a carpenter's shop erected in the back garden, size always boiling over on all the lower fires, Stanfield perpetually elevated on planks and splashing himself from head to foot, Telbin [who was responsible for the all-important lighting effects] requiring impossibilities of gasmen, and a legion of prowling nondescripts forever shrinking in and out. Calm amidst the wreck, your aged friend glides away on the Dorrit stream, forgetting the uproar for a stretch of hours, refreshing himself with a ten or twelve miles' walk, pitches headforemost into foaming rehearsals, placidly emerges for editorial purposes, smokes over buckets of distemper with Mr Stanfield aforesaid, again calmly floats upon Dorrit waters.

His transformation of the children's school-room in Tavistock House was radical. Frustrated by the lack of depth in the room, he removed the bay windows and built a cabin in the garden outside the school-room window, to create what was in effect a thirty-foot stage. Each of the three settings – drawing room, Antarctic hut and, for the last act, cave from which ships in the harbour had to be visible – was individually painted on canvas by Stanfield, who, as well as being the most distinguished marine painter of his time and an RA, had earlier been the chief scene-painter at Drury Lane. Costumes came from Nathan's, the premier theatrical costumiers, new gas-lines (to the disapproval of the fire office-surveyor) were laid down, machinery and props were loaned from the Theatre Royal Haymarket. Paper snow, endlessly problematic, was made to fall during Act II; and Francesco Berger, Charley Dickens's chum from Leipzig, where he had been studying business, wrote an overture and incidental music that was played by a small band with Berger at the piano. All this was rehearsed, re-rehearsed and re-re-rehearsed. And by way of reward, after all this work, Berger reported, suppers on a suitably Dickensian scale were conjured up: 'a huge joint of cold roast beef, a tongue, a ham, several cold roast fowls, a few raised pies, tarts and jellies, dozens of bottled Guinness and Bass'. They ended with Punch brewed by 'the manager's own hand'. This Punch was a speciality of Dickens's, consisting of rum and brandy, spice, sugar and lemon-juice, ladled from a bowl 'the size of a small bath'. The entire company, plasterers and gasmen and carpenters and all – even the prowling nondescripts – were invited, along with the actors, who were drawn from his usual floating company; this time with the addition of his daughters Katey and Mamie, with Charley in a small part. Dickens was never happier than as the Director of the Tavistock House Theatre: 'joiners are never out of the house, and the carpenter appears to be settled (or unsettled) for life … all day long a labourer heats size over the fire in a great crucible. We eat it, drink it, breathe it and smell it. Seventy paint pots adorn the stage.' He said that the sounds in the house reminded him of Chatham dockyard: the Golden Age.

There was nothing remotely amateur about any of this, except that no one was paid. For the first performance of this little family entertainment, on 6 January 1857, Dickens had invited all the leading critics and an audience that included Cabinet Ministers and High Court judges – indeed, the Lord Chief Justice himself, as well as half of the literary and theatrical establishment. Over a hundred people were crammed into the school-room. There was a feeling of something momentous in the air; the critics took it as some sort of manifesto about the art of the theatre. From the moment that the Overture sounded, and Forster, behind a screen, intoned the Prologue, the show held the audience in vice-like grip. It is a testimony to his skill as a director that the feeble first Act, in which Wardour does not appear, and which is dominated by the absurd vatic statements of the old Scottish nurse (played by the wife of Henry Wills, sub-editor of *Household Words*), cast an immediate and a powerful spell over the spectators. The prompt copy reveals the elaborately calibrated effects Dickens had arranged:

> *Lower gas. Setting Sun worked. Red light. Music, piano in next room, heard at intervals. The melody from the adjoining room, which has hitherto been heard indistinctly below the voices of the speakers, stops for a moment then changes to 'Those Evening Bells'. A pause in the dialogue until the second verse has been sung.*

The gas got even lower, the red effect was withdrawn and then moonlight flooded the stage – all, needless to say, without electricity. 'There is nothing to be seen at present on the English stage that equals *The Frozen Deep*,' said the *Saturday Review*.

The general level of acting was high, with Egg brilliant in a comic cameo, Collins sympathetic as the best friend and Lemon impressive in what might be called the John Mills part as the decent, heroic Lieutenant Crayford. But it was Dickens's performance as Wardour that astounded people. They were shaken palpably by it; during his scenes, there were audible sobs onstage and off. 'It *is fearfully fine* throughout,' said *The Leader*,

> from the sullen despair in the second Act, alternating with gusts of passion or with gleams of tenderness … down to the appalling misery and supreme emotion of the dying Scene. Most awful are those wild looks and gestures of the starved, crazed man; that husky voice, now fiercely vehement, and now faltering into the last sorrow; that frantic cry when he recognizes Clara; that hysterical burst of joy when he brings in his former object of hatred, to prove that he is *not* a murderer; and that melting tenderness with which he kisses his old friend and his early love, and passes quietly away from Life.

Dickens, the reviewer asserts, is not simply a great Novelist, but a great Actor. 'Both, indeed, proceed from the same intense sympathy with humanity, the same subtle identification of the individual man with the breadth and depth of our general nature.' The only way in which the dross of Collins's text – 'Dear Crayford! Come nearer! I recollect now. My mind stays clear but my eyes grow dim. You will remember me kindly for Frank's sake? Poor Frank! Why does he hide his face? Is he crying? Nearer Clara – I want to look my last at *you*. My sister Clara! – Kiss me sister! Kiss me before I die!' – could have been made into the gold discerned in it by Dickens's audiences is by intense and detailed connection with emotional truth as opposed to mere theatrical effect.

The playwright and critic John Oxenford wrote of Wardour's appearance in Act II that

> such a man as Mr Dickens presents – a man strong in the command of his voice, but weak in suppressing the language of his eyes and facial muscles, a man whose constant attempts to

hide the internal storm by slight simulations of good fellowship only renders more conspicuous the vastness of that which he would conceal – a man who has a habit of losing his temper in a manner that mere external circumstances do not warrant – such a man is a just object of terror. Richard Wardour, as depicted by Mr Dickens, is the most perfect representation of dogged vindictiveness that the imagination could conceive.

This suggests a positively Stansislavskian degree of many-layered inner life. When melodrama is taken as seriously as this, it can become overwhelming, as it evidently did in this case. In the reviewer's opinion, Dickens's performance 'might open a new era for the stage, if the stage had the wisdom to profit by it'. It was a deeply creative process for him, not unlike that of writing: 'the interest of such a character to me is that it enables me, as it were, *to write a book in company*, instead of my own solitary room, and to feel its effect coming back at me freshly from the reader.' This was the direct relationship he craved, the stimulus he needed, as the writing got harder. It is also, as it happens, the ideal state in which an actor should act: out of immersion in and direct contact with the characters, their actions and their world, so that eventually the actor is actually thinking their thoughts. All else follows from that. It is to some extent a reproduction of the writer's work, a reconstitution of the original creative process: so here, in *The Frozen Deep*, Dickens was the writer as actor as writer.

The audience was genuinely shaken by the performance: after a half-hour break, the actors ended the evening by plunging into the popular Buckstone farce, *Uncle John*. Hilarity was unconfined, and the audience and the actors went home happy. Interestingly, at the beginning, Dickens found that he was unable to recover sufficiently from the intensities of Wardour, and ceded his part in the farce to Frank Stone. Later he found how to manage himself so that it became possible, and he then delighted in the release it afforded him. There were three, equally acclaimed, repeat performances of the double bill at Tavistock House; and then the theatre was dismantled and the school-room returned to its proper function. Dickens was, he said, 'shipwrecked'. There had been rumours of a Royal Command performance, but nothing materialized. 'The theatre has disappeared, the house is restored to its usual conditions of order, the family are tranquil and domestic, dove-eyed peace is enthroned in his study, fire-eyed Radicalism in its master's breast.' But Dickens had been violently aroused and could not settle. He demanded of Wilkie that they go somewhere, do something. Mostly they went to theatres, spending a lot of time with actresses ('little periwinkles') in green rooms. 'Any mad proposal you please will find a wildly insane response ... if the mind can devise anything sufficiently in the style of Sybarite Rome in the days of its culminating voluptuousness, I am your man.' Thus they played out the roles of Hal and Falstaff, but with the roles reversed, Wilkie as a younger, elfin Falstaff, Dickens an ageing Hal, with thinning hair. An interesting pair they must have made. Alas, we have no eye-witness accounts by any of the periwinkles. 'If you can think of any tremendous way of passing the night, in the meantime, do. I don't care what it is. I give (for that night only) restraint to the Winds!' Quite how much Dickens gave into these hedonistic impulses is uncertain; but clearly domestic life was entirely insufficient to him.

All this wild energy, as well as his post-show blues, was given a legitimate channel with the sudden death of Dickens's friend Douglas Jerrold, which shocked him deeply – Jerrold was only fifty-four. Dickens immediately determined that they must do a subscription revival of *The Frozen Deep* to benefit the family (despite their protests that they were perfectly well-off and neither needed nor wanted the begging-bowl to be passed around on their behalf); in addition, he performed *A*

Christmas Carol for them at the St Martin's Hall. He approached Queen Victoria to ask her whether she would lend her name to the Jerrolds' subscription tour, but she declined on principle, asking instead whether he would give the play at Buckingham Palace; Dickens, always a little wary in his dealings with royalty, demurred, saying that it would place his daughters in an awkward position socially, instead offering a private performance at a London venue. This took place, and was triumphantly successful; the audience included not only the Queen and the Prince Consort but also the King of Belgium and his retinue. A slight shadow was cast over the event when Dickens politely but firmly declined, not once but twice, Her Majesty's invitation to be received by her after the performance, on the interesting grounds that he had already changed into his costume for the farce, and preferred not to be presented wearing 'motley and a red nose'. This was Dickens and the monarchy: courteous, but never compliant. When he met her, it was going to be on his own terms. Despite this borderline *lèse-majesté*, the Queen wrote an enthusiastic letter to him, praising both play and performance.

The great Danish storyteller Hans Christian Andersen was also present at the performance; he had been staying as a guest at Dickens's new country house, Gad's Hill Place, in which the family had only just taken up residence. The visit (supposedly for two weeks, but in the end it was five) had not been a success. The encounter of these two geniuses, both with a very special connection to childhood, each intensely admiring of the other, should have been made in heaven, but it was not. Andersen was altogether too fey for Dickens – 'cutting paper into all sorts of patterns … and gathering the strangest little nosegays in the woods'. There was nothing childish about Dickens. He was the child without a childhood, bustling furiously towards manhood. Even Dickens's own children took against Andersen, though he spent some time playing with them: he was, they said, with the brutality of youth, 'a bony bore'. Dickens made wicked fun of Andersen's linguistic inabilities. 'His translatress,' he told Angela Burdett-Coutts, 'claims he cannot speak Danish.' When he finally left, Dickens put a card on his dressing-room mirror: *Hans Christian Andersen slept in this room for five weeks, which seemed to the family ages.*

There were three more highly successful public performances of *The Frozen Deep* at the intimate Royal Gallery of Illustrations Theatre in Regent Street in London, which seemed to be the end of the current run. Then a last-minute invitation from Manchester took them to the Free Trade Hall – a massive space, which meant that the girls, Katey and Mamie, and Georgina and Mrs Wills, none of whom had any experience of playing in large theatres, would have to be replaced. Arthur Smith, authorized stage adaptor of Dickens's Christmas Books, had been managing the revival, and he recommended a once-distinguished Shakespearean actress, Frances Ternan, to play the Nurse, and she suggested her very experienced twenty-year-old daughter, Maria, for the crucial part of Clara, the young woman who rejects Wardour's love; as an afterthought, Mrs Ternan's youngest girl, eighteen-year-old, Ellen, who had recently been appearing at the Theatre Royal Haymarket, was asked to play the small role of Lucy Crayford.

The crisis that had been so long coming was now imminent.

FOURTEEN

Going Public

The Ternans rehearsed with Dickens in London. Maria, who had seen the show at one of the performances at the Gallery of Illustrations and been overwhelmed by it, was worried about becoming over-charged emotionally in performance. And indeed, at the first performance in Manchester, she broke down totally during the final scene, so that Dickens, in his death throes as Wardour, had to whisper reassurances to her. The whole performance was even more intense than usual; Maria's tears unleashed those of the rest of the cast. Dickens seemed possessed, and when he pushed violently past Collins in the last act, the younger man 'turned to jelly'. Collins thought it the greatest performance Dickens ever gave: 'he literally electrified the audience'. The reason for this startling intensity was almost certainly his encounter, not with the over-emotional Maria Ternan, but with her younger sister, Ellen, which concentrated all his feelings of domestic entrapment and his longing for release. Photographs are a poor guide to personal charm, and the ones we have of Ellen, all taken slightly later than the time of Dickens's meeting with her, suggest a young woman of some self-possession, not especially angelic, in the manner that Dickens favoured, nor outstandingly beautiful, but poised and trim. 'Small, fair-haired and rather pretty,' is how Katey Dickens described her, 'of no special attraction apart from her youth.' Ellen flattered him, Katey said, and 'though she was not a good actress, she had brains, which she used to educate herself, to bring her mind more on a level with his'. Whatever it was that Dickens saw in her – and we have not one word on the subject from his own pen – she was the opposite, both physically and mentally, of poor Catherine, about whom his feelings had inexorably turned from indulgent exasperation to deep resentment. From this point forward, consciously or unconsciously, Dickens sought to supplant her with Ellen.

Writing in 1872, just two years after Dickens's death, Forster could not mention Ellen, but what he says is powerfully expressive of the emotional chaos within his friend: 'An unsettled feeling greatly in excess of what was usual with Dickens, more or less observable since his first residence at Boulogne, became at the time almost habitual. And the satisfactions that home should have supplied, and which were indeed essential requirements of his nature, he had failed to find in his home.' Nor did he derive any pleasure from Society: 'he would take as much pains to keep out of the houses of the great as others take to get into them'. Fame had not bred in him any taste for the supposedly glittering salons of the rich and titled; indeed, he was inclined to be uncharacteristically rebarbative or – more often – sullenly silent, in such company. 'The inequalities of rank which he secretly resented took more galling as well as glaring prominence from the contrast of the necessities he had gone through with the fame that had come to him,' said Forster in a passage of searching analysis, 'and when the forces he most affected to despise assumed the form of barriers he could not easily overleap, he was led to appear frequently intolerant (for he very seldom was really so) in opinions and language.' The price of his escape from the shadow of the blacking warehouse was becoming apparent.

His early sufferings brought with them the healing powers of energy, will and persistence, and taught him the inexpressible value of a determined resolve to live down difficulties; but the habit, in small things as in great, of renunciation and self-sacrifice, they did not teach; and, by his sudden leap into a world-wide popularity and influence, he became master of everything that might seem to be attainable in life, before he had mastered what a man must undergo to be equal to its hardest trials.

Dickens was most at ease within his own immediate circle, and his office staff at *Household Words*; but felt most completely himself in front of an audience. Forster was increasingly suspicious of his relationship to the theatre, which, he claimed, expressed only

the craving which still had possession of him to get by some means at some change that should make his existence easier. What was highest in his nature had ceased for the time to be highest in his life, and he had put himself at the mercy of lower accidents and conditions. The mere effect of the strolling wandering ways into which this acting led him could not be other than unfavourable. But remonstrance was as yet unavailing.

He might have more strongly argued that the satisfaction that Dickens derived from these activities gave him no lasting relief; and indeed, the moment the *Frozen Deep* tour was over, making a substantial £20,000 for the Jerrolds (whether they wanted it or not), he was again desperate for diversion. 'Have you any idea tending to any part of the world?' he wrote to Wilkie Collins, whom he now saw as his official partner in truancy.

Will you rattle your head and see if there is any pebble in it which we could wander away and play marbles with? We want something for *Household Words* and I want to escape from myself. For when I *do* start up and stare myself seedily in the face, as happens to be my case at present, my blankness is inconceivable – indescribable – my misery amazing.

They went on a tour, the ostensible objective of which was a series of articles for *Household Words*; the ulterior purpose was to go and see Ellen Ternan in a play she was doing in Doncaster. The pieces, co-written by Dickens and Collins, were serialized as *The Lazy Tour of Two Idle Apprentices*. Eventually collected into a volume, these mere shavings from Dickens's workbench are full of extraordinary perceptions and pen sketches, and filled with the emotional restlessness Forster so vividly describes; above all they record the curious relationship between the two men. The inspiration for the book is an engraving by Hogarth depicting the two apprentices, Thomas Idle and Francis Goodchild; in the articles, Collins appears as Idle, Dickens as Goodchild. In a remarkable passage in one of them, Goodchild/Dickens sets out to explore the country from the tops of all the steep hills in the neighbourhood. On his return, Idle/Collins asks him whether he really did go up those hills, and bother himself with those views, and walk all those miles, just for pleasure.

'Because I want to know,' added Thomas, 'what you would say of it, if you were obliged to do it.'

'It would be different then,' said Francis. 'It would be work then; now it's play.'

'Play!' replied Thomas Idle, utterly repudiating the reply. 'Play! Here is a man who goes systematically tearing himself to pieces, and putting himself through an incessant course of training, as if he were always under articles to fight a match for the champion's belt, and he calls it Play. Play! … you can't play. You don't know what it is. You make work of everything.'

Idle/Collins continues, pitilessly:

> 'To me you are an absolutely terrible fellow. You do nothing like
> another fellow. Where another fellow would fall into a footbath
> of action or emotion, you fall into a mine. Where any other
> fellow would be a painted butterfly, you are a fiery dragon.
> Where another man would stake a sixpence, you stake your
> existence. If you were to go up in a balloon, you would make for
> Heaven; and if you were to dive into the depths of the earth,
> nothing short of the other place would content you. A man who
> can do nothing by halves appears to me to be a fearful man.'

The most extraordinary thing about this unsparing assessment
is that it was written, not by Collins, but by Dickens. They
took turns in writing, but Michael Slater has determined
beyond doubt that this particular passage was written by
Dickens himself. It betokens an uncommon degree of self-
knowledge; moreover, it foreshadows Dickens's behaviour in
the very near future.

In another striking section of the book, Goodchild has
gone to a lunatic asylum during the course of his walk, and
seen a man who obsessively pores over the matting. He is
gently dissuaded by the medical staff from doing this.
Goodchild says that it occurs to him that the matting is now
all the man can understand. 'Then I wondered,' he
continues,

> whether he looked into the matting to see if it could show him
> anything of the process by which *he* came to be there, so
> strangely poring over it. Then I thought how all of us, GOD help
> us! in our different ways are poring over our bits of matting,
> blindly enough, and what confusions and mysteries we make in
> the pattern.

In the midst of perhaps the greatest turmoil of his life, and in some fairly inconsequential material, we catch a sudden shaft of Dickens's genius at its most profound. This slight volume brilliantly illustrates Chesterton's provocative comment that 'you cannot discuss whether *Nicholas Nickleby* is a good novel, or whether *Our Mutual Friend* is a bad novel. Strictly speaking there is no such novel as *Nicholas Nickleby*. There is no such novel as *Our Mutual Friend*. They are simply lengths cut from the mixed substance called Dickens.' On their tour, Collins proved the idler of the two apprentices. But there was no keeping up with Dickens: trying to do so, Wilkie sprained his ankle, and from then on had to be carried everywhere by his friend. 'Wardour to the life!' cried Dickens of himself.

No doubt as he strode heroically up the mountains and over the hills on his tour with Wilkie, Dickens, like the man obsessed by the matting, was studying the pattern of his own life with unusual intensity. On his return, he initiated radical changes to it. From Gad's Hill, where he was staying with the children, he wrote a letter to Catherine's long-standing servant, Anne Brown. It was just the sort of workaday letter he might have sent to Stanfield or Teblin on some detail of the construction of the set for *The Frozen Deep*, proposing a good sensible solution to a pressing problem: in this case, the repulsiveness to one of one's wife.

My dear Anne,

I want some little changes made in the arrangement of my dressing room and the Bathroom. And as I would rather not have them talked about by comparative strangers, I shall be much obliged to you, my dear friend, if you will see them completed before you leave Tavistock House. I wish to make the Bathroom my washing-room also. It will be necessary to carry into the bathroom, to remain there, the two washing-stands from my Dressing-room. Then, to get rid altogether, of

the chest of drawers in the Dressing-room I want the recess of
the doorway between the Dressing-room and Mrs Dickens's
room, fitted with plain white deal shelves, and closed in with a
plain light deal door, painted white … the sooner it is done,
the better … the chest of Drawers shall come down here, when
the van comes down to bring our luggage home at the end of
the month. They all send you their love.

Ever faithfully yours.

Just as one of his characters might do, and with equally expressive symbolism, he was dividing the marital bedroom in two, with a bookcase.

Catherine was given no notice of this development. Life at Tavistock House presumably carried on regardless, though he kept out of it as much as possible. His loathing for his wife had attached itself to his in-laws, or maybe it was vice versa. They frequently came to stay, leaving the place dirty and disordered: 'I think my constitution is already undermined by the sight of a Hogarth at breakfast'. Once, when the Hogarths were in residence, something upset him so badly that he was unable to sleep, so he got up, dressed and walked to Gad's Hill, a distance of some thirty miles. Anyone might have walked out into the night, and then come back half an hour later. Not Dickens. A man who could do nothing by halves, indeed.

He had by now confided his marital unhappiness to Forster and to Angela Burdett-Coutts; it is the familiar litany of complaints that follow on the death of love. 'No two people were ever created, with such an impossibility of interest, sympathy, confidence, sentiment, tender union of any kind between them, as there is between my wife and me,' he wrote to Burdett-Coutts.

> Nature has put an insurmountable barrier between us, which
> never in this world can be thrown down ... she is the only
> person I have ever known with whom I could not get on some-
> how or other, and in communicating with whom I could not
> find some way to come to some kind of interest. You know that
> I have many impulsive faults which often belong to my impul-
> sive way of life and exercise of fancy; but I am very patient and
> considerate at heart, and would have beaten out a path to a
> better journey's end than we have come to, if I could.

He has re-written the script; all the sweetness and loving, the
fun, the joy, the intimacy of the past have been deleted.

Could any woman have been an adequate Mrs Charles
Dickens? Probably not: but poor Catherine was, Dickens now
convinced himself, wholly ill-suited for the job – over-parted,
not up to the role. She was not intellectual, like Angela
Burdett-Coutts; she was not intuitive, like Lavinia Watson;
she was not sharp and perceptive like Georgy; she was not
pretty like, well, like Ellen; and she was jealous. She had
'obtained proof positive', he wrote to Augusta de la Rue, 'of
my being on the most intimate terms with at least fifteen
thousand women of various conditions in life since we left
Genoa'. Finally, and decisively, he says that she has failed as a
mother: 'she has never attached one of them to herself, never
played with them in infancy, never attracted their confidence,
never presented herself before them in the aspect of a mother.'
He says that he has seen them fall away 'in a natural progress
of estrangement'. Mamie and Katey 'harden into stone figures
of girls when they can be got to go near her, and have their
hearts shut in her presence as if they were closed by some
horrible spring.' Every one of the children denied this in their
later recollections, Katey most vehemently, even though the
presence of Georgina in the household was clearly a compli-
cating factor.

He had decided that the relationship between him and Catherine was over. At first he was inclined to be reasonable, to think it six of one and half a dozen of the other: 'poor Catherine and I are not made for each other, and there is no help for it. It is not only that she makes me uneasy and unhappy, but that I make her so too – and much more so,' he wrote to Forster.

> God knows, she would have been a thousand times happier if she had married another kind of man, and that her avoidance of this destiny would have been at least equally good for us both … I know too well that you cannot, and no one can, help me. Why I have even written, I hardly know … the mere mention of the fact, without any complaint of blame of any sort, is a relief to my present state of spirits – and I can get this only from you, because I can speak of it to no one else.

To Forster's sensible reply, Dickens responds:

> To the most part of what you say – Amen! You are not so tolerant as perhaps you might be of the wayward and unsettled feeling which is part (I suppose) of the tenure on which one holds an imaginative life, and which I have, as you ought to know well, often only kept down by riding over it like a dragoon – but let that go by. I make no maudlin complaint. I agree with you as to the very possible incidents, even not less bearable than mine, that might and must often occur to the married condition when it is entered into very young … but the years have not made it easier to bear for either of us; and for her sake as well as mine, the wish will force itself upon me that something must be done … I claim no immunity from blame. There is plenty of fault on my side, I dare say, in the way of a thousand uncertainties, caprices and difficulties of disposition; but only one thing will alter that, and that is, the end which alters everything.

And then, without transition, he says: 'What do you think of my paying for this place, by reviving that old idea of some Readings from my books. I am very strongly tempted. Think of it.' Forster vehemently opposes the idea, but Dickens is resolved.

> Too late to say, put the curb on and don't rush at hills – the wrong man to say it to. I have now no relief but in action. I am become incapable of rest. I am quite confident I should rust, break, and die, if I spared myself. Much better to die, doing. What I am in that way, nature made me first, and my way of life has of late, alas! confirmed. I must accept the drawback – since it is one – with the powers I have; and I must hold upon the tenure prescribed to me ...

While these feelings were hardening in his breast, Dickens was stomping round the country, giving more and more charity readings of *A Christmas Carol*, his parable of kindness, generosity and the melting of the frozen heart. In fact, he was more or less demented, driving himself harder and harder. 'I am the modern embodiment of the old Enchanter, whose familiars tore them to pieces,' he wrote to Lavinia Watson.

> I weary of rest, and have no satisfaction but in fatigue. Realities and idealities are always comparing themselves before me, and I don't like the Realities except when they are unattainable – *then* I like them best of all things. I wish I had been born in the days of Ogres and Dragon-guarded castles. I wish an ogre with seven heads (and no particularity of brains in the whole of them) had taken the Princess whom I adore – you have no idea how intensely I adore her! – to his stronghold on the top of a high series of mountains, and there tied her up by the hair. Nothing would suit me half so well this day, as climbing after her, sword

in hand, and either winning her or being killed. – *There's* a frame
of mind for you in 1857.

In some ways he knew himself very well indeed. He needed to
cast someone in a certain kind of role, so that he could enact
another sort of role. And he now had an ideal actress in mind
for the role of the Princess. But where would that lead? What
would happen to the adored Princess? What life could they
lead together?

For the present, he simply wanted perpetual motion. He
more and more saw a paid reading tour as a way of killing
many birds with one stone. Money was part of the motive. It
is possible he was anticipating having to make some kind of
financial settlement if and when he and Catherine were to
part, but the main purpose of the tour was to blot out his
misery. 'The domestic unhappiness remains so strong upon
me that I can't write, and (waking) can't rest, one minute,' he
wrote to Wilkie Collins. He was quite clear about the underlying cause of his agitation: 'I have never known a moment's
peace or content since the last night of *The Frozen Deep*,' and
had, he said, 'a turning notion that the mere physical effort
and change of the Readings would be good, as another means
of bearing it.' Forster was adamantly opposed to the idea of a
financial reward; Dickens pointed out that everyone thought
he was being paid anyway. But that was not the point: 'I must
do *something* or I shall wear my heart away. I can see no better
thing to do that is half so hopeful in itself, or half so well
suited to my restless state.' Then at the end of March: 'It
becomes necessary … to consider and settle the question of
the Plunge.' He urged Forster to 'quite dismiss from your mind
any reference whatever to circumstances at home. Nothing
can put *them* right till we are all dead, buried and risen … it is
all despairingly over. A dismal failure has to be borne, and
there an End.' It was, after all, merely a relationship between a

man and a woman: there was a much more important relationship to consider.

> Will you then try to think of this reading project (as I do) apart
> from all personal likings and dislikings, and solely with a view
> to its effect on that particular relation (personally affectionate
> and like no other man's) which subsists between me and the
> public.

At the beginning of 1858, he became President of the Great
Ormond Street Children's Hospital Appeal: on 9 February, he
read *A Christmas Carol* for them. Before the reading, he made
a superb speech, one of his finest, instinct with all his unique
power of compassion. In it, he described an incident he had
witnessed as he roamed the city at night:

> There lay, in an old egg-box, which the mother had begged from
> a shop, a feeble, wasted, wan, sick child. With his little wasted
> face, and his little hot worn hands folded over his breast, and his
> little bright attentive eyes, I can see him now, as I have seen him
> for several years, looking steadily at us. There he lay in his little
> frail box, which was not at all a bad emblem of the little body
> from which he was slowly parting – there he lay quite quiet,
> quite patient, saying never a word. He seldom cried, the mother
> said, he seldom complained. He lay there, seeming to wonder
> what it was all about. God knows, I thought, as I stood looking
> at him, he had his reasons for wondering – and why, in the
> name of a gracious God, such things should be.

Then he read for them; thousands of pounds were raised. The
reading was so popular that the Hospital had taken bookings
for possible future readings. 'This closed the attempt at farther
objections.' Accordingly, he commissioned Arthur Smith to
manage a short London season for him, consisting of seven-

teen readings at the St Martin's Hall in Covent Garden. The season started with *The Cricket on the Hearth* on 22 April 1858. The acclaim, rapturous and sustained, was beyond his most optimistic expectations.

Just one month later, his marriage finally unravelled. The end was precipitated by an incident that would not have been out of place in one of the French boulevard comedies he so despised. By mistake, a jeweller had sent to Catherine a bracelet inscribed by Dickens to Ellen Ternan. She confronted him with it; insisting that it was merely a souvenir of *The Frozen Deep*, he became deeply angry and resentful. She backed down, but that was not enough: he demanded that she demonstrate her confidence in him – and her respect for Ellen – by going to visit Ellen and her mother. Katey, overhearing her sobs, found her seated at her dressing-room table in the act of putting on her bonnet; Katey, 'angrily stamping her foot', absolutely forbade her to go to the Ternans, but she did, nonetheless: her marriage was at stake. But when Mrs Hogarth, Catherine's mother, heard about this humiliation, she told her what was patently the case: her marriage was over. She must leave Dickens, her mother said, and she did.

Georgy stayed on to look after the children, and Dickens took up residence at *Household Words* while he and Catherine thrashed out a settlement. With Mark Lemon acting as her negotiator, Catherine sensibly turned down Dickens's suggestions that she should stay on as his hostess while they lived separate lives, or that they should take turns living in Gad's Hill and Tavistock House. She counter-proposed that she should be given a house of her own, plus £600 a year, and that Charley would live with her. Dickens indicated his acceptance of these terms. So far, things were proceeding reasonably. Then, on the point of settling, Dickens discovered that Mrs Hogarth and her youngest daughter Helen had been putting it about that Ellen was Dickens's mistress. This rendered him predictably paroxysmic. He refused to pay Catherine a penny until they had publicly retracted their comments, which they finally did at the end of May 1858. 'We solemnly declare,' they wrote, 'that we now disbelieve such statements. We know they are not believed by Mrs Dickens, and we pledge ourselves on all occasions to contradict them, as entirely destitute of foundation.' Dickens saw Catherine behind her family's rumour-mongering: 'the weak hand that could never help or serve my name in the least has struck at it – in conjunction with the wickedest people, whom I have loaded with benefits.'

Literary London was agog, thinking that the affair must be with Georgina; oh, no, Thackeray casually remarked on the steps of the Garrick, the affair wasn't with Georgy, it was with a young actress. When Dickens heard this, he fired off a letter furiously upbraiding his fellow novelist; shortly after, his young protégé Edmund Yates savagely attacked Thackeray in a gossip column. Sensing that everything he had built up over the last twenty years was in danger of falling apart – above all the relationship of trust he had with his public – Dickens exploded like a nail bomb. He wrote a hysterical public statement for publication in leading newspapers and journals, declaring that '... all the lately whispered rumours touching the trouble at which I have glanced, are abominably false'. He wrote that 'whosoever repeats one of them after this denial, will lie as wilfully and as foully as it is possible for any false witness to lie, before Heaven and earth.' Forster strongly advised him against publishing the statement, but another friend, John Delane, editor of *The Times*, was in favour. Dickens went ahead, putting it on the front page of *Household Words*. Mark Lemon refused to print it in *Punch*, on the entirely reasonable grounds that it had no place in a comic miscellany; Dickens cursed both him and Bradbury and Evans, who, as well as being Dickens's own publishers, also published *Punch*. Other papers did print the statement, often with adverse comment; it was received by the general public with utter bewilderment: they had no idea what he was talking about.

Meanwhile, he wrote another statement for Arthur Smith, the manager of the reading tours, to show 'to anyone who might benefit from reading it'. Smith accordingly let a reporter of his acquaintance read it; the reporter got it to the *New York Tribune*, who published it with alacrity, and from there it was immediately copied by British newspapers. It was widely condemned, and with reason: it is a hateful document, a calm dismissal of Catherine at every level – as a wife, as a mother, as a woman – climaxing in a lyrical defence of Ellen, whom he does not, of course, name: 'there is not on earth a more virtuous and spotless creature than that young lady.' The statement ends pompously and self-servingly: 'I am quite sure that Mrs Dickens, having received this assurance from me, must now believe it, in the respect I know her to have for me, and in the perfect confidence I know her in her better moments to repose in my truthfulness.' The statement had begun with the words 'in the manly consideration towards Mrs Dickens which I owe to my wife …' Commenting on the statement, the *Liverpool Mercury* went for the jugular:

> This favourite of the public informs some hundreds of thousands of readers that the wife whom he has vowed to love and cherish has utterly failed to discharge the duties of a mother; and he further hints that her mind is disordered. If this is 'manly consideration' we should like to be favoured with a definition of unmanly selfishness and heartlessness.

There can be no great man who has ever so completely let himself down as Dickens at this moment. His latent sense of personal injustice, which enabled him to identify so strongly and to such beneficent effect with the disadvantaged, was always simmering just below the surface; now it boiled up and over. His feelings were intensified by the fact that of course he wanted very much to be Ellen's lover, and that all of this would perhaps ruin the chances of that ever happening. The widespread dissemination of the statement enraged him, though to be disseminated was precisely why he had written it: forever after he would refer to it as 'the violated letter', though if anyone was violated by it, it was not him.

The fallout from these events would continue for many years – for the rest of his life, in fact. His deep friendship with Lemon was over, as was the more equivocal one with Thackeray. And he resolved to sever his long and fruitful relationship with Bradbury and Evans. This had immense repercussions; his new venom towards Frederick Evans extended to his refusing to attend his son Charley's marriage to Evans's daughter Bessie. He never again saw Catherine, with whom he had shared his life for twenty years and who had given birth to their ten children. His subsequent twelve-year-long relationship with Ellen Ternan was pursued furtively, unacknowledged by all except his very closest associates; there could never be any question whatever of his regularizing it. The truly astonishing thing is that, despite his fears, the entire ugly incident made so little impact on the key relationship of his life, the one with his readers. He approached the reading at the St Martin's Hall on 17 June, just five days after his first statement appeared on the front page of *Household Words*, with the deepest trepidation. In the event, he was greeted, if anything, more warmly than ever. Remarkably, he remained cool and focused throughout the evening, as he would do for the rest of the run, and throughout the provincial tour, which lasted till November of 1858. Privately, he wrestled with black depression. 'I had one of those fits yesterday,' he told his friend Mary Boyle, 'and was utterly distressed and lost. But it's gone, thank God, and the sky has brightened before me once more.'

In all he did 125 readings across the British Isles; from July 1858 to October 1859 the enterprise was conducted on a properly Dickensian scale. The build-up to each appearance was immense; everyone in the hall felt immensely privileged to be there. Ticket touts outside the auditorium were soon racking up ever-greater profits. Dickens exercised considerable ingenuity to ensure that the poor should be present in large numbers, but he was defeated by the market demand. Since the early readings in Birmingham, he had refined his performances; indeed, very early on he started memorizing the texts, rehearsing them for hours on end. 'I have tested all the serious passion in them by everything I know,' he wrote to Forster, 'made the humorous points much more humorous; cultivated a self-possession not to be disturbed; and made myself master of the situation.' He began to cast his net widely through his published work: he carefully selected the characters and the situations that would be most effective in performance, then he shrewdly worked the texts, ruthlessly cutting and re-shaping them; sometimes he added a telling new phrase, an irresistible new joke; now and then he changed the whole sense of a passage.

Dickens brought all his long-honed skills as a director to bear on the readings. Attired in evening dress, with a rose in his buttonhole, he entered the stage to an ovation that would satisfy a pop star. He then calmly proceeded to pour himself a glass of water while the audience fell into a deep and concentrated silence as he looked at them. 'If ever a look spoke it was just in that moment,' said a contemporary reviewer. 'It felt as if he were making friends with us all. His eyes seemed to have the power of meeting those of every separate person in the audience.' Everyone was spellbound by the eyes: 'he has the look of a man who has seen much,' a reviewer remarked, 'and is wide awake to see more.' He stood at an ingenious lectern of his own devising, on which sat the text from which he was supposedly reading, a carafe of water, and a paper-knife that he sometimes used as a prop. Above the lectern was a gas-filled frame of metal piping that lit up during the reading, both illuminating and focusing Dickens, almost as if he were projected on a screen. He used his hands a great deal in the performance, sometimes with the paper-knife, but he never stepped out from behind the lectern. Above all it was his face and his voice that worked the magic. He learned to understand the acoustical properties of buildings, quickly assessing each venue when he arrived, and discovered how to use his voice so that he reached every single individual in the vast halls in which he played; some of them held two or three thousand people, each of whom he reached out to, personally, individually, without, needless to say, the aid of microphones.

At first, the readings were relatively low-key: he maintained a conversational narrative voice, the characters lightly sketched in. Increasingly, however, his desire to escape into full character prevailed. In all he did sixteen different readings, summoning into living, breathing existence no less than eighty-nine characters. His hope as a writer, he had said long before, was that his characters would take their place 'among the household gods'. They had done exactly that, and to see them brought to life by their creator was an intense joy for his audiences – and for him. His characters were, Forster says, 'living speaking companions to him'. He refers to them constantly in his letters as if they were personal acquaintances. He heard every word his characters uttered, he told G. H. Lewes. 'Only a lunatic could do that,' commented Lewes, accusing Dickens of hallucinating. 'He was a seer of visions. His types established themselves in the public mind like personal experiences. Their falsity was unnoticed in their blaze of illumination. Every humbug seemed a Pecksniff, every jovial improvident a Micawber.' This is exactly the way they had insinuated themselves into the readers' consciousness, to Lewes's intense disapproval. 'In vain critical reflection showed these figures to be masks; not characters but personified characteristics ... even critical spectators who complained that these broadly painted pictures were inartistic daubs could not wholly resist their effective suggestiveness.' If this was so on the page, how much truer it was in the flesh: 'the vividness of their presentation triumphed over reflection,' said Lewes. 'Their creator managed to communicate to the public his own unhesitating belief.'

In the Readings (and they were now definitely Readings, and not mere readings), Dickens's abandonment of himself to the characters drew the astonished admiration of his audiences, which often included professional actors. There was a sense of liberation on Dickens's part that transcended mere theatrical effectiveness: this was a form of catharsis for the performer. 'Assumption has charms for me,' he said. 'Being some one in voice &c not at all like myself.' And multiple-assumption – on a scale not even attempted by Mathews, or by himself, in *Mr Nightingale's Diary* – was the most charming of all. Before the audience's very eyes, and without the aid of props or costume, he would become David Copperfield, Mrs Gamp, Fagin. 'The impersonator's very stature,' reported Charles Kent, 'each time Fagin opened his lips, seemed to be changed instantaneously. Whenever he spoke there started before us – high-shouldered with contracted chest, with bird-like claws, eagerly anticipating by their every movement the passionate words ... his whole aspect, half-vulpine, half-vulture-like, in its hungry wickedness.' This description underlines the fact that acting is above all an act of imagination rather than of mimicry: it is an overpowering mental connection that produces a physical result. As Malcolm Andrews finely puts it: 'in order to get the right voice, in a concentrated way, Dickens had to move his full being into that of the character'. This is precisely what the art of acting is, and Dickens's readings, bereft of any external aids, show this in particularly pure form. He explored in the flesh, as he had done in his novels, what Andrews calls 'the fissility of self', the multiphrenia latent in us all. He was ruthless in his adaptation of the novels, deleting anything descriptive that he could show physically, adding dialogue where it would be useful; sometimes he did this on impulse in the heat of performance. Now he really was 'writing a book in company'.

His contemporaries quickly recognized the extraordinary nature of his enterprise. 'Charley,' Carlyle said to him, 'you carry a whole company under your hat.' To his sister he wrote: 'Dickens does it capitally, such as *it* is, acts better than any Macready in the world; a whole tragic comic heroic *theatre* visible, and kept us laughing – in a sorry sort of way, some of us thought – the whole night.' Beyond all of this was the massive affection his audiences bore towards him. The *Times* reviewer who described his Readings as a 'return to the practice of Bardic times' catches the oddly atavistic quality of Dickens. There is something of the carnival spirit in his sense of the interconnectedness of everything. Alienation was what he set out to abolish, in himself as much as in society. At the readings, the surge of affection from the public moved him to tears and helped, however, temporarily, to heal his own sense of internal estrangement. 'In mid-Victorian towns and cities he arrived in person,' writes Malcolm Andrews with outstanding eloquence, 'to conduct people nightly into a world where the great blaze of Christmas celebrations issuing from the red hearth of the Reading platform threw giant shadows around the hall of listeners, and where, as for Scrooge, Past and Present, reality and illusion became therapeutically confused.'

The first Reading tour was a continuous triumph. In Dublin, 'all the way from the hotel to the Rotunda I had to contend against the stream of people who were turned away. When I got there, they had broken the glass in the pay-box, and were offering £5 freely for a stall.' In Belfast, he reported, a man had come up to him and said, 'Do me the honour to shake me hand, Misther Dickens, and God bless you sir; not only for the light you've been to me this night, but the light you've been in mee house, sir (and God love your face!) this many a year!' With *Boots at the Holly Inn* and *Mrs Gamp*, 'it was just one roar with them and me. For they made me laugh so, that sometimes I *could not* compose my face to go on.' In Harrogate at the *Dombey* reading, a man 'really shook with emotion; he was not in mourning but I supposed him to have lost some child in old time'. Another man found Toots from the same novel so funny, that when he came round again, with his catch-phrase 'It's of no consequence,' Dickens reported, 'he gave a kind of a cry, as if were too much for him.'

It was a fierce schedule; often he did a programme twice if it had been particularly successful; sometimes he did two shows a day. He was never off the railway, sometimes arriving at five in the morning. His itinerary would have been gruelling now, but then, puffing up and down the country, changing trains again and again, it was punitive. He was exhausted, but deeply happy. 'Sometimes before I go down to read (especially when it is in the day), I am so oppressed by having to do it that I feel perfectly unequal to the task. But the people lift me out of this directly; and I find that I have quite forgotten everything but them and the book, in a quarter of an hour.' His voice, subjected to this punishing schedule, caused him troubles: 'I think I sang half the Irish melodies to myself as I walked about, to test it.' But his willpower conquered any mere physical frailty. He was exhilarated, too, by the huge financial success; in Scotland he was earning £500 a show. Forster, profoundly disapproving of the whole exercise, nonetheless saw them all; he opines that *A Christmas Carol*, *Dombey*, *Mrs Gamp*, and the trial from *Pickwick* were his greatest successes: 'the quickness, variety and completeness of his assumptions', having greatest scope in these. Here, I think, more than in the pathos or graver level passages, his strength lay.' In other words, he was at his best as a Public Entertainer, the very thing Forster so despised.

Before leaving for the tour, Dickens, implacable to the last, had exacted punishment from Bradbury and Evans for failing to let *Punch* publish his statement about the breakdown of his marriage, by severing relations with them. As well as their loss of him as an author, it also meant the end of *Household Words*. His fury at what he felt to be their betrayal of him now transmuted into cheerful ruthlessness. He asserted his right – as principal owner of the magazine – to change publisher and printer; Bradbury and Evans had been both. Forster suggested to them that it might be sensible to sell the magazine to Dickens; they refused, so Dickens simply resigned as editor, and set up a new magazine. With careful calculation, he found premises for the new magazine two doors down from the *Household Words* office, whereupon Bradbury and Evans threatened legal action. By the terms of their original contract with Dickens, they had no power to appoint another editor without Dickens's permission, so the Master of the Rolls, the second most senior judge in England and the Head of Civil Justice, was called on to make a judgement. He decreed that the magazine must be sold at auction; Dickens bought it at a knock-down price. The banner of the new magazine stated 'with which is incorporated *Household Words*'. The title they eventually settled on was *All the Year Round,* having toyed with *Home-Music, English Bells, Weekly Bells,* and *The Anvil of the Time;* Dickens himself proposed *Household Harmony,* apparently oblivious that the recently and very publicly separated author might not be thought to be the greatest authority on that subject. *All the Year Round* kicked off electrifyingly with a serialization of Dickens's latest novel, *A Tale of Two Cities;* the success was phenomenal. And if that weren't enough to rub Bradbury and Evans's noses in the dirt, the next novel to be serialized was Wilkie Collins's *The Woman in White,* another *succès fou,* with further novels commissioned from Bulwer-Lytton and Charles Reade. It was deeply satisfying revenge, served up, as proverbially recommended, cold, with Dickens in icy control throughout. It was also savage and unjustified, a naked imposition of Dickens's will, and entirely disproportionate to the offence: Bradbury and Evans had been very good publishers, both of the novels and of the magazine. (Pathetically, they tried to create a rival magazine, *Once a Week;* it failed.)

Inspired by yet another reading (his five hundredth, he jokingly said) of his friend Carlyle's *History of the French Revolution, A Tale of Two Cities* – a book that, except in the magnificent savagery of the revolutionary scenes, has been felt to lack the richness of theme and metaphor characteristic of his greatest work – was nevertheless a deeply personal book for Dickens. In the Preface to the novel, he describes how it grew out of *The Frozen Deep,* which was forever sacred in his mind because it had given him Ellen, into whose life he had stealthily but inexorably moved, making arrangements for her sister Fanny to study in Italy, ensuring that Mrs Ternan was provided for, protecting Ellen and her sister Maria from what appeared to be police harassment, and eventually buying Ellen a house near Mornington Crescent in North London. It is impossible to know whether by now they had consummated their relationship; all the evidence suggests that she was still holding out. But she was now central to his life, and it is not for nothing that the heroine of *A Tale of Two Cities* is named Lucie, the Gallicized version of Lucy, Ellen's character in *The Frozen Deep*. Sydney Carton, the man wasted by unreciprocated love, bears striking resemblances to Richard Wardour, with whom Dickens had identified so strongly: the same Byronic nihilism, the same feeling of being immured (*Buried Alive* was one of the alternative titles for the novel). Both give up their lives for love, and in the process redeem themselves. At this point, the comparisons with Dickens break down. He was not ready to sacrifice everything: he would not give up his love affair with the public.

Dickens was convinced that if just one word of a liaison – especially with a younger woman, and an actress at that – got out, the world would condemn him and reject him. Hence the extreme secrecy of everything to do with Ellen. It must have been deeply oppressive for both of them, though there is the possibility that he enjoyed the cloak-and-dagger element of this clandestine affair, the elaborate covering-up of tracks, the coded messages, the obsessive perusal of railway timetables, the aliases (he rented homes for them sometimes under the name Turnham and sometimes Tringham). What it can have been like for Ellen is another matter; adored by the most famous man in England – possibly the world – and financially secure, with her family well looked after, but unable to have a public life or a private one. She was a bird in a gilded cage, seen by no one, acknowledged by no one. Claire Tomalin's title for her superb book *The Invisible Woman* perfectly sums up her situation.

Apart from his secret life, Dickens was more highly visible than ever. While engaged in the constant toil of producing *All the Year Round* every week, he maintained an extraordinary schedule of speech-making. One week, he was helping to launch the Royal Dramatic College Fund, which, with the kind of practical generosity he admired, secured homes and pensions for members of the dramatic profession in reduced circumstances. It also educated the children of actors and actresses; provided a library and gallery of works of art illustrative of the history of dramatic literature and art; and endowed houses for ten actors and ten actresses. Another week, in another speech, he gave an unexpected endorsement for public schools (though of course his boys, notably Charley, had attended them); speaking in Coventry, he responded to the gift of a gold repeating clock by pledging that 'it should be thenceforward the inseparable companion of his workings and wanderings, and reckon off the future labour of his days until he should have done with the measurement of time'. (It was.) In Lancashire he presided over a meeting of the Institutional Association, giving prizes to candidates from 114 local mechanics' associations. There he summed up the philosophical core of *Hard Times*: 'Knowledge has a very limited power when it informs the head only; but when it informs the heart as well, it has a power over life and death, the body and the soul, and dominates the universe.' He knew what he was talking about: dominating the universe was pretty much what he'd been up to himself all these years.

Family life was given its due at Gad's Hill Place, where he had formed warm relations with his fellow citizens in the area, encouraging them to come to him in any difficulty. He slipped effortlessly into the role of Lord of the Manor. When his fiery, proud daughter Katey was finally persuaded, rather against her better judgement, to marry Wilkie Collins's frail younger brother Charles, a gifted writer and illustrator on the staff of *All the Year Round*, they were married in the local church: villagers set up triumphal arches, the blacksmith made a bonfire and fired off a salute from two small cannons.

Katey's mother, whom she always defended and of whom she remained very fond, was pointedly not invited. The feudal pomp and the outward matrimonial jubilation barely concealed the underlying complexities. After the newly weds had gone off to Dover en route for their honeymoon in France, Mamie found Dickens on the floor, sobbing over Katey's wedding dress: 'But for me, Kate would not have left home.' He knew perfectly well that she didn't love Charles, and had only married to get away from him. It is an almost unique example of Dickens recognizing the malign effects of his will-power, the way in which he manipulated the people in his orbit like a puppet master.

Mamie, who adored her father unreservedly (and who never had anything to do with her mother until after Dickens's death), in turn fell in love with a young man, but Dickens thought him unsuitable; she submitted to her father's disapproval. She never married, a source of deep guilt to Dickens, who thereafter tried to contrive situations in which she might meet a suitable spouse. The boys were for the most part doing well, the older ones scattered around the world in a sort of Dickens diaspora: Charley, fresh from business studies in Leipzig, and planning to set up his own firm, was in the Far East; Walter had been promoted to lieutenant and was in India. Seeing him off, Dickens said, was like having 'great teeth drawn out with a wrench'. Frank laboured under a stammer that would have barred him from most professions: Dickens worked long and hard with him to try to cure it, with only partial success. The boy had entertained dreams of being a gentleman-farmer; these came to nothing, and he now hoped to join Charley in his business. Alfred was studying for an Army commission; Sydney, nicknamed 'Ocean Spectre' because of the faraway look in his eyes – as if gazing out to sea – was a cadet in Portsmouth; the two youngest, Harry and Plorn, were students at Rochester Grammar School, near home in Gad's Hill. He loved them all deeply, though he was afraid, he told Forster, that they might have inherited Catherine's 'lassitude'. None of them, with the exception of Harry, had his energy; but then who had?

Dickens himself evidently felt an urgent need to break from the past. In August 1860, he got rid of Tavistock House: for him, bad memories associated with the place now outweighed good. The set for *The Frozen Deep*, which after the run of the play he had re-incorporated into the school-room where it had started life, he brought down to Gad's Hill, along with the dummy book-backs from his study. That was all that he kept from the splendour that was Tavistock House. The following month, in a gesture loaded with conscious symbolic significance, he burned all the letters he had ever received, and all his papers. The conflagration reminded him of *The Arabian Nights*. 'They sent up a smoke like the Genie when he got out of the casket on the sea-shore,' he wrote to Wills, 'and as it was an exquisite day when I began, and rained very heavily when I finished, I suspect my correspondence of having overcast the face of the Heavens.' It was as if he wanted to wipe out all evidence of his intimate life. 'Would to God every letter I had ever written was in that pile!' Somewhere in the back of his mind was his unmollified rage over what he continued to think of as his 'violated letter'. Ten years later he wrote to someone who had asked whether he had any letters from his friend Daniel Maclise: 'A few years ago I destroyed an immense correspondence, expressly because I considered it had been held with me, and not with the public, and because I could not answer for its privacy being respected when I should be dead. I have since allowed no letters from friends to accumulate in my possession.' One can only presume that his corpse underwent several revolutions in his grave in Westminster Abbey on the completion of the publication of the twelve-volume set of his collected correspondence; virtually no one, it seems, ever threw away a letter from Dickens, for which we may be truly grateful. If not a single novel or story of Dickens were to survive, his letters alone would constitute one of the glories of English literature. But Dickens was now committed to a double life, a life in which the secrets of the heart must never be known. He must destroy all possible evidence. And in that, he succeeded.

Oddly enough, in his journalistic writings – in his personal communications with his public, that is to say – he now started to record selected memories from his childhood. From that same year of 1860, he penned a series of essays under the name *The Uncommercial Traveller*, many of which (though not always strictly accurate) had an autobiographical thrust. In *Dullborough Town*, for example, he describes his early life in Chatham; in *Nurse's Stories*, he recounts the tales Mary Weller told him: 'If we all knew our own minds, (in a more enlarged sense than the popular acceptation of that phrase), I suspect we should find our nurses responsible for most of the dark corners we are forced to go back to, against our wills.' Here again, Dickens is a pioneer. Is there anything in English or indeed world literature to compare with this enterprise? A great novelist using a magazine as a forum for his musings, whimsies, fantasies, reminiscences – the incidental music of his *œuvre* – at the same time publishing the work of other writers who might (in the case of Wilkie Collins, for example) be regarded as his rivals? The readership of *All the Year Round* was immense: 250,000 copies sold every week, and rising; the Christmas pieces were, as ever, hugely successful. The greatest gamble was the serial: and in 1860, the Irish novelist Charles Lever's *A Day's Ride*, after a promising opening canter, quickly faltered, and Dickens decided that the circulation demanded the boost of a new novel from him. With a kindness typical of his editorial regime, he allowed Lever's book to continue its run, encouraging him to find the most graceful way of bringing it to a conclusion, while his own serial ran side by side with it, duly securing the circulation.

Within three weeks, he had written the first seven chapters of the novel, which he called *Great Expectations*. He seems to have undertaken the cripplingly hard work of maintaining weekly instalments with equanimity. Despite, or because of, the momentous changes in his life, he wrote with new control and economy, revisiting in a darker key the story of the making of a young man with gentlemanly aspirations. Before starting to write, he re-read *David Copperfield* to ensure that there would be no overlap. After applying himself to it with furious intensity, he finished the novel by June, 'somewhat the worse for wear'. In his far-ranging survey of disappointed expectations, he takes in a minor-key account of a theatrical venture, that of the ex-clergyman Wopsle, who takes to the stage under the name of Waldengarver. Dickens's account of that gentleman's catastrophic performance of *Hamlet* (he insists on interpolating cries of Amen! into the Ghost's speech, and his diction is 'very unlike any way in which any man in any natural circumstances of life and death ever expressed himself about anything') has a certain grimness about it, Wopsle's dreams of Reviving the Drama ending in a pathetic appearance in a pantomime. There is something distressing about his painful fate, a far cry from the cheerful dreadfulness of the Crummles's rackety ventures. The theatre in which he finally appears is a kind of theatrical dystopia, from which one rather wishes to avert one's eyes: even the stage has lost its healing power.

As Dickens originally wrote it, the book ended with a brief unconsoling encounter between Pip and Estella, the girl trained up to break hearts:

I was very glad afterwards to have had the interview; for in her face and in her voice, and in her touch, she gave me the assurance that suffering had been stronger than Miss Havisham's teaching, and had given her a heart to understand what my heart used to be.

Bulwer-Lytton, after reading it in manuscript, persuaded Dickens to let the reader down a little more lightly, with more hope for the future. Against Forster's advice, he published the present ending:

I took her hand in mine, and we went out of the ruined place; and, as the morning mists had risen long ago when I first left the forge, so the evening mists were rising now, and in all the broad expanse of tranquil light they showed to me, I saw no shadow of another parting from her.

It might be ventured that the original version was truer to Dickens's own experience of love, and to Pip's experience of Estella, but the new ending made his readers very happy. Both serialized and between hard covers, *Great Expectations* was a best-seller, and almost universally admired; even Forster exempted it from his strictures on the later Dickens, believing that he had rediscovered his sense of humour and balance in it. Its autobiographical resonances are subtle and distilled; it is another, even more intense, account of 'what my heart used to be'.

During the intensely focused writing of the novel, Dickens had managed to slip in a short second London season of Readings, followed in November by a major tour all over England and Scotland. He had a slightly dodgy start in Norwich when he tried out a new sequence from *Nicholas Nickleby*, which was not entirely successful; thereafter, all was glory, though not without mechanical and logistical problems, some of them caused by the illness of his tour manager, Arthur Smith, who, though incapacitated, couldn't bring himself to relinquish all the paperwork, with the result that Dickens was often unclear as to where he was supposed to be going or who was supposed to be looking after him. Then Smith died, and his successor, Thomas Headland, was simply not up to the immensely complex job. Dickens in effect took charge, as he always did. In Newcastle, the gas-apparatus on his reading desk fell over. The stage management, paralysed, terrified of fire, or – even worse, of panic in the auditorium and a subsequent stampede – looked on in horror. Dickens bought them some time.

> Fortunately a lady in the front row ran out towards me, exactly in a place where I knew that the whole hall could see her. So I addressed her, laughing, and half-asked and half-ordered her to sit down again; and in a moment, it was all over.

The crew positively shook the boards he stood on with their trembling, he said, when they came on to put things right. When they had, the performance continued, to the usual unbridled accolades; afterwards, the gas-man observed that 'the more you want of the Master, the more you'll find in him', a remark that, understandably, pleased Dickens greatly.

He was very clear about what was acceptable and what was not: in Berwick-upon-Tweed, he was appalled by the absurdly over-large Corn Exchange 'so of course I struck'. They had to improvise a new location, but all went brilliantly. In Edinburgh, the second performance was heavily over-booked, so 'I read with the platform crammed with people. I got them to lie down upon it, and it was like some impossible tableau or pic-nic – one pretty girl in full dress, lying on her side all night, hanging on to one of the legs of my table!' Things going wrong were grist to his mill; like the trouper he was, he always rose above it.

Despite the adrenalin-fuelled exhilaration of the tour, however, he realized that he was getting exhausted – 'in shreds,' he said. He hated performing in the moist warm weather of the summer; and some of the new material he had introduced – the tremendous sequence from *Copperfield*, in particular, culminating in the shipwreck and the death of Steerforth – really took it out of him; Lear-like, the Reader has almost to become the storm. 'I might as well do Richard Wardour,' he said. Macready, deep in his retirement, came backstage after seeing *Copperfield* at Cheltenham:

> I swear to Heaven that as a piece of passion and playfulness – er – indescribably mixed up together it does – er – no, really, Dickens! – amaze me as profoundly as it amuses me. But as a piece of Art – and you know – er – that I – No, Dickens! By God! – have seen the best Art in a great time – it is incomprehensible to me. How it is got at – er – how it is done – er – how one man can – well! It lays me on my – er – back, and it is of no use talking about it.

Macready in his expostulatory way immediately identified what was original and uniquely demanding about the Readings: 'the passion and playfulness … indescribably mixed up together'. Every reading was a helter-skelter: the nimbleness of mind, voice and heart needed to pass in seconds from towering emotion to skittishness, from ingénue to gargoyle, from sustained metaphor to verbal fireworks, is peculiarly exhausting, and though Dickens had great natural gifts as an actor, he lacked the steady experience of playing night after night, year in and year out, which alone builds stamina. He entirely relied, every time he performed, on nervous energy – on adrenalin, in fact, and adrenalin is a dangerous drug. It enables you to ignore your physical limitations; but the body pays the price nonetheless, as does the mind. A small infusion of it produces wonderful results, but becoming dependent on it is ultimately debilitating. Dickens's performances were triumphs of mind over matter: real acting is about mind in matter.

For the moment, he was still deeply thrilled by the roar of the crowd; Macready's praise was a wonderful bonus. Such tributes, to say nothing of the financial rewards, were hugely gratifying. He had had an expression of interest from America some while before, and a concrete offer from Australia for £10,000 for an eight-month tour. He was sorely tempted by the thought of exposure to a new country and the generation of possible new material; he went so far as to plan a series called *The Uncommercial Traveller Upside Down*. He turned the idea of Australia over and over – the effect on his domestic life, the children, and indeed himself: would such a tour allow him to write 'a new story'? The novel that was to become *Our Mutual Friend* was already brewing in his mind. Finally, reluctantly, he said no.

Meanwhile, there were ten more Readings at the St James's Theatre, March to June of 1862, three sensationally successful ones in Paris at the British Embassy in January 1863, and thirteen in London from March to June of that year. After the Paris triumph, he stayed on in France, travelling to Arras because he wanted to see Robespierre's birthplace. He spent his fifty-first birthday there, and seized the opportunity of seeing the town's celebrated Religious Theatre. The Story of the Cross was told six times daily, along with the sacrifice of Isaac by Abraham. 'A woman in blue and fleshings (whether an angel or Joseph's wife I don't know) was addressing the crowd through an enormous speaking-trumpet; and a very small boy with a property lamb (I leave you to judge who *he* was) was standing on his head on a barrel-organ.'

Death was all around Dickens in 1863: his ever-poorly friend Augustus Egg finally succumbed, as did his mother-in-law Georgina Hogarth (unlamented), Thackeray (with whom he had a reconciliation only weeks before he died), and his own mother, Elizabeth. His feelings for her, never less than complicated, had resolved themselves into a kind of comic exasperation. 'My mother,' he had earlier written to Maria Beadnell,

> who was … left to me when my father died (I never had anything left to me but relations) is in the strangest state of mind from senile decay; and the impossibility of getting her to understand what the matter is, combined with her desire to be got up in sables like a female Hamlet, illumines the dreary scene with a ghastly absurdity that is the chief relief I can find in it.

She lived with Dickens's sister Letitia, by then widowed, at Haverstock Hill in North London. On one occasion he had visited her there, to find Letitia and the maid Helen poulticing her poor head. 'The instant she saw me, she plucked up a spirit, and asked for "a pound"'. She died, aged seventy-four, on 13 September 1863; the following day Dickens told Wills that he had an idea for a story that he would call *Mrs Lirriper's Lodgings*. If Mrs Nickleby is Dickens's revenge on his mother, Mrs Lirriper is his absolution of her. Mrs Nickleby's chatter has become a Joycean stream-of-consciousness, her culpable wrong-headedness transmuted into Mrs Lirriper's busy benevolence. This extraordinary outpouring was wildly successful when it appeared in *All the Year Round* as the Christmas Story for 1863, and it became one of his most successful Readings, his impersonation of the verbally incontinent landlady a

comic marvel. It suggests that Dickens had achieved some sort
of closure in his feelings for his mother.

FIFTEEN

The Loadstone Rock

On the last day of 1863, unknown to Dickens, his soldier son Walter died in Calcutta at the age of twenty-three, having fought with distinction in the Indian Mutiny as a lieutenant in the 42nd Highlanders, the Black Watch. In hospital with what was thought to be a minor ailment, he had been talking about his preparations for returning home when, according to Dickens's deliberately understated report, 'he became excited, had a great gush of blood from the mouth, and fell dead'. The news only reached Dickens at the beginning of February – on the seventh, his birthday, as it happens – by which time poor stuttering Frank Dickens – also, of course, not knowing of his brother's death – was on his way to India to join him. Dickens took the news grimly but stoically. Walter had left a small mountain of debt behind him, he gloomily noted.

At the time, Dickens was wrestling with *Our Mutual Friend*, in which London, the city he once celebrated, has become an image of the triumph of materialism, money the index and endpoint of all things. Dust-heaps are the emblem of the waste of society, while the filthy Thames flows sluggishly through the book, a source of income, disease and death. The writing came slowly, Dickens uncertain whether he could 'force an original book out of it … with all this fluctuating distress in my mind'. It was out of the fluctuating distress that the book came, of course. Part of that distress was centred on Ellen. It seems, from the guarded reminiscences of Dickens's children and from Ellen's confidences to her parish priest, that she had resisted Dickens's amorous advances till the early

1860s, when she was in her mid-twenties and he nearly fifty, and that when it finally happened, she had derived no pleasure from the experience; and if she didn't, presumably neither did he, except perhaps fleetingly. Their meetings were irregular and of necessity furtive; she was allowed to make discreet visits to Gad's Hill, and when they met in the house that Dickens had bought for her in North London, Francesco Berger, the young composer who had written the scores for *The Lighthouse* and *The Frozen Deep*, would play the piano for them while they sang duets. Berger suggests a sweetly domestic scene, or rather a sort of enactment of domesticity, brief and temporary, but scarcely, one would have thought, what either of them wanted or needed. Serious doubt has been cast on this reminiscence, but it has a feeling of great probability about it.

It is possible that at some point Ellen became pregnant, and went to France for an abortion; Dickens's daughter Katey bluntly stated that she gave birth to a child, a boy. It has been conjectured, on the strength of elaborate and only partially convincing sleuthing, that the child was born in the house in Slough that Tringham/Turnham had rented; this supposed child is said to have died in infancy. If any of these things are true, the effect on Dickens must surely have been immense, overwhelming; but we have no evidence of any such effect. The veil he drew over this aspect of his life has proved to be impenetrable.

He certainly spent a great deal of time in France on no known business. He writes to Wilkie Collins of 'vanishing into space for a day or two', and to Wills of 'a mysterious disappearance'. He always returned refreshed from these visits. His health in general had not been good: he had been lame in his left foot, which baffled experienced physicians, though he was in no doubt of its provenance himself. He attributed it to a long walk he had taken in the snow with the dogs Turk and Linda. Over the course of the walk, his feet had massively swollen up, laming him, 'to the remarkable terror' of the hounds, who crept along beside him as he struggled to get home. Turk's expression, he said, was 'one of sympathy as well as fear,' while Linda was 'wholly struck down'. He was haunted by this incident, and often referred to it. It is a startling image: the wounded king, crawling through the snow, the leader of the pack disabled. He insisted nonetheless that the problem was purely local, mere frostbite, and behaved as if nothing were wrong. 'I had certainly worked myself into a damaged state,' he told Katey, but he had got better, he said, as soon as he went away to France. He now knew, he claimed, unconvincingly, that he should make 'future dashes from his desk' before he needed them. But the recurring lameness deprived him more or less of 'his inestimable solace of bodily exercise', as Forster put it. A Dickens who could not walk was scarcely a Dickens at all. The exercise was not merely physical, it was mental and spiritual. This was how he re-charged himself. 'Work and worry, without exercise, would soon make an end of me,' he wrote to Forster before another trip to France. 'If I were not going now, I should break down. No one knows as I know today how near to it I have been.'

After one of these restorative sojourns, he and Ellen and her mother, who seems as often as not to have travelled with them, came back to England on 9 June 1865, via Folkestone, taking the 15.11 boat train. As it approached the bridge before Staplehurst station at some thirty miles an hour, a signalman flagged the driver to stop, but the train was too close for it to come to a halt in time and it continued on to the bridge, hurtling over a gap in the line. The engine reached the other side, but many of the carriages plunged through the gap. Dickens's carriage was left half hanging over the bridge; four others were 'smashed to matchwood'. Ten feet below them was the River Beult. Ellen and her mother screamed. Dickens said, 'We can't help ourselves, but we can be quiet and composed. Pray don't cry out.' They promised not to. By now they were all huddled in a corner of the carriage. Dickens told them not to stir – 'they answered quite correctly, "Yes"' – and then carefully extricated himself from the carriage. Until he emerged, he had no idea what had happened. What he saw was alarming: there was open swampy field fifteen feet directly beneath them. The guards were running about distractedly, not knowing what to do. Dickens called out to them, 'Look at me. Do stop an instant and look at me, and tell me whether you don't know me.' 'We know you very well, Mr Dickens,' they replied. He asked them for the key to the carriage and went back and got Ellen and her mother safely out. He next ensured that they could leave the scene immediately; apart from anything else, he had to get them away from possible prying eyes. He then went straight back to the carriage, which was still hanging perilously over the bridge, to fetch a bottle and a half of brandy, which by extraordinary chance he had with him, and his hat. Once he had got them, he climbed down the brickwork of the bridge – this from a fifty-three-year-old man not in the best of health. He filled his top hat with water, and shouted out to whoever needed it, 'I have brandy here.' The first person he encountered had a terrible cut across his face; Dickens could not bear to look at the man, but poured water over his wound, gave him brandy to drink and laid him on the grass. Too late. 'I am gone,' the man said, and died forthwith. A woman was lying on her back, with blood pouring over her face, which was, he noted, the colour of lead. He gave her brandy; the next time he passed, she was dead, too. The brandy he gave to a man called Dickenson saved his life; they travelled back to London together. Someone else ran up to him, imploring him to help him find his wife, but it turned out that she was dead.

'No imagination can conceive the ruin of the carriages,' he wrote to his old friend Thomas Beard, 'or the extraordinary weights under which the people were lying, or the complications into which they were twisted up among iron and wood, and mud and water.' He worked for hours among the dying and the dead. Then he suddenly realized that he had left the manuscript of the current instalment of *Our Mutual Friend* in the carriage, which continued to hang precariously over the bridge. Yet again he clambered back in and retrieved it. His superhuman calm and authority earned him a Resolution of Thanks from the directors of the railway company. He played his heroism down, noting that, 'I have a – I don't know what to call it – constitutional (I suppose) presence of mind, and was not in the least flustered at the time.' But, as so often with Dickens, he paid the price in time. 'In writing these scanty words of recollection,' he wrote to Beard, 'I feel the shake and am obliged to stop.' He refused to be examined at the Inquests, and never wrote about the incident. But when *Our Mutual Friend* was published in volume form, he added a humorous postscript concerning the crash, again demonstrating the extraordinary intimacy and directness of his communication with his readers, and the striking reality his characters had for him:

On Friday the Ninth of June in the present year, Mr and Mrs Boffin (in their manuscript dress of receiving Mr and Mrs Lammle at breakfast) were on the South Eastern Railway with me, in a terribly destructive accident. When I had done what I could to help others, I climbed back into my carriage – nearly turned over a viaduct, and caught aslant upon the turn – to extricate the worthy couple. They were much soiled, but otherwise unhurt. The same happy result attended Miss Bella Wilfer on her wedding day, and Mr Riderhood inspecting Bradley Headstone's red neckerchief as he lay asleep. I remember with devout thankfulness that I can never be much nearer parting company with my readers for ever, than I was then, until there shall be written against my life, the two words with which I have this day closed this book: – THE END.

From that time forward, he found rail travel unnerving. He was obliged to do more and more of it, both in his visits to Ellen, in her various bolt-holes around the country, and on tour with the Readings. Any small increase in the train's speed brought about 'a perfect conviction, against the sense, that the carriage is down on one side' (generally the left side, and not the side on which the carriage in the accident actually went over). Railways assumed an ever more menacing aspect for him. In a freak train accident, one of his deeply loved large dogs, the mastiff, Turk, was killed; Linda, the St Bernard, escaped with minor injuries.

He worked on, despite these apocalyptic omens, toiling over *Our Mutual Friend* 'like a dragoon', as he put it. Finally, in September, he finished it. It had started with tremendous success, but the readership fell off over the course of the serialization. The critics, for the most part, despised it. '*Our Mutual Friend* is, to our perception,' wrote Henry James when it appeared in America

> the poorest of Mr Dickens's works. And it is poor with the poverty, not of momentary embarrassment, but of permanent exhaustion. It is wanting in inspiration. For the last ten years it has seemed to us that Mr Dickens has been unmistakably forcing himself. *Bleak House* was forced; *Little Dorrit* was labored; the present work is dug out as with a spade and pickaxe.

Forster, too, detected a laboured quality in the writing which he believed reflected Dickens's problems and ill-health. The book notoriously contains, in the character of the sublimely pompous Podsnap, a satirical pen-portrait of Forster. Dickens found his old friend increasingly hilarious, 'impregnably *mailed* in self-complacency'. After marrying rather late, he had built himself a stupendously grand mansion, complete with a liveried page boy, whom he loudly berated in front of his guests; at supper, he was given, like Podsnap, to lengthy orations on topics of national significance. He had now ascended from being Secretary to the Lunacy Commission, to being one of its Commissioners, a lucrative if disturbing employment. Forster himself, with Podsnapian obliviousness, was unaware of any lampoon; and indeed, Dickens remained deeply fond of him underneath his superficial irritation.

With his extraordinary flexibility, Dickens had introduced another character into *Our Mutual Friend* as a response to a letter from the wife of the banker J. P. Davis, who had bought Tavistock House from him. The Davises were Jewish, and Liza Davis wrote to reproach him for the anti-Semitism of his portrait of Fagin. Dickens blustered somewhat in his reply to her, insisting that he had 'no feeling towards the Jewish people but a friendly one', and pointing out that in his *Child's History of England* he had 'lost no opportunity of setting forth their cruel persecution in old times'. But when, not long after, he came to write *Our Mutual Friend*, he created, in the character of Riah, a kindly, generous Jew, conscious of his subservience to his employer, which derives from a debt of gratitude he owes the man's son: 'in bending my neck to the yoke I was willing to wear,' Dickens has him say, 'I bent the unwilling necks of the whole Jewish people.' When the novel appeared, Liza Davis sent him a Hebrew/English Bible inscribed: 'Presented to Charles Dickens in grateful and admiring recognition of his having exercised the noblest quality man can possess – that of atoning for an injury as soon as conscious of having inflicted it.'

Writing in general was now much more effortful for Dickens. In particular, he approached the task of producing the annual Christmas Story – 'the Christmas Stone', as he called it – with dread; accordingly, in September 1865, he sat down joylessly to write a story he had sketchily conceived about a Cheap Jack, a travelling salesman, and 'suddenly the little character you will see, and all belonging to it, came flashing up in the most cheerful manner, and I had only to look on and leisurely describe it.' *Dr Marigold's Prescription* is a fully fledged masterpiece, written with all Dickens's youthful exuberance, tempered by the economy he had subsequently learned. It encompasses a vast amount of action within a small space, dealing in rapid succession with child-beating, suicide, loneliness, the problems of the deaf and dumb, all told by Marigold himself in the vocabulary of salesman's patter: everything becomes about buying and selling. Its popularity was immense, both on the page and as a Reading: the fountain of Dickens's invention had by no means run dry. It is worth noting that the piece is a monologue; in writing it, Dickens effortlessly became the character. To the end, he still found joy in, as he put it, assumption: it released him absolutely and restored him to his old buoyancy.

That Christmas of 1865, Gad's Hill was festive in the old Tavistock House way, crammed to bursting with family and guests. Dickens was a superb host: every day, there was a huge breakfast, a sumptuous lunch, and a magnificent supper, very little of which he ate himself. There would be visits to the horses, of which there were six; three large dogs accompanied them on walks. Sultan, an Irish wolfhound, briefly joined the ranks, but proved to be so menacing to everyone but Dickens (of whom he was psychopathically protective) that he had to be permanently muzzled. Even so, he perpetrated a terrible assault on a child, who, though not hurt, was very frightened; Dickens decreed that he should be shot. Dickens supervised his execution with brisk unsentimentality.

The daily walk was *de rigueur* for guests to Gad's Hill, at least when Dickens's foot permitted: four miles an hour was the favoured pace; the walk generally lasted three hours. Not for the faint-hearted. Games were played with equal vigour:

rounders, bagatelle, battledore, bowling, quoits. Dickens played longer and harder than anyone, 'quite the youngest of the company up till the last minute'. Dinner was always awash with hilarity. Dickens did not dominate: he was a wonderful laugher, making his guests feel brilliantly funny. At such moments, his friend and protégé Percy Fitzgerald wrote, his face turned into '*crimpled* wrinkles of enjoyment'. After dinner there would be more games and dancing, especially horn-pipes (his speciality), charades, and memory games, at which of course he always excelled. The punch (lethal) was his responsibility; he never drank more than a glass or two himself, but would not take no from his guests. He was a demon at billiards. He went off to bed at midnight himself, but encouraged the guests to play on, which they did, some-times till dawn. Everybody was expected at breakfast the following morning, regardless of when they had retired. After breakfast, he would withdraw to write, which he did in the extraordinary Swiss châlet his friend the French actor Charles Fechter had sent him, as a present, in ninety-four separate pieces. He had put it up in the shrubbery, which was part of the estate, across the road from the house; it could be reached through an underground tunnel dug to connect it to Gad's Hill Place. There is something peculiarly satisfying about Dickens writing in such a fairy-tale environment, reached by a secret passage. The main house had its own touch of theatri-cal fantasy in the *trompe l'œil* of Stanfield's scene-paintings for *The Frozen Deep* that lined the passage to the rear lawn.

By January of 1866, despite anxiety about his health, Dickens was beginning to plan a new Reading tour on a larger scale than before; maybe he thought he could read himself better. In February, he had a medical examination that revealed degeneration of the heart. 'I was not disconcerted; for I knew well beforehand that the effect could not possibly be without the one cause at the bottom of it.' Quinine, digitalis, and iron supplements were prescribed. In April he kicked things off at the St James's Hall with a virtuoso new Reading drawn from *Dr Marigold*, which rapidly became one of his calling cards. His mastery of the quick-fire patter of the salesman, encompassing wild farce and dark tragic depths, sometimes within seconds of each other, in mercurial succession – the very essence of his 'streaky bacon' philosophy of writing – made it one of his most complete performances.

In June, he set off on the tour, under the proficient management of Chappell's, the London concert agency. The tour manager was the burly Scot Arthur Dolby, tall, bald, with a marked stammer. This unlikely figure proved an absolute stalwart to Dickens for the rest of his life as a performer. The tour inevitably involved railway trains; Dolby would provide a resplendent three-course picnic lunch on the train, with wine and gin punch on ice in the washstand, to distract from the remembered horror of Staplehurst.

Engagements were not well spaced: he played London, Bradford, Edinburgh, Glasgow, Aberdeen, London again, often without days off in between, leaving him very little opportunity to recover; throughout the length of the tour, he managed to get to Gad's Hill just once. He had a more or less permanent cold and quickly became tired and depressed, though he was always cheered by the ringing receptions, the tears and the laughter and the cheers he infallibly provoked; there was never an empty seat at any Reading that he gave throughout his career at the lectern. This no doubt persuaded him to accept Chappell's suggestion of an extension of a further forty Readings. He asked for a rise, which they gave him; over the whole tour, he earned the remarkable sum of £25,000. He was now subject to occasional seizures; he attributed his physical exhaustion to 'too much railway shaking', though he was travelling – thanks to Dolby's good offices – in a carriage of his own, got up with sofas and armchairs, with an *en suite* pantry and a washstand. The travel can't have helped, but it was the show that was draining him. When it was over, he could hardly manage to undress himself. A dozen oysters and some champagne, he said, was 'the best restorative I have yet tried'.

His physical endurance was phenomenal; in Glasgow, he had to have his piles painfully lanced, yet he struggled on, like a marathon runner, determined at all costs to pass the white tape. His powers of recovery are constantly astonishing, reinforced by his unshakeable conviction that energy bred energy. During the Readings in Newcastle-upon-Tyne, the barometric pressure was so oppressive that he and Dolby went for a three-mile walk at Tynemouth. A storm suddenly blew up, which wildly exhilarated him:

> We were in full enjoyment of it when a heavy sea caught us, knocked us over, and in a moment drenched us and filled our pockets. We had nothing for it but to shake ourselves together … and dry ourselves as well as we could by hard walking in the wind and sunshine. But we were wet through for all that, when we came back here to dinner after half-an-hour's railway drive. I am wonderfully well, and quite fresh and strong.

This leg of the tour ended in June 1867, in Cambridge, by which time he had more or less decided, after much cogitation, and despite his now almost complete exhaustion, to accept the frequently pressed offer of an American tour. The money was deeply attractive, of course; he was conscious of the financial needs of his children and relatives, some of whom were feckless, others simply unlucky. The result was the same: he paid. But beyond these practical motives, there was something darker at work. 'I begin to feel myself drawn towards America as Darnay in *A Tale of Two Cities* was drawn towards Paris,' he wrote to Forster. 'It is my Loadstone Rock.'

This is an alarming comparison. *The Arabian Nights*, Dickens's personal Bible, is of course where the original Loadstone Rock is to be found: exerting such force on a ship as to pull all the nails out of its structure, it sinks it. It is impossible to escape the feeling that, at this point in his life, Dickens was pushing himself towards extinction.

'I shall never rest much while my faculties last,' he wrote to Wills, justifying the American tour, 'and (if I know myself) have a certain something in me that would still be active in rusting and corroding me, if I flattered myself that it was in repose.' Moreover, he continues, his work itself is a source of renewal. 'I think that my habit of easy self-abstraction and withdrawal into fancies, has always refreshed and strength-ened me in short intervals wonderfully.' He was right; it had. But for how much longer? 'I do really believe,' he continued, in a remarkable image, 'that I have some exceptional faculty of accumulating young feelings in short pauses, which oblit-erates a quantity of wear and tear.' Earlier in the letter he had written, 'When I went to America in '42, I was so much younger but (I think) very much weaker. I had had a painful surgical operation shortly before.' His self-delusion was becoming dangerous. For many years he had had uncommon energy and powers of recuperation; for a long time he seemed unnaturally young. But now – though he refused to acknowl-edge it – his body was patently failing him. On the top of Dickens's letter Wills had written: 'This letter – so illustrative of one of the sides of CD's character – powerful will – I think ought *decidedly* to be published in justice to Forster and myself, who dissuaded him from America – which killed him eventually.'

Rumours of his ill-health were everywhere, to the extent that he wrote a letter to *The Times* insisting that he had never been in better health; to another paper he wondered whether their suggestions of his being in a 'critical' state of health may not have been a misprint for 'cricketing' since the Gad's Hill team had lately won a match. To the *Athenaeum*, he wrote drolly to say that he combined his 'usual sedentary powers with the active training of a prize-fighter'. It was all bluster; he was in fact 'in tortures' from a left foot so swollen that he was unable to get his boot on. The doctors told him that it was an erysipelas, caused by friction on a bunion. Despite the agonies he was in, he travelled to Liverpool to see Dolby off to America, where Dickens had sent him to sound out the arrangements; he was able to check out the boat at the same time.

He took advice from everyone in his circle about the advisability of going to America, and he ignored it all. There was huge pressure from the American side to go before the upcoming Presidential elections. Dolby having given a good report of the management, on 30 September 1867, the telegram of confirmation was sent. Dickens was hell-bent on it, knowing that he would be acclaimed on a level that England, for all its adulation, could never match. He seemed to entertain the notion that Ellen might come with him, though it is altogether impossible that her presence could have been kept secret from the American press. He arranged a code by which he would notify Wills on arrival whether it would be possible or not; of course it was not, and Ellen went to stay with her sister in Italy while he was away. He had a sweet and intimate farewell gathering with his children and their children, to whom he was known as Wenerables. Meanwhile, a Farewell Dinner on a stupendous scale was being arranged for him. It is quite inconceivable that any other writer – or any other man or woman of his time – or any time – would have been given a comparable send-off. He was only going to America, after all, not the moon, or Heaven. The monumental Freemasons' Hall in Holborn was everywhere draped with British and American flags: golden laurels on a deep red background surmounted the arched panels, at the top of each of which was the name of one of his books, in gold letters. There were 450 guests, among them the Lord Mayor of London, the Lord Chief Justice, the distinguished literary patron, Lord Houghton, the Crimean hero Sir Charles Russell, and pretty well the whole of the artistic world, painters, poets, writers, including a veritable phalanx of Royal Academicians. Disraeli and Gladstone had both, admittedly, turned down the invitation, but they were conspicuous by their absence.

Edward Bulwer-Lytton and Dickens entered arm in arm; Lytton presided over the event. In his speech he referred to 'the royalty of genius'. 'Seldom,' he said, 'has that royalty been quietly conceded to any man of genius till his tomb becomes his throne, and yet there is not one of us now present who thinks it strange that it is granted without a murmur to the guest whom we receive tonight.' Cheers throughout greeted his remarks (though it was the dyspeptic view of the *New York Tribune*'s correspondent that Lord Lytton, as he now was, 'should appear only in print'). Dickens stood, and the place erupted. Everyone rose to their feet; many people jumped up on to their chairs, waving serviettes, bottles, decanters. He raked the hall with his eyes, tears coursing down his face, barely able to speak: 'Twice his throat faltered as he began ... and all felt that it was a sacred moment with him.' Finally he spoke:

> Your resounding cheers just now would have been but so many cruel reproaches to me if I could not here declare that, from the earliest days of my career down to this proud night, I have always tried to be true to my calling ... I trust that I may take this general representation of the public here, through so many orders, pursuits, and degrees, as a token that the public believe that, with a host of imperfections and shortcomings upon my head, I have as a writer, in my soul and conscience, tried to be as true to them as they have ever been to me.

He asserted the decency of the literary profession; the love of art of the British ('I *can* say that of my countrymen, though not of my country'); the goodness and greatness of the American people. He ended:

> If I may quote one other short sentence from myself, let it imply all that I have left unsaid, and yet most deeply feel; let it, putting a girdle round the earth, comprehend both sides of the Atlantic at once in this moment: 'And, as Tiny Tim observed, "God Bless Us Every One!"'

SIXTEEN

On the Ground

Dickens travelled to America on the *Cuba*. The ship left Liverpool on 9 November and finally arrived in Boston ten days later, where he was met by Dolby: he had been given the Second Officer's cabin on deck, which had been entirely satisfactory. Indeed, everything about this return visit was an improvement on the first, except for the weather and his health, which were of course connected, though it was his underlying physical problems that were at the root of his persistent malaise. Journalists were less pushy than they had been before, though not much more observant:

> my eyes are blue, red, grey, white, green, brown, black, hazel, violet and rainbow-coloured. I am like a well-to-do American gentleman, and the Emperor of the French, with an occasional touch of the Emperor of China, and a deterioration from the attitudes of our famous townsman, Rufus W. B. D. Dodge Grumsher Pickville.

As before, enterprising capitalists had produced whole new lines for sale: there were Little Nell Cigars, Pickwick Snuff, and Mantalini Plug, a delectable chewing tobacco. Hospitality was warm, but not, this time, oppressive. In Boston, where he stayed for a fortnight before beginning the Readings, he was greeted by a trio of triple-barrelled giants of American Literature: Henry Wadsworth Longfellow, Ralph Waldo Emerson and Oliver Wendell Holmes. The first Reading there, which they all attended, was a success 'beyond description or exaggeration'.

In fact, the commercial success of the tour became a problem in itself: the scramble for seats reached hysterical proportions. In New York speculators fielded up to fifty people to buy tickets; they started queuing at midnight. At 2 a.m., bona fide buyers begin to arrive. By five in the morning, there were two lines of 800 people each; at nine, each line was more than three-quarters of a mile long. Family members relieved each other in the queue, waiters served breakfast on the chilly December pavements, and people offered $5, sometimes $10, just to exchange places with someone higher up in the queue. Dolby, trying to control all this firmly but fairly, became 'the most unpopular and best-abused man in America'. 'It is time,' thundered the *New York World*, 'that pudding-headed Dolby retired into the native gloom from which he has emerged.' This delighted Dickens, who referred to him from then on as P. H. Dolby. The response to the Readings was everywhere extraordinary, but in New York, Dickens said, it was 'beyond all precedent or description'; *Dr Marigold* was especially brilliantly received. The 33-year-old Mark Twain, then just at the beginning of his literary career, gave the readers of *The New York Times* a vivid account of the physical impact of the man: 'Promptly at 8 p.m. ... with side hair brushed fiercely and tempestuously forward, as if its owner were sweeping down before a gale of wind, the very Dickens came – straight across the broad stage, heedless of everything, unconscious of everybody, turning neither to the right nor the left – but striding eagerly straight ahead, as if he had seen a girl he knew turn the next corner.'

As curious and interested as ever, Dickens was full of admiration for the changes he saw in the city: Broadway had been completely rebuilt, and Central Park newly created out of what in the 1840s had been a series of rundown villages. But he shrewdly decided not to come back to New York every week, as the promoters wanted, instead taking off around the country, in order to make the return to the city in April all the more eagerly awaited. The four-month tour involved hair-raising train journeys, sometimes in steamers across rivers; his luggage was regularly trashed by rough porters. He had become more realistic about his stamina, and never read more than four times a week, but early on he caught a cold that he was unable to throw off. The catarrh plagued him throughout the tour, utter misery for a performer of his kind, blocking his resonators and limiting his vocal range; his voice was all he had to work his magic, that and his eyes and his hands. Often he had no voice whatever when he woke up in the morning, and had slowly to coax something out of his poor over-taxed larynx. As usual, his willpower finally produced a result, and by the end of every Reading, he was in full flood. The catarrh became his sworn enemy: 'It distresses me greatly at times, though it is always good enough to leave me for the needful two hours. I have tried allopathy, homeopathy, cold things, warm things, sweet things, bitter things, stimulants, narcotics, all with the same results. Nothing will touch it.' He was hardly eating or drinking – or rather, he was eating and drinking according to a diet of his own devising:

> At seven in the morning, in bed, a tumbler of cream, and two tablespoonfuls of rum. At twelve, a sherry cobbler [a drink made of wine, sugar, lemon, and pounded ice, imbibed through a straw] and a biscuit. At three (dinner time) a pint of champagne. At five minutes to eight, an egg beaten up with a glass of sherry. Between the parts, the strongest beef tea that can be made, drunk hot. At a quarter past ten, soup, and anything to drink that I can fancy. I don't eat more than half a pound of solid food in the whole twenty-four hours, if so much.

No diet known to man could have been better calculated to make his vocal problems worse.

His good humour and natural curiosity remained intact, nonetheless. In Washington, on his fifty-sixth birthday, he was given a most courteous welcome by President Johnson, who had met him during his previous visit, twenty-five years before. (Dickens cannot be said to have been good luck for American presidents: shortly after meeting President Tyler in 1842, Tyler's own party expelled him; weeks after meeting Dickens, Johnson was impeached.) Backstage, so to speak, Dickens relished an evening of very high-level gossip among senior politicians. One of them had been at Lincoln's death-bed, and described the cabinet meeting at which the President had, Caesar-like, told them of an ominous dream he had had the night before; that same evening he went to the Ford Theatre and was shot dead.

Everywhere Dickens was fêted; rarely was he pestered. Even when huge crowds met him at the station, which they usually did, they offered a great cheer when he arrived, followed him to the hotel at a respectful distance, and then quietly departed. The camaraderie Dickens enjoyed with Dolby was a constant support, too; the giant Scotsman was tenderly considerate to the man he called 'the Chief', checking him at regular intervals through the night, and generally finding him wide-awake, immersed in a book. By March, though, Dickens's health started to get seriously worse. Both feet were now in agony; he had a savage cough, and could neither sleep nor eat. He took laudanum, which helped him to sleep, but then he felt nauseous all morning. Every performance was now touch and go. No one understood, he wrote to Forster, that 'the power of coming up to the mark every night, with spirits and spirit, may co-exist with the closest thing to sinking under it'. After ten days of one-night stands in upstate New York, he was, unsurprisingly, shattered. His left leg swelled up during Readings, blood rushed into his hands so that they became almost black. After one of the last Readings, his friend Kate

Field discovered him with his head thrown back without support, the blood suffusing his throat and temples where they had been white before.

At last the tour came to an end, leaving only the final New York Readings. As he had predicted, the anticipation was redoubled by his having been out of town so long, but he was scarcely the buoyant showman who had made the calculation all those weeks ago. He rose to the nightly challenge and thrilled and beguiled the audiences, who had no idea what it cost him, and who would scarcely have recognized the trium-phant entertainer who stood before them in the prematurely aged, croaking and hobbling figure who painfully made his way to the theatre each night.

Before the very last Reading, a huge Farewell Banquet was planned for him. On the day, his right foot was monstrously swollen; there was no hope of getting a boot on it. Dolby scoured New York for a gout-stocking to draw over the band-ages, but was assured that gout was unknown in the United States of America. It seemed that Dickens would have to with-draw from the event. In the end, Dolby borrowed a stocking from an English gout victim who happened to be in town. Finally Dickens arrived at the banquet, an hour late, and was led in to the accompaniment of loud cheers by the *New York Tribune*'s Horace Greeley, who had so stoutly defended Dickens twenty-five years earlier over copyright; Greeley proposed the toast. In his reply, Dickens talked affectionately about his life as a newspaperman, making jokes about how he had been reported in America, and about his cold.

> I have for upwards of four hard winter months so contended about what I have been admiringly assured was a 'true American catarrh', a possession which I have throughout highly appreci-ated, though I might have preferred to have been naturalised by any other outward and visible means.

But then he turned serious, bearing testimony to 'the national generosity and magnanimity' and the changes he had seen all around him. 'Nor am I, believe me, so arrogant as to suppose that in five-and-twenty years there have been no changes in me, and that I have nothing to learn, and that I had nothing to learn and no extreme impressions to correct, from when I was here first.' A single voice cried out 'Noble!', which provoked a burst of applause. In future and in perpetuity, he said, he would append to *Martin Chuzzlewit* and *American Notes* a passage on the kindness and consideration he had everywhere experienced. 'And this I will do and cause to be done, not in mere love and thankfulness, but because I regard it as an act of plain justice and honour.' He ended, to further applause, with a peroration asserting the friendship and community of interests of the British and American peoples. The following night, after the final Reading of the American tour, he said:

> I shall often, often recall you as I see you now ... I shall never recall you as a mere public audience, but rather as a host of personal friends, and ever with the greatest gratitude, tenderness and consideration. Ladies and gentlemen, God bless you – and bless the land in which I leave you.

The wound opened twenty-five years before had been healed.

As he spoke those words, a representative of the Inland Revenue Service was hovering waiting to arrest Dickens, on the grounds that he owed the American government tax. Dolby only just managed to fob him off with a combination of bluster and cunning; the man was reprimanded by the superiors he had been seeking to impress. Had Dolby not prevailed, Dickens might have faced a perp walk to the local precinct. Instead, he was seen off at the dock by a large crowd; there were flowers and friends and cheers. Dickens's still painfully swollen right foot was raffishly swathed in black silk. A tugboat took Dickens and Dolby to the *Russia*; another followed behind, firing salutes from a miniature cannon.

During the trip home he recovered wonderfully: the catarrh disappeared, the foot shrank to normal size. Meeting him from the ship, his doctor tells him that he looked seven years younger. On his arrival at Gad's Hill, the villagers turned out in force, the choir sang, bells rang, and the dogs came running to greet him. Forster reported him to be fully restored to health. Perhaps it was this, as well as his continuing determination to make as much money as he could, that influenced his almost incredible decision to accept Chappell's suggestion of an extensive new Reading tour in London and across the country; he agreed to a pulverizing further hundred sessions.

Meanwhile, he swung back into his busy life as if he had never been away: he took over the business affairs of *All the Year Round* from an incapacitated Wills, dealing with his contributors firmly but kindly, as ever; he painstakingly edited the abstruse theological writings of a deceased clerical friend, knowing that no more than a handful of people would ever read them; he went to see, both in London and in Paris, productions of the dramatization of *No Thoroughfare*, the Christmas story he and Wilkie Collins had written together, offering sound practical advice to the producers and actors; he entertained American friends, among them Longfellow; and he saw off his youngest son Plorn when he departed for Australia, to join his brother Alfred, who was doing well there.

This farewell upset him deeply. Despite Dickens's special affection for him, the boy had not succeeded in any endeavour on which he had embarked. As with his other boys, Dickens determined that Plorn should do something useful. Australia, he thought, had 'a freedom and wildness more suited to you than any experiment in a study or an office would have been ... I need not tell you that I love you dearly, and am very, very sorry in my heart to part with you. But this

life is half made up of parting, and these pains must be borne.'
He gave him some Polonius-like wisdom:

> Never take a mean advantage of anyone in a transaction, and
> never be hard on people who are in your power. Try to do to
> others as you would have them do to you, and do not be
> discouraged if they fail sometimes. It is much better that they
> should fail in obeying the greatest rule laid down by our saviour
> than that you should.

He put a New Testament in Plorn's luggage 'because it is the
best book that ever was, or ever will be, known in the world;
and because it teaches you the best lessons by which any
human creature, who tries to be truthful and faithful to duty,
can possibly be guided.' He had done the same for each of his
sons as they had gone away, entreating them all to be guided
by the book, 'putting aside the interpretations and inventions
of Man'. He urged Plorn to maintain 'the wholesome practice'
of saying his prayers, morning and night. 'I have never abandoned it myself and I know the comfort of it.' He ends touchingly: 'I hope you will always be able to say in after life, that
you had a kind father.'

Charley, having failed in his business ambitions, took over
Plorn's office duties at *All the Year Round*, and proved to be a
great success; Henry, meanwhile, got the best possible math-
ematical scholarship to Cambridge. When Henry told him
about it, Dickens simply said 'Capital, capital.' Disappointed
to find his big news received so lightly, Henry took his seat
beside his father in the pony carriage he was driving.

> Nothing more happened until we had got half-way to Gad's
> Hill, when he broke down completely. Turning towards me with
> tears in his eyes and giving me a warm grip of the hand, he said,
> 'God bless you, my boy; God bless you!' That pressure of the

hand I can feel now as distinctly as I felt it then, and it will remain as strong and real until the day of my death.

There is a sense that Dickens was beginning to loosen the iron grip on himself that had so triumphantly propelled him through life. But in order to survive the rigours of the Reading schedule on which he now embarked, he was more dependent than ever on his willpower. Already, in Manchester, almost at the beginning of the tour, his voice was failing, and he was overcome with nausea; he wrote to Georgy that 'I cannot get right internally'. In Liverpool, half a dozen Readings on, he was no better. Being Dickens, he opted for the obvious solution: he would add a new Reading, more demanding than any he had so far attempted: the murder of Nancy from *Oliver Twist*. He had carved out a section of the book that offered him opportunities for a degree of violence and emotional realism he had never attempted before in a Reading; his son Charley, chancing to overhear him rehearsing it, broke into his room, thinking that someone was, quite literally, being murdered. Dickens was nervous that it might prove too disturbing to the public, knowing that he had never exposed his public to such ugliness before, so he decided to try it out first in front of an invited audience. In mid-November 1868, he hired the St James's Hall, where a hundred people, including a handful of journalists and various theatre people, saw him perform it. He appeared to be a man possessed.

'Bill, Bill! For God's sake, for your own, for mine, stop before you spill my blood!!! I have been true to you, upon my guilty soul I have!!!' The housebreaker freed one arm, and grasped his pistol. The certainty of immediate detection if he fired it, flashed across his mind; and he smashed it down twice upon the upturned face that almost touched his own. She staggered and fell, nearly blinded with the blood that rained down from a gash in her forehead, then raising herself on her knees, she drew a white handkerchief from her bosom and holding it up towards Heaven, breathed one last prayer, for mercy to her Maker. It was a ghastly figure to look upon. The murderer staggered back towards the wall, and shutting out the sight with his hand, seized a heavy club, and struck her down!!

Dickens's handwritten stage directions to himself convey something of what he was attempting: 'Beckon down. Point. Shudder. Look Round In Terror. Murder Coming. Mystery. *Terror To the End*'. The violence with which he mimed the clubbing was, according to many witnesses, almost unendurable to watch, rising up out of some terrible darkness and rage within him.

As people sat there after the performance in the St James's Hall, ashen and quailing, two flanking screens behind him were suddenly whisked aside to reveal a sumptuous banquet and overflowing champagne bottles, while the man who, minutes earlier, had clubbed poor Nancy to death, passed chattily among his audience. All his stage-managerial genius was lavished on this try-out. Opinion as to whether he should perform it publicly was fairly evenly divided between those against – Forster, Dolby, Charley – and those for – Wilkie Collins and their *All the Year Round* colleague Charles Kent, who urged him to continue the extract up to the death of Sikes. As always with Dickens, the consultations were a formality; he had already decided to go ahead. After further intensive rehearsals over Christmas, he gave the first public reading of it in London on 5 January 1869; he was still shattered from the exertion the following morning. It was a phenomenal success; when Macready saw it in Cheltenham he burst into the dressing room: 'No, Dickens, er – er – I will NOT – er – have it – er – put aside. In my – er – best times – er

– you remember them, dear boy – er, gone, gone! – no – it comes to this – er – TWO MACBETHS!'

Dickens programmed it as often as he could, though it was taking a terrible toll of him, both physically and emotionally. But it gave him something he needed: a sense of overwhelming power not even his previous triumphs had tapped. 'It is quite a new sensation to be execrated with that unanimity,' he wrote merrily to Forster, but that novel experience was secondary to the cathartic, almost sexual, release it seemed to afford him. On one occasion, a concerned Dolby tried to dissuade him with calm reason from programming the Murder so often, pointing out that he performed it at three out of every four Readings. Dickens listened in glowering silence, then demanded 'Have you finished?' angrily bounding up from his chair, and throwing his knife and fork down on to his plate with such force that it immediately smashed into atoms. 'Dolby!' he shouted. 'Your infernal caution will be your ruin one of these days!' Dolby left the table, then turned round to find his Chief crying; Dickens came towards him sobbing, and affectionately threw his arms round the burly Scotsman, promising to be more sensible in future, which he genuinely tried to be.

He cancelled a couple of Readings on doctors' orders, but then resumed the heavy schedule, flogging himself round the country, in an increasingly emotional state. On one occasion, Dolby found Dickens, just before he was to take the train from Manchester to Hull, in 'paroxysms of grief': he had just been told of the death of Sir James Tennent – a good friend, but not an especially close one. This was not simply grief; something else was going on. He determined to attend the funeral, though he loathed such occasions. In order to be able to catch the last train from York, where he was performing, to London, where the funeral was being held, he did the show without the brief interval he so sorely needed to recover his energies, then dashed to the train and travelled through the night. At the service that morning, Forster found Dickens dazed and worn. A few days later he was doing four shows in a row, one after another with not a day off, and each in a different city. In Liverpool, though he was in considerable distress, he made a lovely knockabout speech at a civic banquet in his honour; it was greeted with roars of laughter and grateful applause. Then he was back on the road, reading in London, in Leeds, in Blackburn. He reported feelings of giddiness, an uncertainty of footing, and an inability to lift his hands above his head; he felt numb all down his left side.

Finally, Dr Beard came to see him in Preston, and instantly ordered him to cancel the remaining twenty-eight Readings, including that night's. Like all the Readings, it was completely sold out and eagerly anticipated. They were major events, and levels of expectation were dangerously high. Dolby, accompanied by police on horseback, staged a brilliant operation to intercept ticket-holders from out of town, making repayments to local people with the Mayor at his side, while Dickens and Beard made a clandestine departure to Liverpool where they stayed overnight before heading back to London. In the event, with minor exceptions, people were calm, and 'nothing was heard but words expressive of deep sympathy'. Dickens loathed having to cancel the performances, and wept 'big tears'. Only Beard's warning that if he performed that night he would drag his foot behind him for the rest of his life – he, the great walker – finally swayed him.

Just ten days after the cancellation, in May 1869, he made his Will. It is an extraordinary, emotionally charged document, the first item of which is a bequest of £1,000 to 'Miss Ellen Ternan'. The children are of course provided for, and Catherine's annual payment of £600 is guaranteed. Dickens seizes the opportunity to note that he has continued this payment to her over the years, 'while all the charges of a numerous and expensive family have wholly devolved on myself'. And then, as if to publicly reprove Catherine further, he lavishly praises Georgina – 'the best and truest friend man ever had' – solemnly enjoining 'my dear children always to remember how much they owe her, for they know well that she has been, through all the stages of their growth and progress, their ever-useful self-denying and devoted friend.' As for himself, he 'emphatically' directs that he be buried in

> an inexpensive, unostentatious, and strictly private manner; that no public announcement be made of the time or the place of my burial; that at the utmost not more than three plain mourning coaches be employed; and that those who attend my funeral wear no scarf, bow, long hat-band, or other such revolting absurdity.

His name must be inscribed 'in plain English letters on my tomb, without the addition of Mr or Esq'. He rests his claim to remembrance, he says, on his published works, 'and to the remembrance of my friends upon their experience of me, in addition thereto'. He commits his soul 'to the mercy of God through our Lord and Saviour Jesus Christ', and exhorts his children 'humbly to try to guide themselves by the teaching of the New Testament in its broad spirit, and to put no faith in any man's narrow constriction of its letter here and there'.

It is a combative document, starting with the bequest to Ellen, and it is certainly not the statement of a man who was giving up the struggle. After he stopped doing the Readings, his health returned gradually, though not as quickly as he expected. He had, he told his friend Frances Elliot, 'some distressing indications that I am not yet as well as I had hoped to be'. He continued 'conducting', as he put it, *All the Year Round*, and making speeches. And he felt the stirring, for the first time in over four years, of a new novel; by September he had a title for it, *The Mystery of Edwin Drood*, and by October he was reading the opening chapters to his American friend, James Fields, whom he had taken on a tour of the East End opium dens that figure so strikingly in the first part of the novel. Accompanied by the police, they had come across 'a haggard old woman blowing at a kind of pipe made of an old ink-bottle; and the words that Dickens puts into the mouth of this wretched creature in *The Mystery of Edwin Drood*, we heard her croon as we leaned over the tattered bed in which she was lying'. It is perilously close to voyeurism, yet it proves that Dickens's writing was what he always claimed it to be: the truth – not an invention – nothing but the truth. The writing went vigorously, though he was shaken to discover that the first numbers were, as he wailed to Forster, '*twelve printed pages too short!!!!*' He made good the shortfall.

In addition to editing *All the Year Round* and maintaining his work on *Drood*, he now started rehearsing for the twelve Readings – billed as his Final Farewell Season of Readings – which he had offered to Chappell's as recompense for the lost performances the previous year, whose cancellation still haunted him. Clearly he felt the need of a formal valediction, a farewell to something that had assumed massive, almost mystical, importance in his life. Sensibly, the Readings were spread over January, February and March; he would fulfil his obligations, he assured Forster, 'in a careful and moderate way'. At Christmas he was at home at Gad's Hill, presiding over the traditional Boxing Day sports meeting there, which went swimmingly. He travelled to Birmingham on 6 January – Twelfth Night, occasion of so many sumptuous and joyful past celebrations – to distribute prizes as President of the Birmingham Midland Institute, whose foundation he had encouraged by performing the very first of the public Readings, some sixteen years earlier. The Presidency was renewed annually, and Dickens drolly referred to the temporary nature of his assumption of office:

> It would be useless for the few short moments longer to disguise the fact that I have drawn King this Twelfth Night, but that another sovereign will soon sit on my inconstant throne. Tonight I abdicate, or what is much the same thing in the annals of modern royalty, I am politely dethroned.

Kingly allusions to Dickens were more and more in the air. But though he spoke of abdication and dethronement, he was certainly not resigning his role as Tribune of the People. A few weeks earlier, he had controversially spoken of the people and their government: 'My faith in the people governing us,' he had said, 'is, on the whole, infinitesimal; my faith in the People governed, is, on the whole, illimitable.' He reiterated the remark in Birmingham, quoting the great Liberal historian of Civilization, H. T. Buckle, in his defence:

> 'when lawgivers have succeeded,' wrote Buckle, 'it is because, contrary to their usual custom, they have implicitly obeyed the spirit of their time, and have been, as they always should be, the mere servants of the people, to whose wishes they are bound to give a public and legal sanction.'

These sentiments were widely reported, creating a sensation, to Dickens's great satisfaction. 'I hope,' he wrote to James Field, 'you have met with the little touch of Radicalism I gave them in Birmingham ...? With pride I observe that it makes the regular political traders, of all sorts, perfectly mad.' Dickens's views, it must be acknowledged, are provocatively close to the Jacobinism, the assertion of the Will of the People, which underpinned the French Revolution, and, as Lady Bracknell observed, we know what *that* unfortunate movement led to. Who interprets the People's will? How do the people express it? What if the people are for public hanging (which of course they were, and are)? The political press united to denounce his remarks: 'why do the allwise People submit to be governed by the unwise people?' they asked. Dickens refrained from further comment, but was well pleased with his feather-ruffling excursion into the political arena.

The first of the Farewell Readings took place a week after the Birmingham speech, on 11 January. Public excitement was feverish. Within Dickens's circle, there was only dread. What precautions could be taken? 'Only ascertainment,' as Forster put it, 'of the exact amount of strain and pressure, which, with every fresh exertion, he was placing on those vessels of the brain where the Preston trouble too surely had revealed that danger lay.' Dr Beard was present at every performance, as was Charley Dickens, seated on the front row, with instructions to leap into action if his father were to falter. Beard was backstage, recording Dickens's pulse-rate before and after each performance; after *Sikes and Nancy* it rose to terrifying levels, from 72 to 124. Backstage, after the performance, Dickens could scarcely speak and had to lie down for half an hour before talking to his guests. There were other baleful indications of his physical condition: his arm was in a sling, his hand heavily bandaged, his left foot constantly inflamed. He slurred certain words, including of all things the name of Pickwick, which at times became Pigswick or Picnic or Peckwicks. At a certain point he suffered a haemorrhage, perhaps of the bowels. Walking in the street, he found he could only read the right-hand half of names over shops. Despite all this, Forster said, he had never read better, with a return to all his old delicacy and sense of fun, which had become somewhat coarsened as a result of exposure to the vast auditoria in which he had played in America. He carefully planned the repertoire to ensure that on each programme he took the audience to the heights of dramatic intensity in the first half, and then in the second sent them home happy with a comedy. He allowed himself an interval of only ten minutes; he was so shattered after the first half, Dolby said, that he could not speak 'a rational or consecutive sentence'. After the ten minutes were up, he revived himself with a brandy-and-water then rushed on to the platform to regale his listeners with apparently effortless drollery.

Audiences of all ages were besides themselves with delight. A little boy, the son of a friend of Dickens's, sat on the front row, laughing, roaring, howling, weeping at the performance: 'at least twice I remember very distinctly he looked at me, with a view to having me removed', but at the end, Dickens patted him forgivingly on the head – because, of course, that stage-struck child was him at the very beginning of his extraordinary journey. At the request of a group of working actors desperate not to miss the Readings, he had programmed a number of matinées: according to Dolby he entered with greater zest into these performances – 'for the players,' as he put it – than into any others of the season. 'He wanted to show them,' said Dolby, 'how much a single performer could do without the aid and stimulus of any of the ordinary adjuncts of the stage; how many effects of a genuinely startling character could be produced without the help of scenery, costume, limelight, or mechanical contrivances.' But delight though Dickens might in the response from the audience, each Reading inexorably diminished his health: 'as he wiped them out one by one,' observed Dolby, 'his feverish excitement and bodily pain increased.' It is said that Ellen Ternan attended a performance, incognito – invisible. What complexities of emotion must she not have felt as she watched the man who was both her protector and her captor destroying himself before her eyes?

Finally it came to an end. *A Christmas Carol* had been the very first of Dickens's readings, and it was the last on 15 March

1870; he coupled it with the Trial Scene from the *Pickwick Papers*, the novel that had first made the British public fall in love with him, the beginning of a romance that had never seriously faltered. The event was overpoweringly emotional for both audience and performer. When he appeared on the platform, the two thousand people crammed into the St James's Hall (four hundred above its theoretical capacity) stood and cheered and cheered him to the echo. In palpably frail health – he had to walk on to the platform with the aid of sticks – he sat down to read. To begin with, his voice was hoarse and weak. Once he got into his stride, all that was forgotten. He read the *Carol* with particular fervour; they laughed, they cried, they cheered. In the Trial Scene from *Pickwick*, each character as he or she appeared was cheered, too, as if they were living people who had entered the scene. Dickens was in joyous form, playful and abandoned. When he described Mr Justice Starleigh ('who was most particularly short, and so fat, that he seemed all face and waistcoat'), he naughtily pointed at Sir Alexander Cockburn, the Lord Chief Justice, who, like everyone else of any account, was present. At the end, the audience erupted into cheers. And then, in a deafening burst of tumultuous acclaim, it was over. The Public Readings, that is, were over, but Dolby noted that Dickens seemed to want to defer speaking for as long as he possibly could the few words of farewell he had prepared. Did he think that somehow he might be able to put it off? That, revived and sustained by the palpable adoration of his public, he might somehow carry on? That the applause might heal him and restore him?

After being called back to the platform again and again and again, he finally silenced the applause to make a speech that was more than simply a farewell to public performances: it was a sort of a swansong, and everyone knew it.

Ladies and Gentlemen, it would be worse than idle, for it would be hypocritical and unfeeling, if I were to disguise that I close this episode of my life with feelings of very considerable pain. For some fifteen years in this hall, and in many kindred places, I have had the honour of presenting my own cherished ideas before you for your recognition, and in closely observing your reception of them, I have enjoyed an amount of artistic delight and instruction which perhaps it is given to few men to know. In this task, and in every other I have ever undertaken as a faithful servant of the public, always imbued with the sense of duty to them, and always striving to do his best, I have been uniformly cheered by the readiest response, the most generous sympathy, and the most stimulating support. Nevertheless, I have thought it well in the full flood tide of your favour to retire upon those older associations between us which date much farther back than these, and thenceforth to devote myself exclusively to the art that first brought us together.

He spoke with perfect composure, and, despite his visible emotion, there was not an instant's hesitation. Only when he spoke the last words of his carefully composed speech, with their precise, significant succession of adjectives, Dolby said, was it possible to detect something of the inner anguish that he felt: 'from these garish lights I vanish now for evermore, with a heartfelt, grateful, respectful, and affectionate farewell.' Having uttered them, he returned to his dressing room on the back of a roaring ovation; tears coursed down his cheeks. He had to return, to an even greater explosion of applause, capped by the entire audience waving their handkerchiefs at him. He blew them a kiss and disappeared, the consummate conjuror to the last; but backstage he recollected to Dolby, 'with a pathetic comment', the words he had uttered in Boston, at his farewell performance there, two years earlier: 'in this brief life of ours, it is sad to do almost anything for the last time'.

Performing had becoming an addiction to Dickens and, like many addictions, it was killing him. Perhaps he knew that he had broken the habit too late.

In the speech, he made it clear that he fully intended the relationship to continue by other means, even slipping in a plug, in entirely characteristic terms, for the new book: 'in two short weeks from this time, I hope that you may enter in your own homes on a new series of readings at which my assistance will be indispensable.' The idea of his almost physical presence in people's homes was the essence of his relationship with his public. He had said that he aspired to 'live in the household affections' and hoped his characters would take their place 'among the household gods'; this goal he achieved to a degree unchallenged by any writer of his time, or perhaps of any other, his appeal encompassing every social class, and only excluding the intelligentsia, who continued to regard him with suspicion and condescension. With that exception alone, from the backstreets to Buckingham Palace, he was embraced and adored.

The Queen herself, whose reign exactly coincided with his fame – *The Pickwick Papers* appeared in book form the year she ascended the throne – insisted that she was his greatest devotee. She had, rather daringly, as a newly crowned eighteen-year-old, read *Oliver Twist* when it first came out, though her real enthusiasm was less for his writing than for his acting, *The Frozen Deep* having shaken her to the core. The Clerk to the Privy Council, Arthur Helps, was close to Dickens and arranged a meeting between them, presciently suggesting to the Queen that 'it really would be right that the author, whose name will hereafter be closely associated with the Victorian Era, should have been presented to Queen Victoria'. He also felt it necessary to remind her that Dickens's first name was Charles, and proposed that, to mask her ignorance of his work, she might 'playfully ask whether *David Copperfield* was the work of his which he should wish Your Majesty to read next', on account of its perceived autobiographical content.

The meeting, so long deferred, finally occurred during the last week of the Farewell Season at the St James's Hall, the ostensible occasion being an opportunity for the Queen to thank Dickens for the loan (via Helps) of some photographs he had acquired in America that had interested her. Dickens expected a brief encounter – perhaps ten minutes or a quarter of an hour – with the now middle-aged Queen, still in deep mourning since the death, nine years earlier, of Prince Albert. In the event, the audience lasted an hour and a half, during which, as protocol required, the chronically frail and pain-wracked Dickens stood; so did the Queen, in a rare mark of favour. When the audience was over, an almost boyishly excited Dickens, now very late for supper, joined Dolby at the appointed restaurant, and regaled him with the details of their conversation: the Queen's regret that she had never seen one of the Readings, how touched she had been by his remarks about leaving the garish footlights, how indelible an impression his acting in *The Frozen Deep* had made on her. Dickens found it impossible to refrain from pointing out that the play had been revived, but had failed, and the Queen told him that of course it would have done, without him in it. They talked about Americans' attitudes to the monarchy (Dickens assured her, somewhat disingenuously, that all Americans deeply respected and admired her and her family), and then they passed on to general topics, the Queen memorably asking Dickens to account for the fact 'that we have no good servants in England as in the olden times'. Dickens murmured something about failures in the education system and, after they had dutifully trawled through the conversational doldrums of the price of meat and bread, the encounter 'rippled on agreeably to an agreeable end'. In parting, the Queen presented Dickens with a copy of her recently published magnum opus,

Leaves from our Life in the Highlands, requesting in turn a set of his Collected Works – a somewhat uneven exchange, to which Dickens of course graciously acceded; the books arrived at Balmoral, signed and inscribed, the day he died.

His embrace by royalty, so long resisted, continued with his being invited to a Levée given by the Prince of Wales, for which he had to wear eighteenth-century court attire, complete with sword; the trouper in him effortlessly took to it, though he drew the line at wearing the cocked hat. At the subsequent reception in the Drawing Room he had been invited to present his daughter Mamie. Her continuing husbandlessness guiltily troubled him to the extent that he kept a London base near Regent's Park, throwing occasional soirées there in the hope that she might meet someone to whom she warmed, his attempts to get her interested in marrying Percy Fitzgerald, one of his little court at *All the Year Round*, having failed. 'What a wonderful instance of the general inanity of Kings, that the Kings in the Fairy tales should have been always wishing for children!' Dickens wrote with mock exasperation after his matchmaking had come to naught. 'If they had but known when they were well off, having none!' But the soirées at Regent's Park were not the answer: they were such grand events, and Dickens was so much the dynamic centre of attention, frail though he was, that it is hard to see how Mamie could ever have met a beau in those circumstances. In the party in April 1870, the musical entertainment was provided by no lesser luminaries than Joseph Joachim (the dedicatee of Brahms's Violin Concerto), Sir Charles Santley (for whom Gounod wrote Valentin's 'Avant de quitter' in *Faust*) and Charles Hallé, founder of the great orchestra of the same name. Music perhaps more to Dickens's own taste was provided by the Vocal Glee Union, though he took particular pleasure in Joachim's performance of Tartini's *Devil's Trill* Sonata.

Dickens made such a hit with Prince Edward at the Levée that he was invited to supper with him and the King of Belgium later the same month. Soon after, he had breakfast with Gladstone, the Prime Minister of the day, and dinner with Disraeli, the leader of the opposition. There is a distinct sense, both on Dickens's part and that of the establishment, that they were trying to fix his place in the scheme of things, to make due acknowledgement of his significance. But if there was any thought that he was somehow being seduced by the world of the Court and Society he had so sedulously avoided all his life, he conclusively scotched it when rumour of an impending baronetcy reached his ears: 'If my authority be worth anything, believe on it that I am going to be nothing but what I am, and that includes my being, as long as I live – Your faithful and heartily obliged Charles Dickens.'

He was devastated, as he so often had been in recent years, by the mortality of his friends. When Mark Lemon died, Dickens observed to Forster how many of their companions in art had fallen from the ranks since they acted in Ben Jonson twenty-five years earlier. None of them was sixty years old, Dickens lamented, some not fifty. 'Let us not speak of it,' said Forster. 'We shall not think of it the less,' returned Dickens, grimly. A grateful reader sent him a silver bowl, in the form of the Four Seasons, but, out of tact, left winter blank. One death hit him with terrible force: that of the companion of his young manhood, 'Mac', the Irish painter Daniel Maclise. Perhaps their relative estrangement over the previous decade made the loss the more painful. Though in dismal health, Dickens volunteered to return the thanks on behalf of Literature at the Royal Academy Dinner to give him an opportunity of paying tribute to his old companion. In the speech, he noted how many of his friends had been RAs, and how many of them had died too soon:

> They have so dropped from my side, one by one, that I already
> begin to feel like that Spanish monk of whom Wilkie tells, who
> had grown to believe that the only realities around him were the
> pictures he loved, and that all the moving life he saw, or ever had
> seen, was a shadow and a dream.

In closing, he said this of Maclise: 'no artist of whatsoever denomination, I make bold to say, ever went to his rest leaving a golden memory more pure from dross, or having devoted himself with a truer chivalry to the art-goddess whom he worshipped.' His hearers were deeply moved. Arthur Helps was there and observed: 'Mr Dickens's was the speech of the evening ... when he read, or when he spoke, the whole man read, or spoke.' Forster, reporting the speech, felt that Dickens had spoken his own epitaph.

He never stopped thinking of one who had died so many years before: Mary Hogarth, who, he wrote to Forster in the last year of his life, 'is so much in my thoughts at all times, especially when I am successful, and have greatly prospered in anything, that the recollection of her is an essential part of my being, and is as inseparable from my existence as the beating of my heart is.'

He continued to put in long hours at his office in Wellington Street, doing the daily grind of editing *All the Year Round*, helped out on the business side by Charley, who had finally found his niche there. Dickens kept a sharp eye on his contributors' work. He was very keenly focused on his 'young men', the group of journalists that included Charles Kent, George Sala and Percy Fitzgerald. Fitzgerald, Mamie Dickens's snubbed swain, recounted how generously Dickens encouraged his young colleagues: if what they brought in seemed at all promising, the piece in question would be expensively set up in proof to see how it looked. If it didn't look right, then the proofs would be scrapped, but the writer would have learned something important. 'Few sensible writers but would have welcomed the opportunity of learning their craft under such a teacher,' wrote Fitzgerald. 'The pleasant ardour with which he followed the course of a story, anticipated its coming, debated its name, and helped the writer over various stiles, and even extricated him from bogs, was all in the same spirit.' When a story was accepted, it was advertised on great yellow posters that Dickens would lay across the floor for the young writer to see before they were distributed across London. 'The cost of this system of advertising was enormous,' said Fitzgerald, 'but everything was done magnificently in "the office"'. The essence of Dickens's advice to his writers is contained in a few lines from an *Address to Working People* he had given in the mid-1850s:

> I must say, above all things – especially to the young people writing: 'Don't condescend! Don't assume the attitude of saying "See how clever I am, and what fun everybody else is!" Take any shape but that.'

His passion for the causes he had supported all his life continued unabated; his focus at the office was absolute. Away from it, his step was less certain. When Blanchard Jerrold, the son of Dickens's lamented friend Douglas, who had known Dickens all his life, ran into him in the street around this time, he at first doubted that the white-haired, slow-moving man ahead of him, solemn and earnest of mien, could be Dickens. The moment Jerrold addressed him, though, 'the delightful brightness and sunshine swept over the gloom and sadness; and he spoke cheerily, in the old kind way – not in the least about himself – about all that could interest me.' His delight in plays and players, too, remained undiluted, though due to further 'neuralgic affection' of the foot – 'my foot,' he said, 'is just a bag of pain' – he was obliged with deep regret to cancel his much-anticipated address to the General Theatrical Fund. But he was well enough not much later to go to the theatre with Lord Redesdale and his slightly batty friend Lady Molesworth: Redesdale reported him 'so full of droll thoughts … that he kept himself and his companions laughing at the majesty of his own absurdities … his talk had all the sparkle of champagne.' Right to the end, it is Dickens's laughter that people remembered: 'not poor, thin, arid, ambiguous laughter, that is ashamed of itself, that moves one feature only of the face,' his friend Helps wrote, 'but the largest and heartiest kind, irradiating his whole countenance, and compelling you to participate in his immense enjoyment of it.'

At the end of May 1870, shortly before the theatre jaunt, and during a time of especial and persistent physical pain, he supervised, with all his familiar fanaticism and all his usual abandon, the production of a triple bill of the sort of comedies he adored, *The Prima Donna*, *A Happy Pair*, and *Le Myosotosis* ('a *bouffonerie*'), at Cromwell House, the residence of his friends the Freakes. He had fully intended to appear in the plays himself, but resigned himself to merely directing them, securing the services of the painter John Millais, then one of the most fashionable artists in England, as designer. He rehearsed the actors at his rented London house with unflagging energy, with his usual technique, 'acting all the parts *con amore* one after another,' said Herman Merivale, who was in the show, 'passing from "the old man" to "the young lover" with all his famous versatility and power'. At the performance itself, on 2 June, he was both prompter and stage manager; he rang the bells and worked the lights, 'all with infectious enjoyment'. It was a stifling night, and, unusually, Dickens did not join the audience after the show. He was eventually found backstage by his son-in-law Charles Collins in 'a dreamy state and abstracted'. He had thought, he said, that he was at home.

In a sense, he was. The theatre, he often claimed, was where he had known his happiest times.

It was his last such venture, the final affirmation of a life-long passion: theatre was the other art-goddess he had served. Literature was his wife, the theatre his mistress, and to the very end he was tempted to leave the one for the other. A few weeks before he mounted *The Prima Donna*, he had been walking, a little gloomily, near Westminster Abbey with his friend and *All the Year Round* contributor, Charles Kent, when he suddenly asked him, 'What do you think would be the realisation of one of my most cherished daydreams?' Without waiting for a reply, he answered himself:

> To hold supreme authority in the direction of a great theatre, with a skilled and noble company ... the pieces acted should be dealt with according to my pleasure, and touched up here and there in obedience to my own judgement; the players as well as the plays being absolutely under my command. *That's* my day-dream!

The theatre as escape, as diversion, as fable – but also the theatre as workshop, as forge, as ship of which he was captain. Even as late as the show at Cromwell House, he was telling people that he planned to revive Buckstone's hoary old 1830s Adelphi melodrama *The Wreck Ashore*, and play the leading part; but, lame and dazed as he was, he must have known that that would never be.

He returned to Gad's Hill the day after the performance of *The Prima Donna*, 3 June, and continued work on *The Mystery of Edwin Drood*. The book had started to appear, as he had said it would, just two weeks after the last of the Readings, on 1 April, and it had been an instant and an unprecedented success, having, he exultantly wrote to his American friend Fields, 'very, very, far outstripped every one of its predecessors'.

The first episode quickly reached sales of 50,000. Writing it had not been easy; by the end of April he reported himself 'making headway but slowly' despite being 'most persever-ingly and ding-dong-doggedly at work'. The book betrays none of this effort; Forster, who had felt that Dickens in his most recent books had allowed his genius to be overwhelmed by his despair at the human situation, noted with delight that, despite the sombreness of the central narrative, he was writing in a new vein that incorporated all his old virtues. Even the reviewers (not that Dickens ever read them) welcomed it; it was fully five years since *Our Mutual Friend*, and they rejoiced that his immersion in the Readings had not been a sign of creative barrenness. To Longfellow, eagerly consuming the episodes as they appeared in America, the book was 'certainly one of his most beautiful, if not the most beautiful of all'. Beauty is the *mot juste*; an entirely new note of restrained lyri-cism, in a minor key of autumnal eloquence, sounds through its pages, alongside the familiar melodrama and the accus-tomed high spirits. The central character, the opium-addicted choirmaster, John Jasper, is peculiarly enigmatic: 'Is John Jasper Dickens's vision of the artist as a secret misfit in the world?' asked Dickens's biographer, Edgar Johnson. 'Is the artist a traitor in society's midst, a subverter of its standards, or is he a heroic rebel, fighting its corruptions and its charnel decay?'

Dickens had high hopes for *Drood*, he told his daughter Katey when she came down on Saturday, 4 June, the day after the Cromwell house show, for the weekend, 'if, please God, I live to finish it – I say *if*, because you know, my dear child, I have not been strong lately.' She noted his frailty, but was glad to see that he was in good spirits. The long-mooted conserva-tory had finally been built at the back of the house: 'POSITIVELY the last improvement at Gad's Hill!' he said, jest-ingly. They laughed at dinner; after it, he smoked his customary cigar while they listened to Mamie singing. When Mamie and Georgy had gone to bed, they talked, the father and the daughter who so resembled each other, her will almost as indomitable as his. Like others in his circle, she had tried to modify the intensity with which he was applying himself to writing *Drood*, 'but any attempt to stay him in a work that he had undertaken,' she wrote, half-admiringly, half-despairingly, 'was as idle as stretching one's hands to a river and bidding it cease to flow.'

She wanted his advice: she had been approached by an actor-manager who – on the strength of her performance in the original Tavistock House production of *The Frozen Deep* twelve years before – had offered her work as an actress; she was tempted by the possible financial rewards. He gently disabused her of the idea, telling her that, though she was pretty and charming, her nature was far too sensitive to endure what she would come across: 'although there are nice people on the stage, there are some who would make your hair stand on end'. She was clever enough, he said, to do something else. The idea that Kate might have the kind of life Ellen Ternan had lived, would no doubt have been deeply abhorrent to him. He closed the matter by telling her that he would 'make it up to her' financially. He then spoke at great length, in a low voice, of many subjects he had never broached before, 'as if his life were over and there was nothing left'. He wished, he told her, that he had been a better man and a better father. Not until the early summer dawn broke did they make their way to bed; and when she got up the following morning he was already at his desk in the Châlet, writing. On an impulse, she ran back to see him before leaving, and, uncharacteristically, he got up and embraced her tenderly.

Mamie left the next day, and on the seventh, some Chinese lanterns Dickens had purchased were hung and lit in the conservatory, and after dinner he and Georgina sat looking at them, a little corner of Gadshill translated to old Peking, as if Aladdin or Abanazar or even Widow Twankey might turn round the corner at any moment. Who knows what intimation of mortality they suggested to him, but contemplation of them somehow reminded him to tell Georgy that he wanted to be buried in Rochester Cathedral (although only a few weeks earlier he had been highly critical of the slack way the liturgy was conducted).

It was of Rochester Cathedral, in its guise as Cloisterham Cathedral, that he was writing the following day, the eighth, as he resumed work on *Drood*:

A brilliant morning shines on the old city. Its antiquities and ruins are surpassingly beautiful, with a lusty ivy gleaming in the sun, and the rich trees waving in the balmy air. Changes of glorious light from moving boughs, songs of birds, scents from gardens, woods, and fields – or, rather, from the one great garden of the whole cultivated island in its yielding time – penetrate into the Cathedral, subdue its earthy odour, and preach the Resurrection and the Life. The cold stone tombs of centuries ago grow warm; and flecks of brightness dart into the sternest marble corners of the building, fluttering there like wings.

Unusually he stayed at his desk all day, with a short break for lunch, until he left off work on the novel, with that most Dickensian of things: food.

Mrs Tope's care has spread a very neat, clean breakfast ready for her lodger. Before sitting down to it, he opens his corner cupboard door; takes his bit of chalk from its shelf; adds one thick line to the score, extending from the top of the cupboard door to the bottom; and then falls to with an appetite.

He then knocked off a couple of letters: to his son Henry; to Charles Kent, who was in love, he quoted *Romeo and Juliet*: 'You really must get rid of these Opal enjoyments: "These violent delights have violent ends". I think it was a father of your church who made the wise remark to a young gentleman who got up early (or stayed out late) at Verona'; and then, finally, angrily, to someone who has detected an impiety in something he has written.

> I have always striven in my writings to express veneration for the life and lessons of Our Saviour; because I feel it; and because I re-wrote that history for my children – every one of whom knew it from having it repeated to them – long before they could read, and almost as soon as they could speak. But I have never made a proclamation of this from the housetops.

Perhaps he recollected his own words about Jesus in the little book he had written for his children: 'Everybody ought to know about Him. No one ever lived who was so good, so kind, so gentle, and so sorry for all people who did wrong or were in any way ill or miserable, as He was.'

He then descended to the dining-room, a look of acute pain on his face. He announced that he had been ill for an hour, but that they must carry on. Then he suddenly said he had to go to London; everything he said after that was unintelligible. He pushed back his chair and stood: Georgina tried to hold him, but he was too heavy and he sank to the floor. 'On the ground,' he seemed to say. Servants moved him on to the sofa where he lay, unconscious. The family were sent for – Mamie, Charley, Katey – and his doctor, Frank Beard; it seems that Georgina notified Ellen, who was there for the end, which came at 6 p.m. on the evening of 9 June. His breathing became laboured, he gave a sigh, a tear rolled out of his eye, and it was over. He was fifty-eight years old. Millais was summoned to draw him on his deathbed; Thomas Woolner, another pioneer Pre-Raphaelite, took the death mask – the last two of the many images made of one of the most famous faces in the Western world.

His death was as he would have wished it. Some years earlier, he had been striding exultantly through Kensington Gardens as lightning flashed around him. His companion urged caution. Dickens replied: 'of all the fears that harass a man on God's earth, the fear of sudden death seems to me the most absurd, and why we pray against it in the litany, I cannot guess.' As the lightning flashed and the thunder rolled, he quoted the pirate in Byron's *Corsair* at the top of his voice:

> Let him who crawls enamoured of decay,
> Cling to his couch and sicken years away;
> Heave his thick breath, and shake his palsied head;
> Ours – the fresh turf, and not the feverish bed;
> While, gasp by gasp, he falters forth his soul,
> Ours with one pang – one bound – escapes control.

Despite his ill-health, he had retained his powers virtually to the end, still treading the fresh turf; he had not faltered forth his soul, but been felled in action. And after one pang and with one bound, he leapt straight into immortality. The world was shocked by the brutal suddenness of it: Carlyle, writing to condole Forster, went to the heart of things: 'It is an event world-wide; a *unique* of talents suddenly extinct.'

He was not buried in Rochester Cathedral.

Within days, there was a demand, orchestrated by the newspapers, for him to be buried in Westminster Abbey: 'very few are more worthy than Charles Dickens of such a home,' said *The Times*. 'Fewer still, we believe, will be regarded with more honour as time passes, and his greatness grows upon us.' It turned out, as it happened, that there was nowhere for him to be buried in the parish church at Higham, close to Gad's Hill, or any other local graveyard. The Dean of Rochester offered a plot, but Arthur Stanley, Dean of Westminster, made a tactful proposal for a private burial ceremony at the Abbey, to be attended by no more than a dozen people. Despite the clear provisions of the Will ('I emphatically direct that I be buried in an inexpensive, unostentatious, and strictly private manner'), the family felt they had no option but to accept Stanley's invitation.

Accordingly, at 6 a.m. on 14 June 1870, Dickens's mortal remains left Gad's Hill; the coffin was brought by train to Charing Cross, where it was transferred to a hearse without funeral trappings, as he had decreed. The hearse was then accompanied by the three plain mourning coaches he had specified on its journey down Whitehall to the Abbey. In the first of the coaches, the family – Katey, Mamie, Charley, Dickens's sister Letitia and Charley's wife Bessie – travelled; Forster, the Collins brothers Wilkie and Charles, Dr Beard, and Dickens's solicitor, Mr Ouvry, filled the others. Nobody wore a 'scarf, bow, long hat-band, or other such revolting absurdity'. On arrival, the body was conveyed to Poets' Corner, where, in an austerely simple ceremony, the coffin was lowered into the grave, in the 'stillness and the silence of the vast Cathedral,' said Forster. There was no choir, and precious little music: at the conclusion, the organist played the 'Dead March' from Handel's *Saul*. And that was that. It was all oddly unDickensian. Needless to say, neither Ellen nor Catherine, the two invisible women in his life, was present.

Punch, setting aside satire for a moment, noted with satisfaction that

He sleeps as he should – among the great
In the old Abbey: sleeps amid the few
Of England's famous thousands whose high state
Is to lie with her monarchs – monarchs too

Monarch of the imagination he might have been, but – and here the provisions of his Will were scrupulously adhered to – his coffin bore the simple inscription CHARLES DICKENS. No further explanation or qualification was needed, or ever would be. Mourners appeared at the graveside the following day and for three days, until the grave was closed, they unceasingly streamed past, laying flowers and ferns all around it. And for three months after that, all day and every day, the constant procession of mourners continued, all of them leaving flowers.

At the service at the Abbey, the Sunday following the burial, taking his text from the parable of the Rich Man and Lazarus, the Dean spoke of Dickens:

Through his genius the rich man who fares sumptuously every day was brought to see Lazarus at his gate. On people in the workhouse, neglected children, and starved and ill-used boys in remote schools far off from human sight, a ray of hope was thrown: for an unknown friend had pleaded their cause with a voice which rang through the palaces of the great as well as through the cottages of the poor.

At the evening service, Benjamin Jowett said:

He whose loss we now mourn occupied during his lifetime a greater space in the minds of Englishmen than any other writer. We read him, talked about him, acted him; we laughed with him, were roused by him to a consciousness of the misery of others, and to a sympathetic interest in human life ... no one was ever so much beloved or so much mourned. Men seem to have lost, not a great writer only but one whom they had personally known. And so we bid him farewell.

It was in order to be personally known to his readers that Dickens had striven so long and so arduously, always reaching out to them, inviting himself into their parlours to put on a show. 'A story of his is like a drama for the fireside,' said *Fraser's Magazine*,

> furnished not only with situations and dialogue, but with appropriate scenery, gestures, action, by-play; the author, scene-painter, stage-manager, and moreover the whole company, tragic and comic, male and female, from 'stars' to 'supers', being one and the same skilful individual. The figures impress one rather as impersonations than persons. But how telling they are, and what a list of dramatis personae is that of the *Theatre National Charles Dickens*!

Yes, they knew him all right. And yet he concealed a great deal from them. Latterly, of course, Ellen Ternan, but throughout his life the facts of his childhood. No obituary notice – and they were all, without exception, fulsome in praise of his character and his achievements – made any reference to these great secrets. Indeed, in his *Daily Telegraph* obituary of his old Chief, George Augustus Sala, who had been as close to him as anyone in his circle, wrote that

> he had not been born in poverty, but in a respectable middle-class family. He had never known – save, perhaps, in early youth, the occasional harduppishness of a young man striving to attain a position – actual poverty. He had no terrible experiences to tell … of days passed in slavish toil, or dirt, and destitution, and opprobrium – or in pacing the stony-hearted streets, bedless and

breadless. He had never, like Goldsmith, 'lived in Axe Lane among the beggars', or eaten his meals in a ragged horseman's coat, behind a screen, being thought unfit to join Mr Cave's well-dressed-contributors at table. From youth to age, he lived in honour, and affluence, and splendour. It was a calm, peaceful, and, I should say, happy life.

In a sense, Dickens was a greater mystery to his contemporaries than he is to us: they had absolutely no clue as to where it all came from – the darkness, the passionate empathy with the disadvantaged, the massive driving energy, the overwhelming willpower. Only two years after Dickens's interment at Westminster Abbey, John Forster, exactly as Dickens had intended, in a masterly piece of posthumous stage-management, let the cat out of the bag: the source of so much in his work – and his life – suddenly became clear. But nothing can account for a man like Dickens. Not that there ever has been any man like Dickens: quite aside from the stupendous scope of his writing, his personality and his life are of almost overwhelming richness. It is one of the greatest of English Lives, both humbling and heart-warming, despite titanic flaws. It would be wonderful to think that there might be a second Dickens, but there have so far been no sightings.

After his death, his books continued to be read and his characters relished by young and old, across the classes. Despite the stubborn resistance of the literary critical fraternity, they were considered an indispensible feature of a basic education. As late as the 1970s, as they had been at regular intervals since his death, readily affordable hardback sets of his complete works were widely promoted, and found themselves on the shelves of what Dickens might have termed ordinary households. Eventually, the literary critics decided that he might be rather interesting after all, and that his popularity did not automatically disqualify him from being either complex or profound. To an even larger audience, his name became a household word (as he himself might have put it) through media unknown and probably inconceivable to him. The nascent cinema eagerly seized on his work: more silent films were made from his work than from that of any other author; even without words, his characters and his stories made a huge impact. With words, in the new talking films, they were sumptuously successful. Television seized on him from the beginning, and has continuously and provocatively interpreted and reinterpreted the novels. The theatre continued to adapt his work: it inspired not just big commercial productions in the Victorian and Edwardian theatre – and a few not always successful Musicals in the twentieth century (including an *Edwin Drood* with several optional endings, voteable on) – but the Russian Art Theatre of the 1920s and British experimental companies of the 1970s. Hollywood regularly returns to his work, whether in the period in which it was set or in modern transpositions.

None of this should be in the least bit surprising. Dickens's uniquely vivid sense of the theatre informs every page of his writing: his people leap off the page, as if they were eagerly clambering up onto a stage to strut their stuff; his personal compulsion to perform is present throughout his work, his desire to communicate personally with us, to look us in the eye and thrill us, astonish us, amuse us, is as urgent now as it was for his first readers. As long as men and women want to hear stories, Charles Dickens remains and will always be a leading player on the stage of our imagination.

ACKNOWLEDGEMENTS

To begin with, I must thank my publisher, Martin Redfern, whose idea this book was in the first place, and who has calmly and enthusiastically supported it through its many evolutions into its present form, almost never blanching at the inevitable frustrations of working with an author who was stomping round the country in various plays throughout the period of composition. Next, as always, I must thank my agent, Maggie Hanbury, for her support, wisdom, generosity, appreciation and telling criticism. I am very grateful to Andrew Pinder for patiently listening to my amateurish thoughts about the illustrations and turning them into such a splendid feature of the book. Anne O'Brien was the eagle-eyed and learned copy editor, checking and double-checking facts, quotations, dates, quietly favouring sentences that were grammatically correct over those that were not, generally exuding strong support. Kerry Enzor skilfully and tirelessly co-ordinated all our activities. Katherine Josselyn of HarperPress's publicity department laboured day and night to ensure that everybody knew of the book's existence. My old friend Carol Murphy and her colleagues at that peerless Dickensian emporium, Jarndyce and Co., in Great Russell Street, supplied me with many of the books that I needed; my secretary Fiona Wilkins was inexhaustible and indispensable in making hundreds of phone calls and sending dozens of emails in connection with the book. Another friend, Dr Florian Schweizer, put the wonderful resources of the Dickens House Museum, of which he is director, at my disposal, and

Acknowledgements

helped me at very short notice to assemble a complete set of
the letters, on which I have so heavily relied. Sir David Hare
read an early version of the manuscript and was as penetrating
as ever; his observations considerably influenced the final text.
Professor Michael Slater did me the enormous favour of a
thorough critical reading of the text, correcting many errors,
making many excellent suggestions which were eagerly acted
on and encouraging me to believe that I had something useful
to say about the writer about whom he knows more than
anyone alive. For the paperback edition, a number of errors,
repetitions and other infelicities have been corrected thanks
to the sharp observation of Professors Malcolm Andrews and
Stanley Wells, and my friends Nicholas Walsh and Matthew
Hurt.

354

SELECT BIBLIOGRAPHY

Allen, Michael, *Charles Dickens' Childhood*, Basingstoke: Macmillan, 1988

Amerongen, J. B. van, *The Actor in Dickens: A Study of the Histrionic and Dramatic Elements in the Novelist's Life and Works*, London: Cecil Palmer, 1926

Ackroyd, Peter, *Dickens*, London: Sinclair-Stevenson, 1990

Andrews, Malcolm, *Charles Dickens and His Performing Selves: Dickens and the Public Readings*, Oxford: Oxford University Press, 2006

Aylmer, Felix, *Dickens Incognito*, London: Rupert Hart-Davis, 1959

Brannan, Robert Louis, ed., *Under the Management of Mr Charles Dickens: His Production of the Frozen Deep*, Ithaca, NY: Cornell University Press, 1966

Collins, Philip, ed., *Charles Dickens: The Public Readings*, Oxford: Clarendon Press, 1975

Cruickshank, R. J., *The Humour of Dickens*, London: News Chronicle Publications Department, 1952

Dickens, Mamie, 'My Father as I Recall Him' (1897), in *Charles Dickens: Family History*, ed. Norman Page, vol. 5, London: Routledge, Thoemmes Press, 1999

Dolby, George, *Charles Dickens as I Knew Him: The Story of the Reading Tours in Great Britain and America (1866–1870)*, London: T. Fisher Unwin, 1885

Field, Kate, *Pen Photographs of Charles Dickens's Readings: Taken from Life*, Boston, MA: Loring, 1868

Fitzgerald, Percy, *Memories of Charles Dickens: With an Account of Household Words and All the Year Round, and of the Contributors Thereto*, Bristol: Arrowsmith,1913

Fitzsimons, Raymund, *The Charles Dickens Show*, London: Geoffrey Bles, 1970

Forster, John, *Life of Dickens*, 3 vols., London: Chapman & Hall

Furniss, Henry, *Some Victorian Men*, London: John Lane, The Bodley Head, 1924

Hardwick, Mollie, *Charles Dickens (as They Saw Him): The Great Novelist as Seen through the Eyes of His Family, Friends, and Contemporaries*, London: George G. Harrap & Co., 1970

House, Madeline and Storey, Graham, *The Letters of Charles Dickens*, Pilgrim edn, 12 vols., Oxford: Clarendon Press, 1965–2002

Hughes, William R.M, *A Week's Tramp in Dickens-Land*, London: Chapman & Hall, 1891

Johnson, Edgar, *Charles Dickens: His Tragedy and Triumph*, 2 vols., London: Gollancz, 1953

Kent, Charles, *Charles Dickens as a Reader*, London: Chapman & Hall, 1872

Matz, B. W., ed., *Dickens in Cartoon and Caricature*, Boston, MA: The Bibliophile Society, 1924

Sala, George Augustus, *Charles Dickens*, London: George Routledge & Sons, 1870

Schlicke, Paul, ed., *Oxford Reader's Companion to Dickens*, Oxford: Oxford University Press, 1999

Slater, Michael, *Charles Dickens*, New Haven and London: Yale University Press, 2009

Slater, Michael, *Dickens and Women*, London: Dent, 1983

Slater, Michael, ed., *Dickens on America & the Americans*, New York: The Harvester Press, 1979

Tomalin, Clare, *The Invisible Woman: The Story of Nelly Ternan and Charles Dickens*, London: Viking, 1990

INDEX